Praise for
Family Outing

"Part memoir about a daughter coming to terms with being gay in the spotlight of famous parents and part how-to for the average family coping with coming-out issues . . . *Family Outing* comes alive with Bono's own story. There is sincerity in the telling, a straightforwardness that lets the reader connect with the real people behind the tabloid headlines."
— Lydia Martin, *Hartford Courant*

"A comprehensive guide to the coming-out process: to self, to friends, to family, and, eventually, to the world. . . . Through the example and dissection of their subjects' fears of coming out, behaviors of self-destruction, and the reactions of others, the authors honestly find a universality to such much-pondered issues as building self-esteem and, in particular, mending familial relations."
— David Drake, *Lambda Book Report*

"Chastity Bono writes about gay life and its impact on families — including her own. . . . *Family Outing* uses more than a dozen real-life examples to show young gay people the rewards and pitfalls that go with being open about their sexuality."
— *People*

"This is an eloquent account of the pain that young gay and lesbian people experience, and how love and courage can lead them and their families to overcome homophobia. It is impossible for any sensible person to read this book and still hold to the notion that the young people who deal with this terrible prejudice do so voluntarily by 'choosing' their sexual orientation."
— Congressman Barney Frank

"A helpful, step-by-step guide . . . Bono is particularly good at describing the struggles of gay and lesbian teenagers, and she offers the kind of guidance and encouragement that for many of them is desperately hard to find."
— Caitlin Flanagan, *San Francisco Chronicle*

Dedicated in loving memory to my father

Family Outing

Little, Brown and Company
Boston   New York   London

Originally published in hardcover by Little, Brown and Company, 1998
First Back Bay paperback edition, 1999

Library of Congress Cataloging-in-Publication Data
Bono, Chastity.
    Family outing / by Chastity Bono with Billie Fitzpatrick. —
1st ed.
        p.   cm.
    ISBN 0-316-10233-4 (hc) / 0-316-11596-7 (pb)
    1. Coming out (Sexual orientation) — United States.   2. Gay
men — United States — Family relationships.   3. Lesbians —
United States — Family relationships.   4. Heterosexual parents —
United States — Attitudes.   I. Fitzpatrick, Billie.   II. Title.
HQ76.3.U5B65   1998
306.76'6'0973 — dc21   98-7348

10 9 8 7 6 5 4 3 2 1

MV-NY

Book design by Barbara Werden Design

Printed in the United States of America

Contents

Acknowledgments

We would like to acknowledge Loretta A. Barrett and Sarah Burnes for their faithful efforts during the creation of this book. We would also like to thank Fredi Friedman for her initial interest, which made this book possible. In addition we would like to extend our warmest appreciation to the gracious members of P-FLAG and to those individuals and families, including our own, that let us into their lives and shared with us their most intimate stories — thank you.

Introduction

As a child, I always felt there was something different about me. I'd look at other girls my age and feel perplexed by their obvious interest in the latest fashion, which boy in class was the cutest, and who looked the most like cover girl Christie Brinkley. When I was thirteen, I finally found a name for exactly how I was different. I realized I was gay. And suddenly I made much more sense to myself. This first realization was just the beginning of a process that continues today. I started coming out to a few close friends, got involved in relationships, sought out other lesbians, and made friends. Then, when I was eighteen, I came out to my parents. At the time, my father was immediately supportive; it took my mother much longer. But as we as a family began the arduous, confusing, often frustrating process leading toward acceptance, I was derailed by an uncontrollable outside force.

In the winter of 1990, I was outed by the tabloid the *Star*, which published an unauthorized article that disclosed my sexual orientation to the public. At the time, I was far from ready to have this still-private matter exposed to people other than those I chose to tell. I felt so violated and vulnerable to other people's judgment of me that I retreated into the closet: for over four years, I went into virtual hiding, constantly afraid of being exposed again by the tabloids. I rarely went out in public, especially to places where I might be photographed.

This was an extremely difficult, painful time that exacerbated all my self-doubt and negative feelings about being gay in a mostly straight world. It wasn't until I became involved with an older woman and then, soon after, lost her to cancer that I began to reevaluate living in the closet. I then made the decision to come out publicly: I needed to take my power back.

In April 1995, I appeared on the cover of *The Advocate*, and for the first time told my version of my coming-out story to a national audience. Though I knew that this act would forever change my life, I had no idea how positive the outcome would be. I received piles of letters from lesbians and gays across the country telling me that they admired my courage and saw me as a role model. While coming out in public began as a personal decision, it catapulted me into a political role that has transformed my life, providing me with affirmation as a lesbian, as a woman, and as an individual. And not only has this public role provided enormous personal and professional fulfillment, it also allowed my family to accept me in a much healthier way. Even my father, with whom I had political differences, felt proud that I had become an activist. And because I now truly accept myself, my family is able to do the same.

There is a vital connection here: a family's acceptance of a gay or lesbian child or sibling is directly tied to the gay person's ability to accept him- or herself. As gay people we can't expect acceptance from those close to us and the world at large until we are completely comfortable with being gay ourselves. Coming out, then, is a dual process that both individuals and families struggle through and ultimately learn to appreciate.

By August 1996, one year after I came out publicly, my mother had progressed so far that she agreed to "come out" herself on the cover of *The Advocate* as the proud mother of a lesbian daughter. The response to my interview with my mom was tremendous. I remember one letter in particular. A woman

I'll call Chloe, a single mother with two young children, wrote that she had known she was gay for many years but was afraid to tell anyone — even though her brother was gay too. After picking up a copy of *The Advocate* because my mother was on the cover and reading the article, Chloe finally felt ready to tell someone she was a lesbian.

I was stunned yet again. There was *no one* she could tell she was gay before reading the article?

As I had begun feeling more and more comfortable about myself, I had begun to assume that coming out was becoming less of an ordeal, less of a struggle. I was wrong. I keep thinking that society is making it easier for gay men and women to come out and live a free and fulfilled life without censoring themselves and without the risk of rejection, harm, and discrimination. But clearly, though society has changed remarkably in the twenty-seven years since Stonewall (and my birth) in 1969, and we have made legal and political strides, being gay in America is still not easy.

Chloe is one of many people I have come across in the past several years who either revealed complete emotional paralysis about their homosexuality or were still firmly in the closet. Before taking on an activist role as a spokesperson for the Human Rights Campaign and more recently as entertainment media director for GLAAD (Gay and Lesbian Alliance Against Defamation), I had only experienced the difficulty and rewards of coming out on a personal level. But when I began to meet people from all different backgrounds and hear their stories, I discovered with surprise and sadness that men and women are still afraid to come out.

What became clear as I listened to the stories of others and shared my own is that although the gay community is diverse, the desire to tell our various coming-out stories is a constant. And as I became aware of the individual struggles, I was confronted with a general need for more understanding of how and when to make the journey. These men and women from diverse ethnic, racial, religious, and socioeconomic backgrounds were at different stages of self-discovery. Some had told their families; some had only told a best friend; some had only told their lovers; some had told no one at all. Some women and men had come out to their families and close friends but still hid their sexual orientation from their coworkers, their bosses, and some of their straight friends.

I realized then that maybe I could make a difference, that by sharing my story and especially my experience with my family, specifically my mother, Cher, I might be able to help other people arrive at the happy place I am now.

The goal of *Family Outing* is not only to guide gay women and men through the closet door but also to give them the tools with which they can complete the process by bringing their families, especially their parents, along with them.

The book as a whole traces the stories of gay individuals and their parents, allowing the reader to follow these families, including my own, as the coming-out process unfolds. In the first part of the book, I introduce the various issues we as lesbians and gays experience in coming to terms with our homosexuality by first telling my own story and then bringing in the stories of many others, taken from extensive conversations with people who vary in age, gender, race, ethnicity, religion, and geographic location. These narratives illustrate the universal themes and stages that form the coming-out process for all gay people. Yet within this framework a myriad of different feelings exist.

In the next part of my book, I share my conversations with my mother about my coming out, which introduce the issues most families and friends confront when someone they love tells them they are lesbian or gay. Again, this material is organized thematically, mirroring the process itself, and includes experiences of other families of gay people. As in the first part, a central framework emerges here as representing the universal stages in moving toward acceptance. But again, the individual feelings and experiences vary.

The social and political environment has become more accepting of homosexuals and our need to be honest and open about who we are. We are at the point now where people in high-profile positions in entertainment, sports, and politics have taken the risk and come out to overwhelming positive response. Elton John, Ellen DeGeneres, Melissa Etheridge, k. d. lang, David Geffen, Amanda Bearse, Greg Louganis, Barney Frank, and Colonel Margaret Cammermeyer: these men and women have helped to break down the stereotype that openly gay and lesbian men and women cannot succeed.

Family Outing reflects this spirit of change — but it also challenges both those still in the closet and those wanting people to stay in the closet to overcome their fears. I hope this book will demystify the coming-out process for gay people and their families and allow them to see that sexual orientation does not limit people in any way. Once we learn to define homosexuality in positive, life-affirming terms, lesbians and gays will move beyond acceptance to true empowerment. I hope that by sharing my story and experience, as well as the stories of others from across the country, I can help all readers reach their own sense of freedom and personal pride in who they are.

Part One
Coming Out
Ourselves

Chapter 1
Feeling "Different"
When We Were Young

"The real world was suspicious of girls who did not want to play Jane."

BLANCHE MCCRARY BOYD,
from *The Revolution of Little Girls*

No More Frilly Dresses

Like most of us, I don't remember much from my early years. As hard as it may be to believe, I barely remember my parents' television show, or being brought on stage with them. In fact, I don't even remember my parents as a couple. My mom tells me that we were very close when I was little, that we'd play dress up together, that I went everywhere with her, attached to her hip. I have a photo of us together in matching black cat suits. She's smiling at me, and I'm clapping my hands. The picture is vivid, but I have no recollection of this moment, or any other until I was around seven.

I have a blurred memory of the emotional chaos that followed my parents' divorce when I was four years old. My parents decided that I should spend equal time with each of them, so I'd stay with my mom for a week or two and then move to my dad's. I'm sure they thought this was best for me, but the constant shifting was overwhelming.

When I'd arrive at one house, I would begin to get anxious. Sometimes it would take me a full day to adjust. I would cry and not be able to sleep, wishing that I were still at the other house. After a day or so, I'd settle in and feel fine, only to be uprooted in a week or so. Like most kids of divorced parents, I felt torn, with no one place to call my own. Even though I had doubles of a lot of toys and clothes, it wasn't twice as good: instead, I wanted one room, one set of toys, one household.

For a few years after they divorced, my mom and dad continued to work together in a nightclub show that moved around the country. I remember once they were doing a show in Buffalo. After the performance, someone threw a bouquet of roses on stage for my mother. From the wings, I looked out desperately at the forgotten flowers. I felt so sorry for the flowers, I ran out to save them. But my act of rescue only annoyed my mother, who admonished me for running out on stage. Her reaction confused me. Didn't she feel sorry for the flowers too? I think this image sticks in my mind because it captures how sensitive I was to both the pain of others and to my mother's reaction to me.

My most vivid memories of my childhood begin when I became conscious that I was somehow "different," specifically different from who my mom expected me to be.

Another memory, which shows how I was beginning to feel different, is from when I was seven and a half. My brother, Elijah, had just been born, and we were living in a big Spanish-style house in Beverly Hills. I was sitting on a high stool in the kitchen. Instead of a table, we had a kidney-shaped island — at home it was never my mom's style to sit down and eat in a formal way. I was small. I'm sure my hair was an unruly mess, that my knees were scraped, that my jeans were covered in grass stains. I was planning my birthday party while my mom was making one of her health shakes. Her back was to me, her long dark hair cascading across her shoulders and back. She was probably in sweats and barefoot.

"Mom," I said, "here's my list. There are ten."

My mom glanced at the sheet of paper quickly and then said, "These are all boys, Chas. Don't you want any girls at your party?"

I looked up at her and saw this strange expression on her face, a look that I'd begun seeing more and more frequently. Her face was still, her lips drawn a bit more tightly. "*All* my friends are boys," I explained.

"You must have *some* friends who are girls."

I shook my head. "No." But I'd begun to feel bad: there was something wrong with not having girlfriends.

"Just ask a few girls from your class, okay?"

"Okay," I said, wondering how I was going to come up with three girls I could even tolerate. My mom brushed the top of my head, pulled the hair out of my eyes, and kissed my forehead.

I had always been a well-behaved, quiet kid who never gave my mother any trouble, so her anger, which was clearly directed at me, confused me. I began to feel nervous around my mother, which stirred up some of the anxiety I used to feel right after the divorce.

By the time my brother was two or three, my mother no longer worked with my dad. Most of the early confusion of shuffling between my parents' two houses had stopped. I saw my dad regularly, but I no longer had nervous reactions when I moved from one house to the other. I was getting older and began to assert some independence and choose my own clothes. I began my transformation into a tomboy, and as I did, I became aware that I was somehow different from other girls, and definitely different from what mom expected me to be.

I remember an incident vividly from around this time. My mother was traveling a lot for her career, and we were living in temporary housing while our house on Carolwood in Beverly Hills was being renovated — never a simple matter for my mom, who has always been slightly obsessed with decorating every corner and corridor of a home. I was about ten and just beginning to get my sea legs as my own person. My brother was about three and starting to terrorize everyone, especially me.

I came downstairs, ready for my nanny to drive me to school.

My mom came into the hallway to kiss me good-bye. She took one look at me and said, "Chas, you're wearing *that* to school?" I looked down at my red-decaled T-shirt, my gym shorts, and my beat-up Nikes. This was my uniform at home, so I didn't understand my mother's problem with what I was wearing. I thought I looked okay. My clothes were clean. I had even combed my hair.

"But Mom —" I began.

She cut me off. "Chas, you're going to school. Don't you want to wear something a little nicer? What about the blue-jean skirt I got you?"

"Mom — I can't wear *that*; I'll look like a loser."

But she wanted me to compromise, and I went along with her and wore the skirt with Wonder Woman patches all over it.

When I arrived at school, my friends looked at me in astonishment. Being boys, they started teasing me immediately. They called me a sissy; they wouldn't throw me the ball during recess. I was mortified. How could I be one of them in some silly skirt? I wanted to rip it off. In that instant, I vowed never to wear anything girlie again.

It's funny, but I think I stopped wearing dresses and skirts a lot younger than my mother recalls. It's as if as I began to change and have definite tastes, my mother clung to this image of me in a frilly dress. Like that of many parents, my mother's reaction was in part an unconscious expression of her not wanting me to grow up and become more separate from her. But I was also becoming someone who, on the outside at least, did not resemble either her or who she wanted me to be.

Because my dad seemed so much more at ease with my being a tomboy, I began to spend more time with him. In a way, I think I was the son my father never had. He'd play football with me in the backyard, challenging me to become the first female in the NFL, and take me to the track. He loved taking me to the horse races. I remember one time being dressed in a miniature Pierre Cardin suit to match my father's. I had invited my friend Ricky along, and we stopped at a toy store on the way so that Ricky and I could pick out toys: Ricky chose the Incredible Hulk action figure, and I decided on the Thing — not exactly a Barbie.

When my father encouraged my tomboyishness, my mother would get annoyed. I think in some ways they acted out their frustration with each other through me: my father would aggravate my mother by encouraging my boyish behavior, and my mother became more uncomfortable with me because she saw me as mimicking my father.

My mother is very direct, and it's impossible for her to hide her feelings. As a child, I knew how upset I made her, but I didn't know what to do. I couldn't wear dresses or be more feminine just to please her. Even today, she criticizes how I dress. As she says, "I don't like the way you dress, and you don't like the way I dress."

But the real problem, I now think, was that my mom's idea of closeness was premised on the idea that we had to be similar. As we became more and more dissimilar, she found it more and more difficult to relate to me. She says that she didn't think that I was gay until I was eleven, but I suspect that underneath her anxiety about our being "different" were fears that my tomboyishness hinted at latent homosexuality.

Midway through fourth grade, I met Gina, who was the younger sister of our weekend nanny, Colleen. Gina was three years older than I was, but like me, she was a total tomboy: she loved sports, didn't hang out with other girls, and basically did her own thing. We became instant best friends, and for the next three years, we did everything together. Gina's appearance by my side seemed to relieve my mom. I think the fact that I finally had a friend who was a girl made her worry less about me: maybe it meant I was turning into a "normal" girl after all.

I also remember the first day of sixth grade. I was starting at a Montessori school and was nervous. Having skipped so much school when I traveled with my mom, I had missed a lot of the fundamentals. As a result, school had become an intimidating place for me. To combat my tenseness, I decided to wear my new black leather jacket as a kind of defense. It worked: I didn't want the other kids to bother me, and they didn't.

My mother didn't have a problem with my outfit that day. I think she liked that I showed some interest in clothes that she thought were fashionable or cool and wore herself. That was the same year that she helped me dress up for Halloween as a Hell's Angel. The school was having a Halloween fair, and she came. I was dressed in head-to-toe leather, and she had drawn a tattoo on my arm with "Mom" written in the middle. You can't imagine how cool I thought I was!

I felt much more at ease with myself at the Montessori school. The teachers gave me a lot of individual attention and encouraged creative thinking, and I began to build up my confidence again. My awkwardness with feeling different lessened, and I became more comfortable with myself. I still look back on Montessori as one of the most positive experiences of my life.

Unfortunately, Montessori ended in sixth grade, and I started seventh grade in a new school. Curtis was a very posh, uniform-wearing private prep school, and I instantly hated it. Once again, I felt alienated from the majority around me. I could no longer be one of the boys because my figure was now showing very real signs of development. Yet I still felt as if I had nothing in common with the girls, especially those prep school girls, who were obsessed with fashion and boys.

With the exception of Gina, whom I'd see on weekends, I had no friends. I was again doing poorly in my classes. The one person who made school tolerable was the gym teacher, whom I had befriended. I spent most of my lunch periods with her because she seemed to understand me. I'm fairly sure she was a lesbian. She probably recognized me for the baby lesbian I was and sympathized with my obvious confusion and distress at school — thank God for gym teachers!

At home, my mom's behavior continued to distress me. Sometimes a simple preppy button-down shirt would upset her; other times she wouldn't bat an eye if I wore her black leather vest. When I started wearing her black leather jacket and steel-toed motorcycle boots regularly, she bought me my own. By that time she seemed to have given up trying to make me girlie, but that cloud of disapproval still hovered between us, and a certain distance had begun to creep into our relationship.

These memories of my childhood stand out as the first outward signs that I was somehow different — different from how my mother wanted me to be, and different from other girls. At school I'd look at the other girls with a kind of contempt. They never seemed to do anything, never said anything. To me, they were boring. But I knew my mother wanted me to be more like them. At the time, I didn't understand my mom's reaction to me, and this made me extremely anxious, almost frightened of her.

Part of the way I responded to my mom's questions and criticisms of what I was wearing and how I was behaving is related to the somewhat frenetic way we lived. I had never known anything but the excitement and commotion of my mother's career. She had always been an entertainer, and showbiz was the backdrop of my life from its beginning. But the older I became, the more I needed to have some control over my environment, and the constant motion exacerbated my sensitivity to her disapproval of me.

Seeds of Shame

As a child, of course, I didn't have the words to explain why I preferred dressing in boys' clothes. I didn't understand why I felt different or why my mother seemed so upset by certain things about me. In hindsight, it's obvious that my identifying more with boys than girls was natural for me, but it was very difficult for my mother. Though my mom admits having been a tomboy herself as a child, she didn't understand why her daughter seemed to go to such an extreme. From her perspective, I was being rebellious without cause. What reason did she give me to rebel? Why was I behaving this way?

Somehow my mother's own tomboyishness was acceptable to her, but not mine. I went too far. I was hurt and angry that she didn't accept me for who I was. Why did she have such a problem with my jeans and T-shirts, my long scraggly hair and boys' sneakers? When my mother became distracted by other people or her career, I was convinced that she was withdrawing from me because I disappointed her. Looking back, I see that aside from my mother's confusion about and difficulty with me, she had a lot of other demands in her life. She had to manage a growing career, take care of my younger brother and me, and bear the full responsibility for a large household as a single woman. But like any child, I wasn't aware of my mother's real life. I could only focus on her increasing distance from me.

In the past few years, as my mom and I have closed the gap between us, she has admitted to me that my masculine style of dress and manner made her suspect I was gay way before I had any notion of it myself. Her suspicions are common among parents of children or teenagers who don't neatly fit accepted gender roles. Children like myself who may identify more naturally with the opposite sex provoke anxiety in their parents. But as a child, I didn't understand why my behavior upset my mother. Her disapproval of my clothing choices meant only one thing: she disapproved of me. I heard her comments or questions about how I dressed and how I acted as criticisms of my entire person. I didn't understand the distinction between my mother's love for me and her discomfort with how I was expressing myself. And the end result was that I began to feel ashamed of who I was *because* I was different.

Gender Bending

In my conversations with gays and lesbians over the last few years, I began to uncover a similar map in their stories: first we feel different, then we are criticized or receive negative feedback, and then we internalize the criticism and become ashamed of who we are. This is what happened to me: I felt different, my mother disapproved of me, and I became ashamed. I believe that deciphering this map is the first step toward redefining ourselves in a positive way so that we can not only embrace ourselves as lesbians and gays but be proud of our difference, not ashamed.

As children and even as teenagers, we don't yet possess the language to communicate how or why we feel different, and when we are without the intellectual or psychological tools with which to make sense of our feelings, the feelings themselves can become exaggerated and overwhelming. We not only feel different, we feel ashamed of our difference. In their book *Coming Out of Shame*, Gershen Kaufman, Ph.D., and Lev Raphael, Ph.D., point out the impact of feeling different and its relationship to shame: "It is virtually impossible to be different, particularly in this culture, and not feel deficient for the difference, because any awareness of difference inevitably translates into a devaluing comparison. First we are devalued by others, and then we devalue ourselves." So at ages six, seven, eight, when we are convinced that we are different, we can also be convinced that we are inferior, deficient in some way we have no control over. This acute shame about ourselves is directly related to society's view that homosexuality is not just distinct from the norm, but abnormal.

RICHARD*

I met with Richard in his one-bedroom apartment in Chelsea, a popular gay neighborhood in New York City. Richard is a twenty-seven-year-old urban planner who, much like myself, identified with the opposite sex rather than his own as a child.

Richard was raised in an upper-middle-class Irish-Catholic family in a Connecticut suburb. Richard's father worked on Wall Street and commuted into Manhattan each weekday. His

* Certain names are first introduced with an asterisk to indicate the use of a pseudonym, out of respect for the privacy of individuals and their families and friends.

mother was an entrepreneur and developed several of her own businesses over the years.

The youngest child with four older sisters, Richard describes himself as always having been gentle, soft-spoken, slightly effeminate, and not particularly athletic or interested in sports. Like me, Richard had difficulty relating to his same-sex parent. "My father was in the army, and every time he and my mother would argue, my father's retort was 'I should have stayed in the army.' My father was always frustrated with his life — with his career, his marriage, his children. My mother paid little attention to him, and he hated being a stockbroker. He also had a temper and sometimes became violent. I was spared from his wrath, but not my sisters. There were occasions when he would rap them across their limbs or backsides. We were all scared of him, and I learned very early to be as quiet and docile as possible. You never knew what was going to trigger his outbursts.

"The older I got, the less my father and I had in common. He loved sports, especially football. I avoided contact sports like the plague. I would push myself into tennis or swimming, sports I could do on my own. He tried to encourage me to play sports, but I was just not that interested. He made me go to a real jocky summer camp, and I remember feeling completely out of my element.

"After a while, my father seemed to just avoid me and kept his distance. My mother would always badger him to spend more time with me. I would overhear these conversations and feel humiliated. It was clear that my father didn't know what to do with me because I was so different from him. Nowadays, all we can talk about is business. We have nothing in common. But when I was little, it was even harder."

Richard remembers his sisters actively trying to "toughen him up." "It was like they were obsessed with trying to teach me to be a boy because I didn't resemble one to them. They would curse at me or around me and push me around. Of course this didn't make me change. It just made me feel more ill at ease with myself."

Richard also recalls not fitting in with the majority of boys and feeling much more comfortable with girls. "I remember it always being awkward for me to befriend guys. There were all these things they would talk about, like sports or having sex with girls. I just wasn't interested in talking about those subjects."

When Richard was nine, his parents divorced, and he and his sisters moved to Manhattan with their mother. Living in New York City enabled Richard to feel much more comfortable. "I was in the big city, and there were many different kinds of people. I was exposed to kids who were Asian, Hispanic, Jewish. There were also different kinds of boys — nerdy, not all white-bread sports types. This was a huge relief. My mother was in fashion, so I also met gay men — not that I thought of them as gay at the time. But I could tell there was something different about them."

But his sisters kept on his case. Richard remembers when he was about eleven, two of his sisters took him to the school playground down the street to play basketball. "Terry* was getting more and more annoyed because I wasn't showing any interest in learning how to do a layup. Then she threw the ball at me. It hit me hard in the stomach and knocked the wind out of me. She was furious and I was furious. But I was also afraid of her. She made me feel like I was a total piece of shit."

The older he got, the more his sisters persisted. "I remember once when I was about fourteen, I had just bought all these neat clothes and I was going out to a party. It was summer, and I was wearing white balloon pants, a black satin shirt buttoned to the top, and black suede pointed shoes. I felt very cool and was excited to go to the party. When I came downstairs, my sister Terry shrieked and said, 'Oh, my God — you can't go out looking like that. You look like a' — and then she couldn't finish her sentence. I was devastated. I knew what she meant. I could hear the word *faggot* ringing in the air." Richard not only changed his clothes that evening, but from then on, he became much more self-conscious about how he dressed.

In the same way that my mother questioned my only having male friends, Richard's mother questioned the fact that all of his friends seemed to be girls. When he was about sixteen, his mother remarked that all he seemed to talk about were the girls in his class — how glamorous they were, how smart and interesting. "My mother finally said to me, 'I don't want to hear about those girls anymore. Don't you have any friends who are boys?' I got the message. That's when I started to realize that I had to censor myself."

Soon after, Richard began dating girls. "I think it had to do with proving to everyone and myself that I was capable of it." Like many gay men, Richard felt more comfortable with girls than with straight guys, whose interests he generally didn't share.

Since the acceptable gender roles for boys and men are even more strict than they are for girls and women, Richard received even more criticism for being different than I did.

In her groundbreaking study *Gender Shock*, Phyllis Burke explores this rigidity of gender roles in our society and its effect on the natural development of identity. She writes:

> In our early gender training, we are taught that there is something we are able to do, but are forbidden, because of our sex. Every child has this experience, sometimes consciously, sometimes not. It is a moment when the mind stops, experiencing a break in time, as a crucial facet of our identity is socially decreed: our behavior, or gender role, is determined by our sex, or body. Although

the assigned gender role is declared absolute, definite, permanent and immutable, most of us secretly do not believe in every aspect of the role. A boy is told that boys do not skip, or jump rope, but he knows that his body is capable of skipping. A girl is told not to physically fight because she is a girl, but she knows that her anger is as real as her fist.

My experience and Richard's mirror each other in several ways: we both had a distant, disapproving parent, felt alienated from the other kids, and were generally uncomfortable with feeling somehow different. Both Richard and I were criticized for stepping outside the prescribed gender roles that our parents felt comfortable with. In turn, we responded to our parents' anxiety by becoming uncomfortable with ourselves. Whereas Richard tried to change his behavior (playing basketball with his sister and later dating girls to prove his masculinity), I withdrew rather than force myself to change. But in both cases, we actively suppressed parts of ourselves.

Seeds of Homophobia

BEN

Ben, who is at thirty-one an ordained minister of the United Church of Christ, a mainstream Protestant denomination, grew up in Henderson, Kentucky. He describes his family this way: "We were a well-adjusted, professional, happy household. Both my parents were educators who encouraged my sister and me to be successful. My father played golf and wasn't that involved at home, though that has since changed. We were very close and loving."

Ben seems to embody the spirit of a minister. He is thoughtful, sincere, and guileless. Like Richard, he recalls being aware of feeling different from most other boys while growing up and links that early sense of not fitting in to his eventually becoming a minister. "In hindsight, I remember having a real heightened sense of other people's pain. When I was eleven years old I was part of a children's group that started a child-abuse prevention organization, and we became well-known in the regional area of the state. I devoted hours and hours to it while other kids were outside playing. I see a real connection between my always identifying with people who were hurting and my being gay."

When I asked him to explain this connection, he recalled being teased "all through my elementary school years. They called me 'queer' or 'sissy' or 'faggot.' I was by no means the only kid being teased. It was perfectly accepted and tolerated, not only by the other kids but also by the teachers and other adults. It didn't matter if the child was really gay or not. The words were used as slurs. But for young people who know they are gay or are struggling with those issues, the teasing is even more frustrating and hurtful. There you are in the park or playground, and you have to hide who you are; you're thinking, 'How do they know this about me?' As children, we don't understand that these are words being said indiscriminately to many young people; they're fighting words, street words, playground words."

The teasing made Ben immediately aware that he did not fit in with the others. It made him feel ashamed of himself because even then he knew that the difference he felt was difficult for others to accept. In the same way that Richard's sisters pressured him to be more masculine, the teasing put pressure on Ben to conform. "For me there was a real need to be accepted by my peers. I became more self-conscious with the name-calling. I wasn't especially effeminate as a young person. I played sports. But I was very kind and considerate, always sat up straight in my chair and didn't talk when I wasn't supposed to, I was always real attentive, I was a musician and sang and played the piano, good student, so most of the name-calling came from a set of kids that looked at me as a Goody Two-shoes; I doubt they thought the word *gay* — maybe they did; the term *fag* can mean so many things to a kid — they don't necessarily intend the slur to mean gay or lesbian."

But the words are definitely pejorative, and every kid in school knows that association. In fact, "faggot" and "queer" are some of the few slurs associated with a minority group that are still used with regularity by adults too and are not yet culturally censored, as is the case with "nigger" or "kike" or other defaming descriptions of oppressed groups or minorities. The fact that "fag" and "dyke" are still tolerated terms reinforces the shameful feelings associated with homosexuality.

Ben continues, "I remember always really trying to watch my actions in new situations, such as a class trip or a new school. I would always hope that in the next phase of my life, things would be different. I struggled to not let on that the other kids were getting to me with their teasing, but I could not hide the fact that it did bother me, and this just added to the verbal abuse. I got defensive, I didn't play along, got quiet or upset or nervous. In the process of maturing in high school and finding a group of friends that were supportive, I realized that I was not the class fag, the one who was always excluded. In fact, if they were asked now, I think my peers would probably remember me as popular."

Sometimes the abuse for being different is not limited to hurtful words. All too often homophobia can be expressed with physical violence, and some of this violence is directed at children who not only have little understanding of what *gay* means but cannot defend themselves from attack. And while the nation is becoming less and less tolerant of such hate crimes, their continued occurrence needs to be eradicated completely.

BRUCE

Bruce, who is now nineteen and works at a retail shop in the small Indiana town where he grew up, describes his experience with not fitting in. "Even in kindergarten I felt different from most of the other kids in class. I remember having my first crush in kindergarten; I didn't have a word for it at the time, but I liked being around this kid and smiled a lot when I was around him."

Unlike Richard, the urban planner, Bruce recalls having had a close relationship with his father. "My father and I are very different. He's this big lumberjack kind of a guy, and I'm effeminate." Despite their differences, Bruce and his father spent a lot of time together when Bruce was growing up. "My dad was very involved in my life. We'd play ball, put together my bike, and sometimes he would even play dolls with me. My father didn't treat me any differently than he did his older son, my half-brother."

But throughout elementary school, Bruce was teased by the other kids. "A lot of times I wouldn't go out and play; I'd sit on the swing set and just talk with the girls. I didn't want people to call me sissy or girlie if I wanted to play games like dolls. I think I knew immediately that they were feelings to be ashamed about." Bruce tried to change his behavior but was unsuccessful. "No matter how hard I tried, I could never pass."

Then, in a matter-of-fact voice he says, "The first time I was gay bashed was in third grade. I was walking home from school and I was tackled by three older kids. They were probably in the fifth grade. Two of them held my arms down and one punched me in the stomach and called me a 'fag' and 'queer.' I knew they sensed something about me that they hated, and it scared me because that meant there was something wrong with me. At the time I felt lucky that they hit me in the stomach and not the face, because then I didn't have to tell my mom what happened. I was convinced that she'd have the same reaction. But I remember feeling very scared, lonely, and vulnerable. I had no one to turn to."

Richard, Ben, Bruce, and I all experienced being different in terms of gender: we didn't fit what was generally accepted behavior or appearance for our sex. However, sometimes gays and lesbians feel different in more subtle ways. On the outside they may conform quite neatly to what is considered normal for their sex, but inside they recall feeling nagging doubts about whether they *really* fit in.

JUDY

Judy, who is forty, grew up in Washington state and is the third of four children. Both she and her youngest brother, Dave, are gay. Judy now works in real estate and shares custody of her two children with her former husband. Judy's father, a retired Methodist minister, and her mother raised their family in a comfortable upper-middle-class household. Judy describes her parents as "mainstream liberals."

"My parents were easygoing and approachable. I had a rather nondramatic childhood. But I was always restless," she recalls. "I was a terrible kid. I'd sneak out in the middle of the night. I was the preacher's kid that hated church." In hindsight Judy interprets her uneasiness as a child and young adult as an indication of her prehomosexuality. She continues, "I was very rebellious and had only a 1.2 or 1.3 grade point average." Her low achievement in high school is linked to her internalized negative feelings about being somehow different from her peers. Whereas I didn't fit in with other girls in obvious, concrete ways, specifically choosing to wear more masculine clothes, Judy masked her questions about herself by rebelling against her parents.

"I was definitely a tomboy and had a lot of male friends, but I was very much a girl." But, she explains, she always felt troubled: "I was definitely searching. There was something about myself that I just didn't understand. I thought I'd outgrow the feeling." At the time, her parents only reinforced her shameful feelings about herself. "I remember hearing my dad tell my mom that he didn't think I'd make it through high school," she recalls.

But those feelings of difference didn't disappear; they just went underground. Like many gays and lesbians, Judy pushed away her feelings of inadequacy. She says, "I guess I just started putting my feelings aside. By the time I graduated from college, I had a map of the rest of my life: I was going to be married by the time I was twenty-three, with kids by twenty-six or twenty-seven. I had all my goals in line. I was so focused on where I was going, I didn't let myself have time to think about how I felt about anything."

Her life plan did help alleviate that inner, unnamable anxiety for a while. "Then there I was, married with a couple of kids, and then I was like, 'Oh, now I know how I feel, and I don't feel very good.'" Her lingering doubts were becoming larger, more concrete, but she was still unable to identify the root of her dissatisfaction. "At the time I didn't know why I felt so unsettled. After I was married, I knew I had made a mistake. The problem wasn't my husband. He is a wonderful guy and a terrific father."

Judy seemed to have repressed the source of her dissatisfaction. The thoughts and feelings were too frightening for her to address at a conscious level, so she pushed her feelings aside and didn't deal with them until she was in a more stable place in her life, when she had more to fall back on and had given herself a clear identity as a wife, mother, and professional.

Judy very clearly pushed away her vague, unnerving feelings and tried to live up to the image of a typical woman by marrying, having children, and doing what she thought was expected of her. Although she remembers always feeling "restless" and "unsettled," Judy wasn't able to identify why she felt this way until she was thirty-one, when she fell in love with a woman.

Turning the Shame Inward

Although both Ben and Judy sensed they were different and obviously felt some anxiety about themselves, they turned to positive outlets to sublimate or channel the feelings: they both developed positive feelings about themselves through school activities in the case of Ben, and in Judy's case through work and in her role as a mother.

However, that's not always the case. Often, gays and lesbians turn the shame of feeling different toward themselves and become self-destructive. As Kaufman and Raphael say, "Because of the close connection between the awareness of difference and shame, being gay or lesbian inescapably marks us as lesser."

SARAH*

Sarah, who grew up in a middle-class Jewish family on Long Island and is now a television producer in Los Angeles, said she was "different, but it didn't manifest necessarily in masculine ways. I was definitely more inclined to play with GI Joe than Barbie, but I didn't necessarily look or act like a tomboy. I played sports and was tougher than the other girls, but they all looked up to me. I was a leader, and a lot of my girlfriends wanted to please me," she recalls. "But this was confusing. There was something I wanted from my friends, but I had no way of expressing it — to myself or to them. As a result, there was always friction between us."

But the shame was there. "I got into drugs when I was very young. I think I tried pot when I was eleven, and then got into quaaludes, speed, and acid. The druggie group at school was asexual, so I fit in. I didn't want to deal with my sexuality at all, so I denied it, blocked it out through drugs. In high school I became a Deadhead, an artist, but doing drugs was what pretty much organized my life."

Why did Sarah turn to drugs, an obvious self-destructive behavior? She explains that at the time, in the early 1980s, drugs were plentiful at school. "My two older sisters were following in my parents' footsteps, preparing to get married and settle down. That seemed so boring to me. I knew I was different, but I also think I was naturally rebellious." She sees that even though she thought of herself as "tough" when she was younger, she wasn't able to manage her feelings about being different. "I didn't want to deal with how I was different, so I did drugs."

MELISSA*

Melissa grew up in an affluent Chicago suburb. As she admits, "My parents spoiled me and my brother. There was nothing I couldn't ask for." And like Judy and Sarah, she was popular and a leader of her social clique all through middle school. However, as her internal questions and doubts began to surface in high school, Melissa became promiscuous and self-destructive. "I think I slept around with guys because I didn't want to face the fact that I was really attracted to women. I did a lot of drugs — smoked pot almost every day at school. I just couldn't deal." It took another fifteen years for Melissa to finally be able to accept herself fully.

As we'll see in the stories throughout this book, many gays and lesbians have become self-destructive at one time or another. The threat and reality of being rejected or excluded because of our difference can sometimes be so painful that it's easier to take the pain out on ourselves. In the moment, the drugs, alcohol, even running away, can feel like an escape — but this is only a temporary solution to shameful feelings.

SYDNEY

There is a minority of gays and lesbians who don't recall ever feeling different. One woman I spoke with enjoyed dating men for years before discovering that she was a lesbian. Sydney, who is African American, was born when her parents were both in their forties. Her father spent a twenty-five-year career in the Urban League after receiving his degree from Yale Divinity School. Sydney's mother was an educator before becoming a stay-at-home mom. Now thirty-six, Sydney works in research at a university library in central New York state.

When I asked Sydney if she ever felt different growing up, she declared emphatically no, and then said, "I went to the United Nations school with hundreds of kids from around the world. The only kids who were perceived as different were those who arrived at school not being able to speak English."

In Sydney's case, any possible or latent sense that she was different never developed, because she was exposed to children of so many various backgrounds. This is interesting: it seems to imply that the more narrow our exposure, the more likely it is that we will experience our "difference" as negative or shameful. It also seems to imply that if being different didn't have a negative value, then it wouldn't be a shame-based feeling or characteristic: being different in terms of sexual orientation could be seen as a genetic trait like left-handedness or blue eyes.

When we are younger, before we have any sexual experience, there are few straightforward clues that we may be lesbian or

gay. Many of us don't even possess the words in our vocabu-
lary. We just feel different, and it is this feeling of difference
that is often the first sign that we may be gay. In general, this
stage is associated with the middle school years, before most
of us have a concrete awareness of ourselves as sexual beings,
and has more to do with the trappings of gender: clothes, activities, sports, and other ways of presenting ourselves. Although we can experience sexual feelings from a very young
age, we don't usually have the conceptual framework to categorize such feelings as sexual desires. The most we do is call
our feelings "crushes" — and God knows we've all had crushes,
even as early as first grade!

As we all know, the playground and the classroom can be vicious places, where competition and cliques often rule, and
most kids, even the most popular, feel insecure when confronted with the pressures of fitting in. But many gays and lesbians become overwhelmed with the belief that our difference
is unacceptable. Sometimes it takes years for us to understand
that these early feelings of difference created an inner source
of shame, and the impact of this early shame leaves scars.

When I was growing up, the more I resisted conforming
to my mom's version of being a girl, the further apart we grew,
and the older I got, the more strained our relationship became.
For the next few years, until I came out to myself at thirteen,
we reached a kind of truce that was premised on "don't ask,
don't tell." Neither of us wanted to dwell on the awkward feelings between us. But my distance from my mother, and hers
from me, was painful.

The stress of those early years, most specifically my
mother's reaction to me, stayed with me throughout my childhood and most of my adulthood. It has only been in the last
few years, when as an adult I began to process both my own in-
securities and my difficulties with my mother, that I have

been able to uproot from my heart the shame of being and feeling different. The more I have spoken with other lesbians and gays around the country, the more I realize I have not been alone. Many of us have begun the often long, excruciating process of unraveling our histories so that we can see our difference as positive, not negative. This process, though painful, is not only necessary to accepting yourself, but also essential if you want to be truly happy.

Chapter 2

Recognizing Ourselves
Personal Best

*"Written on the body is a secret code only visible
in certain lights; the accumulations of a lifetime
gather there. In places the palimpsest is so heavily
worked that the letters feel like braille."*

JEANETTE WINTERSON,
from *Written on the Body*

Two Girls Kissing

I realized I was gay when I turned thirteen. Ben realized he was
gay at eleven. Judy didn't realize she was gay until she was
thirty-one. There is no fixed time that someone realizes that
he or she is gay. Many factors contribute to the timing of when
we put a name to why we feel different from those around us.
Everything plays a part: religious or cultural backgrounds, the
extent of our exposure to lesbians or gays in everyday life, the
attitudes of our parents, the media's treatment of homosexuals, and our age.

But still, many gay people speak of a specific moment
when they realized they were gay. We may know gay people,
may even know what homosexuality means, but we don't nec-

essarily put two and two together until we are ready. Being ready may mean our bodies are maturing and as a result we are more sexually aware. We begin to wonder about ourselves as sexual beings. We can experience this consciousness gradually or all at once, as I did.

In the middle of my seventh-grade year, my mom, Elijah, and I moved to New York when my mother got the part of Sissy in the play *Come Back to the Five and Dime, Jimmy Dean, Jimmy Dean*. I was completely relieved to be leaving Curtis, which I hated, and I had always liked visiting New York. Also, whenever my mom began a new project — in this case a four-month run on Broadway — she'd become more focused on work, which conveniently allowed me time and space to do my own thing. And at thirteen I was craving my freedom.

We moved into the Mayflower Hotel, on the southwest edge of Central Park. I was used to living in hotels at that point, and the Mayflower is a low-key, almost eccentric hotel. I loved its location near the park; I could either walk or take the uptown bus to my new school, Walden, which was farther north on the Upper West Side. Similar to the Montessori school I had gone to for sixth grade, Walden was a liberal, progressive school that encouraged individual and creative learning. The school had a casual, artsy atmosphere that made me feel comfortable. I always did much better in this kind of environment. I joined the basketball and softball teams, and instantly I felt better about myself. Playing sports, even football with my dad, always nourished my self-esteem, making me feel stronger and more vital. Walden's students came from various social and ethnic backgrounds, and this diversity lessened my sense that I was different from the other kids, especially from the girls. Soon I had made a few friends, and my life seemed much better than it had been in Los Angeles, where my only friend was Gina.

Though I'd visited New York many times before, I had never really appreciated the city. Now I was old enough to ride the subway, take the bus, or walk, so I was no longer dependent on someone to pick me up or take me where I needed or wanted to go. New York soon became synonymous with freedom. After school, I roamed the city. Any outing seemed like an adventure, whether I went to the movies, downtown to the Village to shop, or to the park to meet other kids. Sometimes I'd visit my mom in the theater district and watch her during rehearsal. I loved being backstage and part of all the commotion among the actors, the director, the lighting guys. The theater was very familiar territory for me.

For my thirteenth birthday in March, my mom surprised me by flying Gina out from Los Angeles for a weekend visit. Gina and I had remained in touch, and I was dying to show her the city. She'd never been to New York. I had been hearing about a new movie, *Personal Best*, starring Mariel Hemingway. All I knew about the film was that it centered on two female athletes, and I was determined to drag Gina with me.

Personal Best was already becoming a lesbian classic; it would also be the catalyst for my realization that I was gay.

The movie opens with the camera on Mariel Hemingway as Chris, in the middle of a long-distance race, which she loses. The winner, Tory (played by Patrice Donnelly), begins to follow Chris with her eyes for the rest of the track meet. Later that night, we see Chris with her father at a restaurant, where everyone but Chris is celebrating. Still upset about her loss, Chris stays behind when her father leaves the restaurant. When Tory observes Chris crying, she invites her back to her apartment. In the next scene, Chris and the winner are relaxing on the floor in front of the television. Then they begin to kiss.

There I was, sitting in the dark movie theater, completely enthralled as I watched two attractive women embracing on the big screen. Not only had I never seen two women kiss, I never imagined that it would look and feel so completely beautiful and natural. I immediately related to the women on screen: suddenly I got it; I got me.

In one dramatic moment, I could put a name to all those feelings from my childhood that I had been unable to categorize. All the questions, the doubts, the not fitting in, suddenly made sense. My identification with the two girls, the situation, the feelings, the desires, was immediate. I knew instantly that I was "gay."

Before seeing *Personal Best*, I was aware that other kids in school were getting together as couples. I knew they were "making out," but since I had no interest in kissing boys, I thought I wasn't very interested in kissing at all — until I saw two girls kissing. Suddenly it was as if my hormones had exploded inside of me. The emerging sexual feelings were no longer abstract or free-floating; instead, they'd become attached to a very real, concrete image: the two girls kissing. It wasn't until my hormones started to kick in that I was able to attach my feelings of difference to the idea of being gay.

In the movie theater, I was both relieved and excited to realize that I was gay. I finally understood myself. This relief, however, was countered with an immediate sense of trepidation: I knew I couldn't breathe a word of my discovery, especially to either of my parents. Besides, I wasn't yet *completely* sure myself.

After my mom's Broadway play closed that spring of 1982, we relocated for the summer to Las Vegas, where she was appearing in a cabaret-style show. As usual, Gina came along to keep me company. We stayed in Caesar's Palace and basically had the run of the place: we ordered room service, played in the pool, watched all the strange people float through the hotel.

Gina and I soon met two busboys at the hotel, and in pure teenage fashion, the four of us arranged ourselves into couples and began to date. For me, deciding to date this young guy was a way of testing the idea of whether I was *really* gay.

When my mom got word through the cast that I had a boyfriend, she was ecstatic. As usual, she didn't say anything directly to me, but I definitely heard about how happy she was from the wardrobe guys and the dancers. Like any child, I felt wonderful knowing that I had made my mother happy.

Meanwhile, after a few short weeks of trying to hold hands and cuddle with my "boyfriend," I lost interest. Thankfully, Gina had lost interest in hers as well, and both of us were just as happy to go back to our routine of hanging around the dancers for my mom's show.

But something about having tried to date this young man made me want to tell Gina that I thought I was gay. I didn't really plan it, but all summer long I had kept thinking it: "I'm gay." The words were always on the tip of my tongue. I kept thinking about certain girls in my class, the gym teacher at school, and friends of my mother's, and realized that my feelings for them were "special." Suddenly I realized that I had had a crush on my mom's friend Kate Jackson, that when I imagined cuddling with her, kissing her, I was having *fantasies*. The more I thought about this new fact about myself, the more tense I became and the more my secret started to weigh on me. I couldn't get the images from *Personal Best* out of my head. I had to tell someone. Finally I took the step.

Gina and I were in the Jacuzzi in my mom's suite, which overlooked the Vegas Strip. The music was blaring, and I had just dunked under the water. I took a deep breath and said softly, "Gina, I have something to tell you."

"What?"

"Well, I think I'm gay?" I said it as a question, afraid of her response, not knowing what she was going to say.

Gina, who was fifteen at the time and going into her sophomore year of high school, just kind of shrugged and said, "What's the big deal?"

I was completely relieved.

Gina and I never really talked about the subject again that summer. Her nonreaction helped me feel more comfortable and sure that I was a lesbian. Like many of us when we are young, I looked to my friend to see if *I* was okay, and since Gina, who was straight then and still is today, never seemed bothered by the fact that I was gay, my immediate fears were allayed. But I still wasn't near ready to share this information about myself with anyone else.

Keeping the Secret

BEN

When I spoke to Ben, the minister, about how and when he realized he was gay, he told me he also felt relieved — and kept it secret. "I remember a distinct moment in sixth or seventh grade of looking in the bathroom mirror and saying to myself that I was gay. I can remember the scene: I was alone in the house; no one was there. I was in the bathroom that I shared with my sister. We each had a sink and a mirror. I stood there and looked in the mirror and said two things out loud: 'You are gay,' and 'You can keep a secret.'

"Both of those were equal affirmations for me at that age. I was not personally condemning myself. I didn't think I was suddenly this awful person. I see that as really central, that I didn't have a lot of self-hatred. I just thought of it [being gay] as a complete inconvenience." But it's significant that, like me, Ben felt he needed to keep his homosexuality secret. No matter how relieved we both felt finally understanding who we were, we also responded to an internalized need to censor this information.

Ben attributes his essential positive feelings about himself, especially his nonjudgmental feelings about being gay, to the fact that his family had always encouraged him and his sister to be aware of and get involved with people less fortunate. He says, "My family was very interested in social justice issues. We ate dinner together and talked about current events. My mother tells me that I always led the discussions. I remember distinctly that we were encouraged to talk freely, to form and express our own opinions."

This openness and ability to speak his mind seem to have helped Ben learn to love himself, and this strong self-esteem affected his reaction to learning he was gay. But he also thought that he had to keep this information about himself hidden. He wasn't yet sure how others would react, but he knew they might not react as positively as he felt. It is this threat of condemnation or criticism that makes most of us keep the knowledge that we are gay secret initially, especially from our parents.

PAUL

Paul grew up in South Carolina, in a strict Southern Baptist household, and realized he was gay in the sixth grade. Now thirty-one, he is a successful computer artist. Paul's manner of dealing with the discovery that he was gay shows again how we can feel at once relieved at the knowledge and frightened of the possible consequences. When I talked to him about his childhood and the years that led up to his discovery that he was gay, I could still hear pain in his voice. "I was the first boy in my class to go through puberty, and I remember feeling extremely self-conscious in physical education class. Sixth grade was also the first year that we were bused to school. The very first day on the bus, the seventh and eighth graders were hassling the younger sixth graders as we got on the bus, saying, 'Are you gay?' By the end of the bus ride, I figured out that *gay* meant you liked boys, and I remember thinking, 'Wow, that's what I am.'

"Later that year, I wrote three notes on two-by-two-inch-square pieces of paper, saying, 'Dear Mom and Dad, I love you very much. I am gay. This is not your fault. I am still your son. Love, Paul.' Then I folded the three pieces of paper until they couldn't get any smaller and hid them in obscure places in the house — one I stuck into the center of a fake plant that had been on display in the center of the dining-room table for years. I stuck the note down in the green Styrofoam among the stems. I put the other on top of my dad's old college textbooks, way up on top of a bookcase with two inches of dust on them. I can't remember where I placed the other. For the next three years, I went along fine. I wasn't racked with guilt, because I felt I had solved the problem for myself. I reasoned that if they were meant to know, then they would find one of these notes; if they weren't meant to know, then the notes would stay where they were."

In one way, Paul's eleven-year-old reasoning helped him gain some affirmation about himself. He wrote the notes as a way to relieve the pressure of the newly discovered part of his identity without risking full disclosure, which could bring negative consequences. At some level, he was aware that his parents would disapprove, and he wasn't ready to handle that kind of rejection. In this way, Paul was testing this new information about himself: he wanted, needed, to control his environment and the possible reactions of others while he became more familiar with his feelings on his own terms. But clearly the threat of rejection and disapproval remained in the air.

Paul continues, "During seventh grade, I was really attracted to an older student. He was a really good athlete but kind of a delinquent. The guy had been left back a couple of times. I never got close to him, but I remember he started noticing that I had a crush on him. Then he told his friends. This was right before my parents found the note. I remember feeling like things could get dangerous for me. I was scared."

Looking back, Paul realizes that he was rightfully frightened. When his parents and classmates discovered that Paul was gay, they did indeed reject him. Paul received such brutal treatment both at school and at home that he ended up running away. As we will see later in the book, it wasn't until Paul's brother, Davis, came out ten years later that their parents began the slow, arduous process of acceptance.

There is no doubt in my mind that coming out to ourselves is one of the most positive, life-affirming events in our lives. The enormous relief, the self-satisfaction, and the sense of being honest with ourselves enables us to take our first steps toward living a full, happy life. However, no matter how old we are, coming out is also frightening. It's a good idea to make sure it's "safe" to tell someone. In my case, telling Gina wasn't a big risk. We were best friends; we'd been hanging out with the gay dancers in my mom's show all summer in Las Vegas. Without fully articulating her attitude to myself, I had been observing her with gay people and watching how she interacted easily and freely with them. When I told her I was gay, I felt fairly certain that she wouldn't reject me. But everyone I spoke with remembers some amount of risk; most of us kept the news secret while we tried to absorb the information ourselves. This kind of surveying is both common and wise. As we begin to try to integrate our homosexuality into our identity as a whole, we need to be aware of the attitudes of those around us and avoid subtle rejection, hurtful words, or outright attacks before we have developed a strong sense of pride in being gay and gained the necessary support from the gay community.

Paul, Ben, and I realized we were gay at the onset of puberty, but for others hormonal surges are not enough to cause the realization. Some lesbians and gays are not ready until much later in their lives. What does "ready" mean? Many things. Ready may mean that a person has amassed enough experience to be convinced that he or she is *really* gay. Being ready can also reflect an intellectual understanding of homosexuality that is necessary before the person is able to reconcile the negative cultural and religious judgments of homosexuality with the fact of his or her sexual orientation.

DAVE

Judy's younger brother Dave is now thirty-two and an insurance executive in Seattle. As the youngest of four children, he remembers "playing games" with other young boys from eight years old through high school. Dave admits that from day one he was more effeminate than other boys in his class. "I had a Dorothy Hamill haircut and wore loose turtlenecks that were almost like cowl necks. I guess I dressed more like a woman, not that I'm into the transvestite thing. But back then I remember feeling more comfortable in clothes that were looser. As early as third grade, I remember going into the local drugstore to glance through the soft-porn magazines like *Playboy* and *Playgirl*. I was curious about both of them, wanting to look at both men's bodies and women's. But when my dad used to take me to the gym, I was always too shy to really take notice of anything. I was already painfully shy about getting naked in front of other men. Junior high was a real nightmare in gym class. I felt incredibly vulnerable, exposed, silly. When they would separate the girls and the boys in gym, and the girls would go do gymnastics and the guys would go wrestle, I would much rather have been doing gymnastics. I didn't want to be scrutinized for how manly I could be; I didn't want to have to demonstrate how masculine I was, how much of a dude I was."

Dave's sense of shame for not fitting in and for his latent homosexual feelings is palpable. It took years for him to unhinge these feelings of self-loathing and learn to like all of himself.

It wasn't until college that Dave actually admitted to himself that he was gay. By that time, he had not only had a number of same-sex experiences, he knew there was a name for those experiences. In retrospect, he says his unwillingness to identify his quite blatant homosexual behavior as evidence of his being gay was fueled by both his disgust with what he was doing and his fear that he would become a social outcast. At the same time, Dave didn't, couldn't, change his behavior. In other words, as much as he was at times filled with self-loathing (internalized shame) for his actions, he couldn't stop himself from wanting to be with or touch other men.

Dave's experience captures the many mixed feelings we have as we begin to assimilate our homosexuality into our self-image. His shyness in the locker room reflected his discomfort with his own emerging sexual feelings toward men. At the time, he'd rather have been separate from other men, because his feelings seemed too big and hard to handle.

For Dave, realizing and then accepting he was gay was a five-year process. This is common. A number of gays and lesbians I spoke with went through similar testing periods, myself included. Dave says, "I dated women in high school and college. I had sex with them. For the most part they were really good relationships, but there was something missing — both emotional and sexual. With a woman I felt like we were two gears that didn't quite click into each other. But I had a very close friend in high school, Kurt*. In our senior year Kurt and I were taking a class together called 'Performance Workshop.' We spent a lot of time outside of school building a miniature set for *Death of a Salesman.*

"Once he spent the night at my house so we could work on the set. At some point we started wrestling around, and all of a sudden we realized that there was something going on between us. We spent the night together, mostly just touching. It got a little sexual, but we never kissed. We both knew that if we kissed it meant we were gay, and at that time I still didn't think I was gay. I didn't think the label applied to me. I just thought of us as good friends. We called ourselves 'flush friends.' We knew there was a boundary we couldn't cross. I think if we'd crossed it, we wouldn't have been able to handle it then.

"I tried to talk myself out of it. At the time it was too intense to take it any further. I felt like Sybil: there was a side of me that was completely repulsed by the whole thing and wanted to put it out of memory. Whenever I saw Kurt, I would get this ache in my back, like this is wrong. But part of me wanted more. Looking back on it, it was magic — if only my other dates now were more like that," he says wistfully. Then he continues, "Two weeks later, Kurt and I ended up getting into a fight over how many steps there were in the staircase in the *Death of a Salesman* set. We never spoke to each other after that. I don't know where he is now." Although Dave sought out and enjoyed his experience with Kurt, he was also disgusted with himself. He no longer feels this way, but he says it took a number of years to feel good about being gay.

He explains the dichotomy this way: "I think a lot of it had to do with the images of gay people in the media at the time; when they would show gay people on the news, it was always that stock footage — men with receding hairlines and mustaches, with their hands in each other's back pockets, dressed in lavender-colored tank tops, walking down the Castro. These were the only gay images I saw then. I remember looking at *The Joy of Gay Sex* in the library and seeing the same men in handlebar mustaches. I just didn't relate to these images — not that I have a problem with *who* they are. They were just so far removed from who I was, growing up in an upper-middle-class suburb outside of Seattle. I felt like I was an ugly duckling looking for myself as a swan."

Given the shame Dave experienced regarding his sexual feelings, his five-year struggle to acknowledge and begin to accept his homosexuality makes sense. A few years later, when Dave was a junior in college, he pushed himself to speak to a counselor in the college's gay and lesbian center. With this kind of support, he was finally able to admit to himself that he was gay and start the process of integrating this information about himself. Now he looks back sympathetically at his former self: "It's such a relief not to be in that place anymore."

NINA

Nina told me a similar story. She too was reluctant to admit that her feelings for women meant that she was gay. Nina, whose mother is African American and her father Caucasian, grew up in New Jersey and now, at thirty-six, lives in Maryland and works for a nonprofit environmental education organization. When I talked to her, she emphasized that she didn't think her coming out was late; rather, she believes that she just wasn't ready until she left home for college. She also didn't think of herself as specifically different from girls or boys growing up. She explains: "Though I was a tomboy, I definitely found a community with other girls who were athletic. When I hit puberty, I had a hard time wearing makeup, but I was still comfortable being a woman." She didn't give much thought to her sexuality beyond dating boys in high school. "I was attracted to the guys I went out with, but I do remember feeling a bit uncomfortable in the sense that I wasn't very interested in or excited by sex — I felt like I needed to be with guys because my female friends had boyfriends.

"As I got older — sixteen, seventeen, eighteen years old — I was spending more time with my female friends. I didn't realize until after I came out that what I had been feeling was much more significant than just friendship — but I didn't know it then." For college Nina decided on a small liberal arts school outside of Boston that had a strong athletic program. "I was playing field hockey and other sports, and spent most of my time with the other women athletes. I knew these women were different from the majority of the women at school, but I still wasn't conscious of *how* they were different. They didn't date guys and hung out among themselves exclusively. I thought I might have something in common with these women, but I didn't know what that was. I was dating a guy, who I really liked, and Bill and I had a lot of fun, but I was still drawn to my women friends like a magnet. When I was with him, I was always curious about how my women friends were spending their time.

"One Friday night a few of the women asked me to join them dancing at a club in Boston. All of a sudden, we're all in the car, and I realize that the other four were two couples! It finally dawned on me that they were gay. I thought, 'Holy shit, these women are together.' I became really anxious but didn't say anything to them. Then we went to the women's club. After a while I started to relax and enjoy myself. It was awesome. I was really comfortable. I loved the atmosphere — just being around all these women. I began to realize that this was what I'd been feeling, this was why I was gravitating to these women."

But Nina admits that she was reluctant to say she was gay right away. "It wasn't like that night completely convinced me I was gay. It was a pretty big night, but there had been and still was a certain degree of hesitation for me. I continued to go to the women's club and sometimes even brought some of my straight friends. That didn't make them gay. And for me, I just wanted to see how comfortable I was. I was still open to the possibility that it was just the environment I liked."

Nina had not known any gay people growing up, but she did have a built-in negative attitude toward homosexuals. "At that time [the sixties and seventies], my mother was involved with NOW, and she apparently knew gay women, but homosexuality wasn't talked about in the family or with my peers. If I heard reference to it at all, the association was always in a negative context, with words like *fag* or *queer.* I didn't really know what it meant, but the person was dismissed quickly."

Nina's hesitation about admitting she was gay seems directly related to the negative cultural associations with homosexuality. She says, "I bet if I hadn't heard the negative stuff about being gay, I may have realized I was gay sooner." As it turned out, Nina identified that she was a lesbian when, later in her freshman year, she found herself interested in another woman. "We were at a party, and I was very attracted to her. Suddenly I was no longer afraid to admit who I was." For me, the meager attempt to have a boyfriend was enough to prove to myself that I am "really" a lesbian; Nina needed to experience real affection for a woman. And this real feeling was transformative for her. Nina's hesitation is common in a culture in which being gay is often perceived as a negative or inferior characteristic.

KARI

Kari, who is thirty-one and works in ticket sales for a sporting events company in southern California, remembers as a child being attracted more to female characters on TV shows, but she didn't necessarily feel different from other girls. "A very good friend of my mom was a gay man, so I knew what it was growing up. It was no big deal. My mother is a psychologist, and she never gave me any impression that there was anything wrong with being gay.

"I started thinking I was gay in high school, in junior or senior year, but I kept the feelings to myself. Around that time, Prince came out with *Purple Rain,* and once I took a look at Wendy [Prince's lead guitar player], that absolutely clinched it for me — I knew my feelings for women were sexual. But I was still thinking that they were *just* fantasies that I could keep separate from the reality of my everyday life. I went out with guys and slept with them until I was about twenty-two. But it wasn't ever right. I'd heard my mother talk about her lesbian friends going to lesbian bars so they could dance. I knew there were places out there; I just didn't know where they were. My fantasies about women continued, but I felt confused and unsure about how to proceed.

"Then I answered an ad in a local paper for a guitar player in a band. I was the only person who responded, so I got the gig. It was this all-female band. After I'd been with them for about a month, the other musicians told me they were lesbians and asked me if I had a problem with that. I said, 'No. Do you have a problem that I'm not a lesbian?' I was very quick about it. I still didn't think I was gay. I thought that I was supposed to be with guys, so that's what I was doing. I certainly didn't have anyone I felt comfortable discussing it with. I had all these feelings, and I didn't have a name for them. How do you know if you like lima beans if you haven't had lima beans?

"Then I started hanging out with the band, and they basically fused me into the gay community. I got to know places to go, see healthy couples and unhealthy couples. The women behaved just like straight couples. I began meeting some great women who were wonderfully supportive of me. Finally I met this woman who I was completely attracted to, and we had this one passionate night. The affair was a miserable failure, but the sexual experience itself confirmed everything for me: this was right, this was comfortable. Sex with men may not have been bad, but it had never felt quite right either. As horrible as this affair ended up being (she was freaked out after our night together), I knew being with a woman sexually was what I wanted. This was lima beans."

Both Nina's and Kari's stories illustrate how the process of coming out to ourselves can be gradual. Both women needed positive, tangible exposure to a lesbian environment, and in Kari's case actual sexual experience, before they felt ready to admit to themselves that they were gay. Judy too didn't put a name to her feelings of difference until she found herself in love with someone who happened to be a woman.

JUDY

Judy was married and the mother of two children when she came out to herself. Like Kari and Nina, the catalyst for her realization was concrete experience. Judy befriended Mary*, a woman who worked in the same office. "When Mary told me she was a lesbian," Judy recalls, "I was like 'Wow!' I think I was in shock at first, then felt excited. I had never known anyone who was gay." Judy was excited and intrigued by her new friend, and slowly Judy started spending more and more time with Mary and other lesbians. Judy began inviting the women to her house, where she lived with her husband. "At first my husband was being supportive and loving, giving me space to incorporate these new friends in our lives. But after a while, he became angry and frustrated and would berate me when I would want to do something with my new group."

Judy had to wrestle with a lot of conflict when it began to dawn on her that she was probably a lesbian. She was married, had made a commitment to her husband; she was also the mother of two young children. But once she fell in love with Lenore, there was no denying the reality of who she was.

Judy believes that if she had been exposed to gay people earlier in her life, she may have confronted her latent sexual feelings for women earlier. Does she regret having married? Did she have a good marriage? She says, "I loved my husband.

I still love him. He's a great guy. Looking back on the relationship, I don't think I was ever in love with him. But it wasn't like I didn't enjoy myself. Sex was fine. But for me, there was a real difference between making love with Lenore and having sex with my husband: being with a woman just gratifies me more emotionally."

It's interesting that Judy had no firsthand experience with any gays or lesbians before meeting Mary. It was not until she began pursuing a friendship with Mary and then met other gay women that Judy even began to question her own sexual orientation and relate it to her dissatisfaction with her life. Once the questions began, she knew right away that she "wanted to explore" what being a lesbian meant and didn't hesitate to act. Judy's experience seems to suggest that she needed concrete evidence of her feelings for women to connect her general, abstract discontent with her sexuality.

Women's Sexuality

The experts say that most men reach their sexual peak at eighteen, and women tend to reach it later, during their mid-thirties. So if women get in touch with their sexuality later in life, it makes sense that some can be relatively adjusted to a heterosexual life and only later come to the realization that they can be happier and more complete with women as sexual partners.

ROBIN*

Robin, who is thirty-five and a writer living in New York City, came out as a lesbian relatively late at thirty-two years old. She explains that even though she had a number of opportunities to experiment while she was in college, she never did. "I would go to these women's bars and look around and not identify with the women at all. They weren't women I would have been friends with outside the bar. One summer, though, I met a woman who I had a complete crush on. I loved hanging out with her — she was tall, very masculine, with a severe short haircut. I thought she was totally cool. But I couldn't do a thing about it. I was convinced that she and her friends thought I was this conservative little straight girl from the suburbs. I couldn't imagine taking the step and saying or doing anything about my feelings."

After college, Robin became involved with Ted*, a man she knew from college. They lived together for five years and then married. After four years of marriage, they divorced. "We didn't get divorced because I was gay. Our marriage split up because Ted could never resolve his ambivalence about being monogamous, and I was finally no longer willing to wait him out." But throughout their relationship, Robin had had fantasies of being with women. "I didn't know what to make of it — I would always conclude that they were just fantasies and leave it at that. I was married; I wanted children. I also loved Ted. We were each other's best friend. At first I didn't say anything about the fantasies; then I told Ted. He was excited by them and encouraged me to share them. Telling them actually became a regular part of our sex life."

After Robin and Ted divorced and she moved to New York, Robin's curiosity about the fantasies increased. "I started to date men because I thought I wanted to get married again. I was now thirty-two and I was beginning to worry that I was going to be too old to have children. I know that sounds ridiculous in this day and age, but I was panicking. Then I was talking to a friend of mine who was gay and told her that I should try to meet some women. I had to do something." Robin's friend came to New York for a visit and took her to a women's party.

"The party was held in a beautiful penthouse apartment overlooking Central Park, the night before the New York Marathon. The terrace had a view of Tavern on the Green, and the runners were assembling for their meal before the race in the morning. It was a clear October night. I can remember exactly what I was wearing: a gray cashmere turtleneck, black wool trousers, and my black leather jacket over my shoulders. I stepped onto that terrace and saw all these sophisticated women. I couldn't stop smiling. No women's bar had ever been like this. All the women I was introduced to were interesting, professional women who were into fashionable clothes and wearing makeup. I felt immediately comfortable, excited too, but I just knew something was right."

Robin continues, "I met a woman that night, and immediately there was tremendous electricity between us. I resisted her at first, saying I just wanted to be friends. But the truth was, I was terrified. Finally lust took over, and we began an intense relationship. Statistically you could call me bisexual, since I used to be sexual with men. But I now identify more with being a lesbian."

Robin says the reasons for her not coming out sooner are complicated. "One factor was definitely because I had not really related to most of the women I had come across. I think I was also afraid to look at some of these real masculine women and say, 'Am I like her?' I'd look around and think, 'This is not me; I'm not into cutting off my hair and wearing no makeup.' I'm not criticizing those women. I just didn't think I had anything in common with them."

Another factor was her own fear of being gay. "I just couldn't seem to reconcile my love for my husband, my desire to have children, and my fantasies about being with a woman. I couldn't make sense of all the seemingly contradictory feelings. They just didn't make sense. No matter what, I couldn't figure out a way not to lose something. But when the marriage finally broke up, I no longer was able to not do anything about the fantasies."

She explains why, when she went to the party in Manhattan, she allowed herself to act on her feelings. "I grew up around women. I have four sisters. Four female cousins. One of the most important activities growing up was shopping and dressing up for parties or restaurants. For better or worse, that was how I learned to be a woman. I felt, just because I am a gay doesn't mean I have to totally change the way I dress, act, or present myself, so when I actually came face to face with gay women who were sophisticated and 'feminine,' the final barriers went down."

In being able to identify with these women, Robin was able to better accept her feelings. The recognition factor is powerful. For me it was *Personal Best*; for Kari, Nina, and Judy it was exposure to a lesbian environment. We were all looking for role models to assuage some of our anxiety about our identities.

No Role Models

This issue of being able to identify with other gay people is especially significant. Because gays and lesbians are a minority (the most recent survey puts the figure at 8 percent of the total population, with a 50 percent higher male homosexual population than female), and since there have been very restricted and negative images of gay people in the mainstream media, it is challenging for a gay person to find an accurate representation of the spectrum of gays and lesbians living in this country.

We cannot underestimate the power of these negative images. Their impact can have traumatic, even tragic consequences.

BRUCE

When Bruce, the Indianan, realized he was gay, he "wanted to die." The fear, shame, and pain of the knowledge stopped him from having a positive outlook. "I was lying in bed saying, 'You're gay, get over it. You're just going to have to deal with it.' I was trying to figure out which would cause my parents more pain — having a dead son or a gay son." Unlike some of us, including me, Bruce was filled with instant and deep self-loathing when he realized he was gay. The very idea of his homosexuality was so disastrous that suicide seemed his only recourse. "When I realized I was gay, I was scared. I was worried about whether I'd lose my friends and family and how my parents would react. I never thought I'd be thrown out, but I thought suicide was my only way out. I contemplated my plan for over two months: I was going to overdose on pills."

He didn't take the pills; as he puts it, though: "I was terrified. A lot of what I knew about gay people came from TV. But what I saw made me feel even more lonely, because there weren't any positive role models that I could look up to and say to myself, 'Well, he's gay and look how wonderful he is.' The only portrayals I had to go on were negative characteristics on such shows as *In Living Color, Saturday Night Live,* or the tabloid talk shows." I don't think we can underestimate the power of negative stereotypes and the lack of positive gay role models in the media. For Bruce, growing up in a small, very conservative town in the Bible Belt, exposure to other gay men was extremely limited. As a result, his definition of homosexuality was both inaccurate and destructive.

Both Bruce and Dave have pointed to the negative and inaccurate images of homosexuals in the media as being partially responsible for why they experienced such fear and self-loathing when they were struggling to come to terms with their own homosexuality. I think it's difficult for nongay people to imagine that the pain and confusion of realizing you're gay or lesbian can make you want to take your own life. But suicide, especially among young people, is common enough: one-third of all young adults attempt it.

As society in general becomes more educated about homosexuality and we as a culture integrate lesbians and gays more fully as an acceptable minority population as opposed to a disenfranchised subculture, the coming-out process will not be so shameful, so painful, even life threatening. Clearly an increase in the number of positive role models or images in the media of gays and lesbians can offset the negative conclusions many gay people come to about themselves.

I consider myself lucky. My generally positive response to my realization was partially a result of having grown up with frequent exposure to gay people. Since my mom never treated them any differently, I never thought there was anything wrong with these men and women.

Looking for Support

We all come out at different times. The way we manage or respond to our discovery that we are gay is often a mixture of excitement, relief, shame, and denial. It's common that after some initial relief at finally understanding this essential part of ourselves, we often go through a kind of testing period during which we keep the knowledge to ourselves as we slowly "research" what it means to be gay.

For me, this testing period felt like being on a seesaw: I would vacillate from excitement to fear and back again. When my mom, Elijah, and I moved back to Los Angeles at the end of that fateful summer, I had to return to the Curtis School, which I was dreading. I knew I wouldn't have any friends. And now that I was carrying around this knowledge that I was gay, I felt even more anxious about going back to a school where I didn't fit in.

We were living in an Egyptian-style mansion in Benedict Canyon. Elijah, who was about five or six at the time, was becoming only more of a towheaded pest, making everyone who took care of us, including my mother, that much more aggravated. And I was in the full throes of my adolescence.

To my dismay, I was maturing rapidly and fully. My body was taking shape in a form altogether different from my mother's: where she was lean and tall, I was short and round. Where she was relatively flat chested, I was full chested. Once again, we couldn't have been more different.

I suffered through the weeks at school, waiting for weekends at Gina's. I'd see my dad occasionally, but he was fairly busy with his restaurant. Like most teenagers, I was finding it harder and harder to relate to adults. And despite my mother's accepting attitude toward her friends who were gay, I still had a feeling that she didn't want *me* to be gay. I didn't have to be told explicitly: her continued criticism of my tomboyishness felt like disapproval of my emerging sexuality. As a result, talking to either of my parents about the "gay issue" seemed out of the question.

But keeping the secret meant feeling as if no one really knew me. I began to feel completely alienated from everyone around me, becoming more and more withdrawn. I'd retreat to my room and close the blinds. I tried to avoid any intimate conversation. One day, trying to go back to that initial feeling of relief when I first watched *Personal Best*, I began writing a screenplay entitled *Jump Shot*.

It was merely a rip-off of *Personal Best* with a basketball setting instead of track. I renamed the characters and retold the story. But it kept me going. It was a way for me to begin to explore my new identity, as well as let go of some of the building pressure. My mom, my aunt Georgeann, and my mother's assistants were excited that I seemed suddenly involved in a project. They encouraged me by giving me books on writing screenplays, and they kept asking to read it. And as much as I liked their attention and support, I was terrified to show anyone the screenplay because it would reveal my secret. Once again, I was confronted with the paradox of feeling good about myself and feeling afraid of rejection.

At Christmas that year, my mom had a tree-decorating party. A number of us were up in her bedroom watching a tape of an HBO special that she had just done. I was sitting on the floor when in walked a woman whom I recognized. It was Joan, an old friend of my mother's. I had always known Joan was a lesbian, but now I saw her through new eyes, and I felt as if she could see right through me.

That night I wouldn't let Joan out of my sight. She was dressed in a sexy black leather skirt and red silk blouse, and I thought she looked gorgeous. She was with a date, but that didn't stop me from following her around for the entire evening. I talked to her, told her jokes — anything to get her attention. I had fallen madly in love, a crush that would later become much more significant.

After that Christmas party, I spent a lot of time with Joan. She became the first lesbian in my life with whom I could identify, and she helped me enormously as I tried to understand what being gay meant to me. I consider myself fortunate that I had someone who was older and more experienced to be a role model for me. Many gays and lesbians have no access to such support.

Chapter 3
Exploring
Birds Do It, Bees Do It

"Perhaps, as we say in America, I wanted to find myself. . . . I think now that if I had had any intimation that the self I was going to find would turn out to be only the same self from which I had spent so much time in flight, I would have stayed at home."

JAMES BALDWIN,
from *Giovanni's Room*

New Territory

Realizing that I was gay enabled me finally to understand why I had always felt so different for all those years, but this realization didn't make all the pent-up, often confusing feelings disappear. In fact, a new kind of frustration set in. I was fourteen and in the eighth grade, and like so many other kids, I had raging hormones. But unlike most of them, I had no one to go steady with, which made me feel as if I had fallen into a void.

Without saying the words aloud, I had come out to Joan and got comfort from my friendship with her. I began to spend more and more time with her. We'd go to the movies, hang out at her place, or go out to dinner. I certainly had a crush on her, but at thirty-six, she was twenty-two years older than I was; needless to say, my feelings for her were a bit different than hers for me.

The real problem for me (aside from still being stuck at the Curtis School) was that I had no idea how to meet gay people my age, especially other lesbians. At that time (1983), the only place gay people seemed able to meet was in bars. I thought I'd have to wait until I was twenty-one before I could even think about having a girlfriend. Luckily I was wrong.

For my fourteenth birthday, my mom enrolled me in acting classes at the Lee Strasberg Theatre Institute in West Hollywood. I loved it immediately and started making friends quickly and easily. The kids were artsy, open-minded, and so much cooler than those at my preppy school. When the school year ended, I signed up for Strasberg's intense summer youth program, which consisted of acting, dancing, and vocal lessons. Midway through the program, we started rehearsal for the original musical that we would perform for a live audience at the summer's end.

Two of my closest friends at Strasberg were Kate* and Gordon*, who were a couple. I had not told anyone that I was gay, but I felt comfortable around the group as a whole because everyone seemed so open-minded.

After the final performance of the musical, the director hosted a wrap party at his house for everyone from the cast and crew. I was in the living room hanging out with some friends and went into the kitchen to get something to drink. When I walked in, I saw Gordon and Kate alone, in what appeared to be a serious conversation. I quickly got a Coke and left the room to give them their privacy. About ten minutes later, Gordon came into the living room. I hurried over to see if everything was all right, and he told me that he and Kate had broken up. Once I was sure that Gordon was okay, I went into the kitchen to check on how Kate was doing. I was ready to console her, but surprisingly she seemed fine. We were facing each other, talking about why they had broken up, when Kate told me that she was in love with me. With the words still lingering in the air and me wondering if I had heard her correctly, Kate leaned in, pinned me against the fridge, and kissed me on the lips.

I was so shocked by Kate's kiss that I didn't know what to do or how to kiss her back. I felt excited and terrified at the same time.

Kate was quite sexually experienced for someone our age; I, on the other hand, was definitely not. I had never kissed anyone before — male or female. As much as I was drawn to Kate's sexual energy, I was also intimidated by her experience. I may have liked the feeling of her kiss, but I was too scared to really enjoy it.

I quickly left the room to try to make sense of what had just happened. I had gone from trying to console my straight friend to being thrust against the fridge and pressed into my very first kiss. To make matters more complicated, Kate and I had made plans earlier that day for a sleep-over that night. I didn't know what to do!

When we got back to my house, I was so nervous that I practically slept with one foot touching the ground. With Kate next to me in bed, I was sweating, my heart was racing, and I barely slept a moment the entire night. My emotions ran the gamut — from excitement to terror to relief to lust. For the next couple of days, I distanced myself from Kate. But as I had time to think about everything, I knew I wanted to kiss her again.

A few days later, Kate came over my house again, and after a little while of feeling awkward, we went outside to talk about what to do next. We were standing up against my grandmother's car when Kate kissed me for the second time — only this time I wasn't afraid. I kissed her back with a vengeance. We went back to my room, locked the door, and spent the rest of the afternoon passionately making out.

As befitted the teenagers we were, our fooling around wasn't very sophisticated, but technique didn't matter. I couldn't believe that I was actually kissing a girl, and I couldn't get enough. I fooled around with Kate for the rest of the summer, until I had to leave for New York.

A typical fourteen-year-old, I shifted my attention from Kate to my next adventure. I had been accepted into the drama department of the High School of the Performing Arts and was thrilled to be returning to New York, where I would be on my own. At Strasberg, I had discovered that I felt passionately about acting, and I was excited about going to a school that was so committed to the arts. For many reasons that are more clear in hindsight, getting accepted into PA was probably the best thing that could have happened to me.

Bright Lights, Big City

My mother was busy working in Los Angeles and couldn't move to New York, so I ended up living with Anna Strasberg and her two sons, Adam and David, whom I had become close to at the Strasberg Institute in L.A. My mother was very comfortable with the Strasbergs and felt I would be in good hands in New York. And frankly, I was relieved to be leaving home. Although my mom had been very supportive of my interest in acting and was glad that I was suddenly so happy after months of being miserable, I was still keeping an enormous secret from her: distance from her meant not having to worry about her finding out that I was gay. At that point, telling her about my newly discovered sexuality was still completely unthinkable.

Though I did miss Kate a bit at first, I got so involved in

the school's intensive drama program that I was able to move on quickly. With the distance of two thousand miles, I realized that though I was sexually attracted to Kate, I had not developed a deep or lasting emotional attachment to her. Thank God.

PA was like nothing I'd ever experienced before, and I instantly loved everything about it — from its location in the theater district to the historic old building itself. I had never encountered a group of young people as serious about acting as I was. As you may remember from the film *Fame*, PA was also known for its melting pot of students. The racial, ethnic, and economic diversity of the students was completely new to me. It was a total relief not being around the spoiled, sheltered kids I had grown up around in private schools in Los Angeles.

I started making good friends at PA and thriving in the creative atmosphere. Because the school was so artistic, there seemed to be a very high level of tolerance, and as I got closer to new friends, I felt comfortable coming out to a few of them and telling them about my summer with Kate.

Though good friends were plentiful during my first two years at school, romance was not. I had some crushes and even dated one girl for a while, but my heart wasn't really in it. All that changed, however, in my junior year, when I fell in love for the first time.

Julie, Julie, Julie, Do You Love Me?

It started at my friend Cecil's sixteenth birthday party, which was held at our friend Delby's house. It was the typical high school party: no parents, about fifty classmates, plenty of beer, good music, and conversation. I was hanging out with my core group of friends, but as the evening progressed, I started to notice that Julie* was finding opportunities to make small talk with me.

At about five-foot three and with a really nice figure, Julie was beautiful. She had long blond hair, blue eyes, and a nice mouth. Though I had gone to school with her for two full years, I had never really talked to her. We had different groups of friends, and I had always thought of her as kind of conservative. My friends were on the fringe of the punk–rude boy scene, buying our clothes at downtown thrift shops and wearing Doc Martens at a time when only two stores in New York imported them from England. Julie had more of an all-American good-girl look about her. Though all my friends were straight, they never seemed to obsess over or get hung up on boys. Julie, on the other hand, always seemed to have lots of boys around her. I can even remember her hanging out with senior boys when we were still freshmen. At that point, I assumed Julie was nothing more complex than some white-bread stereotype. But as with many hasty assumptions, this one was very wrong.

When Julie started talking to me that night at the party, I was immediately taken by her: she was charming, witty, and intelligent. I remember telling her a joke and being captivated by her laugh. For the rest of the night, I made it my mission to make her laugh as much as possible. As the hours passed, I was definitely flirting up a storm with her. To my amazement, she seemed to be flirting back. I can remember telling my friends Delby and Cecil, "I think Julie is flirting with me." They told me I had either lost my mind or that my ego had finally gotten the better of me.

But I knew I was right, and after the party wound down, I was vindicated. A handful of us were spending the night at Delby's house. I slept in one of the two single beds in her room. Just as I was drifting off to sleep, I felt someone get into the small bed with me. It was Julie. Even though there appeared to be other unoccupied places to sleep, she chose to curl up next to me. Though nothing happened between us that night, it was a sign of things to come.

Armed with a joke on Monday, I searched for Julie at school. When I tracked her down in the locker room before drama class, she was as receptive to me as she had been at the party. We made plans to get together with Delby and Cecil that Wednesday, which was Cecil's actual birthday. We all met at Cecil's house in Riverdale. The plan was to go to the movies, then back to her house for cake. Delby and I would spend the night, and Julie, who also lived in Riverdale, would be picked up by her mom later. We went to see *Jagged Edge*, with Glenn Close and Jeff Bridges, and about halfway through the film, I got bold and took Julie's hand. To my delight, she grabbed hold of my hand, and we spent the rest of the film caressing each other. The entire walk back from the movie theater, we alternated between walking arm in arm and holding hands, and Julie seemed totally comfortable.

I was elated. I couldn't believe that she was being so receptive to me. In a million years I would never have thought that I could get a girl like Julie. After Julie's mom called to say she was on her way, I signaled to my friends to give us a couple of minutes alone so I could kiss Julie good night.

Alone with me in Cecil's room, Julie suddenly seemed very uncomfortable. As Julie's mom honked her horn, I stood blocking the door, ready for my long-awaited good-night kiss.

Julie nervously said, "That's my mom — move out of the way. I've got to go."

Dumbfounded, I replied, "You're going to leave, just like that?"

"Yeah, get away from the door, my mom is honking," she replied. It was clear that she had started to panic.

"You're really going to just leave, just walk out the door?" I asked once more.

"Yes," she said strongly.

I moved out of the way, and Julie seemed to hesitate for a couple of seconds before leaving the room.

I was confused and felt terrible because I had obviously upset Julie. After talking with my friends for a while, trying to figure out what went wrong, I decided to call Julie. She was just as confused as I was. She told me that she had previously been to a psychiatrist because she thought she might be gay and didn't want to be. Holding hands with me and flirting felt safe to her, but when I tried to take it to the next level, it brought all her feelings to a head, which was too much for her to handle.

For a few days, things were strained between us. But soon we fell back into the flirtatious friendship we had previously begun. We spent a lot of time talking about our feelings for each other. I was honest about how much I really liked her and how attracted to her I felt. Julie admitted she felt the same way but wasn't ready to act on it. As we became closer, it got harder for me to deal with Julie's constant mixed signals. I remember one conversation we had walking to the subway after school. We were talking about a mutual friend I thought was very pretty.

"Oh, she would be easy to have," Julie said. "I could tell you how to get her."

"Really? You think you could?" I asked sarcastically. "Okay, Romeo, tell me what's your secret."

Julie replied in a seductive way, lowering her voice and tilting her head to the side. "No, I haven't decided if I want you yet."

Julie finally decided she wanted to take our relationship to a physical level in late December, a couple of days after her sixteenth birthday. She had received as a gift two tickets for an Alvin Ailey dance company performance from a mutual lesbian friend of ours. Knowing what had been going on between us, our friend had convinced Julie to take me to the dance concert.

I met Julie for dinner before the concert at an Italian restaurant around the corner from the theater. She looked stunning that night, dressed in a tight black miniskirt, blouse, and pumps that really showed off her figure. Julie was an extremely sexy girl, but that night she was on fire. Along with our dinner, we ordered a bottle of red wine, which we proceeded to drink in its entirety. By the end of dinner, both of us were feeling quite uninhibited. Over dessert, I began to feel Julie's shoeless foot slowly creeping up my leg.

We arrived at the theater as the lights were about to go down and quickly took our seats. Though the performance was entertaining, Julie and I were too engrossed in each other to concentrate on anything else. With the seats next to us empty and the theater dark, we practically made love right there with my coat over her lap. When Julie came back to our seats after using the rest room, she whispered in my ear, "Not only is my underwear wet, but so are my stockings."

After the show ended, we couldn't get out of the theater fast enough. We hailed a cab for the long ride up to Riverdale, and made out ferociously the entire way. When we got to her house, her parents were already asleep. We immediately headed for her bedroom. Once safe inside, we started to undress each other with an urgency that can only come from such a long courtship. As we began to make love, the magnitude of my feelings for Julie was apparent. I had been with other girls, but it had never felt like this. Our passion for each other was overwhelming, and what we lacked in technique, we more than made up for in enthusiasm. I clearly remember her rationale for finally agreeing to have sex with me: near the end of the evening she said we would do it one time, so she could get it out of her system and resume her heterosexual life.

In spite of her pronouncement, Julie and I were involved off and on for the next couple of years. She constantly battled with her sexual ambivalence: she was obviously drawn to me, but she still felt afraid of what that meant. After a few months, she revealed to me that the first night we held hands in the movie theater, she was so frightened she actually contemplated suicide when she got home. To this day, Julie and I maintain a friendship, and she still struggles with questions about her sexuality. Do her sexual feelings for women mean that she is "really" a lesbian who is afraid to come out? That she is bisexual (she dates men)? Or that she is essentially a heterosexual who has had sexual relationships with women? Thankfully, my sexual identity was a lot more clear-cut: I had no sexual interest in men, and I was unquestionably attracted to women.

For me, the relationship with Julie was an emotional roller coaster. My heart was pulled, tugged, and torn. Yet despite the heartache, I consider myself lucky to have been able to explore my sexuality in a relatively open, safe way. In Julie's case, I would hazard a guess that once her parents found out about her and me and took her to a psychiatrist, she became inhibited about exploring her feelings, and that intense anxiety pervaded her involvement with me.

Because of the open-mindedness of my school friends, the relative freedom of New York, and my distance from my family, I was able to think about and act upon my sexual urges in the same way that most young adults do. Most of my friends at PA were straight, but they didn't have a problem with my being gay. My being able to talk about my crushes with my friends made me feel comfortable with myself. Also, my feelings for Julie were so deep and real to me that there was no room to deny them. Falling in love with Julie, as painful and confusing as it was because of her mixed feelings, helped me to acknowledge and accept at a deep level that I was gay.

Of course, this exploration of my identity was premised on keeping my sexual orientation from my parents, particularly my mother. Since she was living in Los Angeles at the time, the geographical distance allowed for a safe barrier between us. When my mother visited me in New York or I went home for holidays or school vacations, we were standoffish with each other. With neither of us communicating directly, the troubling subject of my emerging sexuality was avoided. Instead, she focused on superficial issues that bothered her: my short hair, my mannish clothes, my weight.

Exploring

When gays and lesbians first start to explore what it means to be gay, we are faced with the same problem that many young adults are: how do we learn about our sexual feelings? When we're younger, it's often a question of opportunity. The popular kids in school seem to find girlfriends or boyfriends with ease. But for the less popular and more insecure teenagers, finding romance and sex can seem just about impossible. For gay and lesbian teenagers, the situation can be even tougher. As I said, I was lucky. I felt safe enough to tell my friends I was gay. In dating a couple of different girls, including Julie, I was following the natural inclination of any teenager to want to date and kiss and explore sexual feelings. Sometimes it's fun, sometimes it's scary. Some of us aren't so lucky.

RICHARD

Richard, the urban planner, did not explore his sexual feelings for men until he was a sophomore in college. Indeed, his exploration occurred side by side with his coming out — first to himself and then to others. After graduating from an all-boy Catholic prep school in New England, Richard went west to attend a prestigious private university in northern California. He dated a couple of girls in high school, but never went beyond the merest kiss. He said that although at times

he wondered if he were gay, he never took his thoughts seriously. He just figured he wasn't ready to date.

I took my Catholicism seriously, and I was very aware
the church taught that homosexuality was wrong. I
ght of becoming a priest, that's how intent I felt about my
n. But I had one friend, a guy from South America, who
would always try to kiss me. He was a jokester, so I always
brushed away his come-ons. I tried not to think too much
about them. He was flaming, and everyone at school knew he
was gay, called him 'faggot' and 'queer.' There was no way I
wanted to be made fun of or associated with him.

"When I got to college, I started feeling really depressed.
Here I was at this great school — a lot of really smart, beautiful people — but I felt like I just didn't fit in. Something was
wrong. Finally I called the Gay and Lesbian Student Union and
went to one of their meetings. All the guys there were so
nerdy, I thought I was going to cry. It was so frustrating. I tried
again to date some women, but as much as I liked them, I
could never have sex with them. I just couldn't go through
with it. I was miserable."

Richard was not just closed to his latent homosexuality
but to his sexual feelings altogether. He admits that he'd never
masturbated until he went to college. His sexuality was so
overwhelming to him that he could not even entertain fantasies; having any sexual urges made him uncomfortable. "I
guess I wasn't ready to deal with the fact of being gay," Richard
says, sounding almost surprised. "When I finally told this
shrink at school that I thought I was gay, I felt like my whole
exterior self was about to crumble. I felt like people could see
right through me."

The next people Richard came out to were two of his sisters. "My sisters were both living in Los Angeles, and one of
them had just had a baby and she named me the godfather. After the christening, we went to a restaurant to celebrate. My

sister's husband and his sister and brother-in-law were also there with their two young kids. During dinner I kept looking at the children, thinking, 'I'm gay, I'll never have children.' I was getting more and more upset, and finally I had to leave the table. One of my sisters came after me and asked me what was wrong. She took one look at me and then said, 'Let's leave.' We left everyone at the restaurant, and my sister and I went back to the house. By then, I was crying. She kept asking me, 'What's wrong, what's wrong?' and I would just say, 'Don't you know?'

"Finally my sister said, 'You're gay?'

"'Yes. Well, I mean, I'm bisexual.' She just hugged me and told me she loved me. She wasn't surprised at all; she said that she and my other sisters had figured I was probably gay."

Richard admits that in calling himself bisexual he was still afraid to admit his sexual orientation. However, by the end of that year, he was able to take his first steps toward testing the reality of his sexual feelings. He dated a couple of times, but he didn't have his first sexual experience until he was a senior in college.

Unlike mine, Richard's way of dealing with the unsettling feelings around the idea of his being gay was to suppress all sexual urges. Richard points to his Catholic background as being instrumental in why he shut down such a big part of himself. Until he was able to say, "I am gay," he didn't allow himself to experience any sexual pleasure. But once he had sex with a man, his sexual orientation was confirmed. "I couldn't take any action for what seemed like a long time. I was too afraid," Richard remembers. "When I finally did, all I felt was relief," he says, smiling.

BEN

Ben also separated the knowledge of his homosexuality from his actual sexual feelings. His first same-sex experience

was in the eighth grade, with another boy ⌐
scribes it as a "typical boy experiment, natura⌐
that age. But," he adds, "there was no kissing.
preted kissing as too intimate, romantic, and that wo
made the "experiment" more risky or threatening. As h
older, especially after he came out to himself at twelve, Ben
says that his emotional attachments were with girls. "This
was a real source of confusion for me because a lot of the
people I had strong friendships with were my girl friends; and
I'd enjoy making out with them, kissing, going out on dates,
but I never sexualized those relationships. They were all emotional. I still fantasized about guys, but I wouldn't let myself
have romantic feelings about guys."

This is the same sort of split Julie experienced between
what she felt and what she thought she should feel. Like
Richard, Ben repressed some aspects of his sexual feelings, re-
flecting his mixed attitude about being gay. Richard's separa-
tion between who he was and how he felt was most extreme:
he banished his sexual urges altogether. Ben allowed himself
to experience emotional closeness with his friends who were
girls, but only sexual feelings for the men he fantasized about,
not letting himself experience fuller attachments. I think
what makes their experiences similar is the internalized shame
of homosexuality. As much as each of them had considered or
decided he was gay, each of them was still resisting some part
of what being gay literally meant: being sexual with someone
of the same sex. Julie felt the same way: although she was attracted to me and clearly enjoyed being sexual with me, she
was tortured by her ambivalence.

For me, it was easier, at least at this stage. Since I had
been exposed to gay people and had had some positive role
models, I felt more free to explore my feelings, yet not without
some trepidation. Although in the heat of the moment with
Julie I didn't repress my sexual desire, I still needed to keep my
experience hidden. But those gays and lesbians who grew up in

an environment, either cultural or religious, that communicated an extreme negative view of homosexuality often confront emotional or sexual roadblocks that prevent them from acting on their sexual urges.

Ben remembers "a sting operation in our city to entrap gay men who would hang out in a public park. About twenty men had been arrested, and some were well-known people in our community. I was a senior in high school and at Thanksgiving dinner, my extended family was talking about it [the sting]. Someone said, 'Can you imagine anything worse than being a homosexual?' There was so much pity around it, if not outright condemnation. So much sadness and weakness associated with homosexuality. I remember thinking, 'Well, where are gay people supposed to meet each other in Henderson, Kentucky?'" The negative stereotypes, as well as the lack of opportunity to meet other gays and lesbians, clearly contributed to both men's need to repress some aspect of their sexual identity.

Ben also felt he had to give up early aspirations to be a politician. "I always wanted to be a politician, and part of the problem with coming out was 'How am I going to run for congress as a gay man?' I had to keep this a secret or I'd never be a public person."

Ben now counsels gay and lesbian teens. He says, "Now young people coming out see a lot more of the love aspect than I did when I was first coming out. There are so many more role models, more portrayals of gay people in the media in the last five years. They may not always be accurate, but at least they're out there. The fact that I wasn't really allowing myself to have feelings about romance toward guys shows that I'm a product of my generation, growing up in the nineteen-seventies."

CAROLINE*

Other people I spoke with remembered feeling even more afraid of exploring their sexual identity. This was especially true for those who came out more than fifteen years ago. Caroline grew up in New Hampshire and now works for a sports marketing firm in Colorado. She was the only girl with three brothers, and, like them, she was an athlete. She remembers that her mother showed disapproval of her being a tomboy by not helping her get to practice or workouts. "When I decided to take up competitive swimming, my mom said, 'Fine, but don't expect me to drive you to the pool.' That didn't stop me. I would ride my bike ten miles every weekday morning to practice. I think it actually made me work harder."

Unlike some of us, including me, Caroline began experimenting long before she ever put a name to her behavior or her feelings. "I was a lifeguard at a local pool, and the summer I was seventeen, I started hanging out with this girl Peggy*. Once she kissed me in her basement. At first I pushed her away and then avoided her for a few days, but then we started hanging out again. After a while, we started having sex."

When I ask Caroline how she felt about being with Peggy, she says, "At the time I just didn't think about it. I certainly didn't think I was gay. I didn't know what it meant. I still had Klaus*, my boyfriend." Then I ask Caroline if she remembers the first time she realized that she might be gay. Dropping her eyes and looking suddenly shy, she says, "Well, it was near the end of the summer. As usual, I was hanging out with Peggy. I came into the kitchen to get a soda or something, and my mom just looked at me and said, 'What, are you queer or something?' I was shocked and immediately humiliated." Her mother's angry question didn't stop her from having sexual relationships with women, but for the next eighteen years, she led a double life.

"I was training for a big meet, and Ed* [her swim coach] and I did everything together. Everyone, especially my family, thought he and I were a couple. And we were a couple, but I would never sleep with him. I loved him enormously, and I know he was in love with me. We did everything together but have sex. I knew that by not sleeping with him I was torturing him, and I was tortured myself. But I just couldn't do it. I had girlfriends on the side and always kept them secret. I had this whole other life no one knew about."

Caroline stayed in the closet until she was thirty-five. It's as if her mother's one comment so long ago triggered such intense shame that she was unable to reconcile the pleasure she experienced being with women and the anger and rejection she sensed in her mother's words. The only way Caroline was able to deal with her sexuality was to keep it completely separate; in other words, she stayed in the closet. Even though it felt natural for Caroline to kiss and be sexual with women, her fear of rejection had become so overwhelming she felt she couldn't risk telling people she was gay.

MELISSA

Another woman I spoke with who struggled for a long time with being a lesbian also led a double life. Melissa considers the film *Personal Best* a trigger in her coming-out process, just as I do. Melissa is now thirty-eight and an account executive at an advertising agency in Chicago, her hometown. She admits that while she was attending an all-girl Catholic high school in Chicago, she thought she was gay. But she continued to live a completely straight life until she was about twenty-one. At that time, she was living with a man, Dale*, in a small seaside town in California. "Dale was about ten years older than me; he took care of me. I looked up to him and felt really safe with him. One night we went to see *Personal Best*. When the two girls started kissing, I thought I was going to die. My heart started beating fast, and I could feel my face flush. I was sure that Dale knew what was happening. As excited as I was by the movie, I couldn't get out of that theater fast enough. When we got home, we had really intense sex. I was completely aroused by the movie, but Dale certainly didn't complain."

Melissa had secret affairs with several women before finally breaking up with Dale and moving back to Chicago. She stopped dating men, but she pretended to her family and friends that she was straight, pining over Dale. "I just couldn't believe I was gay. I was very popular with all my friends; I thought for sure they would dump me if they knew I was gay." Melissa tried to deny her sexuality by leading a double life. "Being with women felt so right, so much more intense than sex with men. I would feel so much more connected to a woman. But it took me a long time to trust that feeling. I hated the image of myself as some dyke." In fact, once she got to know other gay men and women in Chicago and became part of a small community of friends, Melissa began to come out to her straight friends and then her family.

Caroline and Melissa are good examples of how some of us can experiment with or explore our sexuality without really admitting we are gay. But being in the closet comes at a price. Lying to our friends and family and the stress of maintaining a double life cause tremendous pain and emotional confusion. I should know.

Are You Sure You Haven't Done This Before?

ROBIN

When I spoke to Robin — who didn't realize she was gay until after she'd been divorced for two years — she explained that despite how satisfying her first sexual experiences with women were, she still questioned whether she was *really* gay. "I remember the first time. I had known Maggie* for a number of years. She'd been the lover of a good friend of mine. I had always been attracted to her but never understood how I was attracted to her. Anyway, that night we were in her cabin out in the woods in front of a fire. We started kissing, and then I couldn't stop. Maggie said to me, 'Are you sure you haven't done this before?' That made me feel good. I was still nervous, but being with her, touching her body, knowing how to touch her, seemed so natural I didn't have to think about it. But it's been three years since that time, and I still question whether I'm a lesbian. If I were in my twenties maybe I would feel less pressure to know for sure. But I'm thirty-five and I want to settle down. I don't have all the time in the world to go out exploring. Recently I spent some time with my ex-husband. We're still very close, and afterward I kept thinking that it would be so much easier being straight. I did it before, why not try it again? In my heart, though, I know I'm gay. It's just so scary at times."

I hear in Robin's words a familiar refrain. It is not easy being gay. In talking to many gay men and women of all ages and backgrounds, I often hear uncertainty masking their fear of rejection and loss. Robin's story also reminds me that coming out is a process, and a gradual one at that. It takes time to sort through all the feelings in order to understand and accept your sexual orientation as one part of you. Straight men and women are not faced with the same kind of challenge; they don't ever have to feel different because of who they are attracted to, so they don't experience their sexuality as a separate, often threatening part of themselves that they have to learn how to integrate. However, despite their pain, struggle, and even paralyzing ambivalence, everyone I have spoken with describes a sense of victory in having come out. Their words, some of them oft-heard clichés, repeat themselves: "a new lease on life"; "now I'm truly free"; "an enormous burden has been lifted"; and "better late than never." No one I have spoken with regrets coming out; all point to the strength and joy the process has given them.

Lost in the Lies

DAVIS

Davis's first sexual experience was when he was a freshman in college in South Carolina. "I was eighteen and I definitely had sexual urges. I thought about men. I had no desire to be with a woman. At USC the dorms opened a week ahead of time. I always worked, so I returned to campus a week early. My fraternity brothers called and invited me to a small get-together. The night before I had called the president of the gay student union on campus (I had seen his name in the paper) and asked him where the gay bars were in Columbia. So after I had had a few beers at this fraternity get-together, I decided to go by the gay club and see what it was like. It was two o'clock in the morning, so there were maybe ten people there. I must have looked like fresh meat; it wasn't hard for me to start talking to someone. I'll never forget the whole experience: I was eighteen, pretty naive, and he was nice enough, but I think he might have taken advantage of me. He pushed me further than I was ready to go, and I felt dirty, guilty, and nasty afterward. That's why I didn't have another sexual experience until my senior year — three years later." Davis admits that he had had a few beers and wanted to play at the time. But he also regrets that because there were no other available outlets to explore his sexuality, he ended up putting himself in a vulnerable position and was hurt as a result.

When I asked him how it felt to retreat into the closet for the next three years, he said, "I led a double life. I couldn't deal with it. I did pretty well playing a straight boy. But in my senior year I worked at this restaurant, and every Friday night I would party with my coworkers, and afterward I would go to a gay bar. I would go there, drink some more, meet someone, usually have sex, fairly anonymous. Even though I never had a real relationship, I so much wanted the sexual interaction I was willing to compromise. That's when I started living a double life; sometimes I would have a date with a guy, and I would go to great pains to come back with these elaborate stories to tell my roommate. I didn't have to tell him anything, but I lied, which made me feel worse. I constantly prayed that the two lives would never meet. If I were out with some of my straight friends and saw someone I knew from the gay scene, and they'd come up to me and say, 'Hey, girl!' I would just freeze and keep walking. The lies I told bothered me. I always thought of myself as an honest person. I would get lost in my lies — it was hard to keep them straight." Like those of Caroline and Melissa, Davis's lies took a toll on his psyche.

Drugs and Drink No More

JAVIER*

Sometimes coming out even to oneself can be so devastating and threatening that people can turn the fact of their sexuality against themselves: they become self-destructive. Javier, a twenty-eight-year-old Hispanic man from Houston, realized he was gay when he was ten. Although he is now a drug and alcohol counselor working with urban teens, Javier had to hit rock bottom before accepting his homosexuality.

As the third of eight children growing up in a poor Mexican-American household, he was often responsible for caring for some of his younger siblings. His parents both worked and were away from home for long hours at a time. When Javier began being harassed and teased at school and by his two older brothers, his parents wouldn't listen. He says, "They didn't want to deal with the problem. I was a sissy."

When he was thirteen, Javier ran away from home. In a city like Houston, it is relatively easy to get lost in a life on the street. It's a city with a large underground population of street kids and other transients, many of whom quickly become hooked on drugs and alcohol, and a large number of whom resort to prostitution at some point.

Javier did. Once he found a niche of gay teenage runaways, he thought he'd found the answer to his prayers. Unfortunately, he didn't understand how the kids were actually surviving. "At first I thought it was just fun. I was thirteen, I liked the attention they were giving me, and I thought they were just playing around, jacking off and shit. But then it got more serious." He was quickly swept into a life of being abused by older street boys, as well as men they'd turn tricks for. Young, naive, and especially vulnerable, Javier began drinking and doing drugs. When I asked him why he didn't just go home, he said, "I couldn't. I felt like I was stained. That my mother and father would know. How could they love me? How could they take me back in?" Javier learned how to survive on the street, and that meant using his body.

"I suppose you don't have to be gay to become a prostitute or drug addict, but for me, well, it felt like that was what was supposed to happen to me. I didn't know any better." It took Javier ten years to hit bottom. Eventually he was arrested and placed in a rehab center. "The guy in charge was Mexican like me. I identified with him, and he saved my life. I got off drugs and drinking. I've been clean for five years." Quietly, Javier tells me that he is HIV positive. "I guess, given the risks I've taken in my life, I should feel lucky just to be alive."

Javier's confining Latino background, with its stress on men being macho, made his homosexuality so incomprehensible and unmanageable to him at thirteen that he had to leave the safety of his home and live on the streets. "At that time, I didn't know one gay person I could turn to. The first gay people I met were on the street; that's who I first identified with."

Unfortunately, Javier's story is not uncommon in Latino culture. Eric-Steven Gutierrez, recalling his great-uncle in Betty Berzon's book *Positively Gay*, says "*Jotin* is probably the worst thing a Mexican father can call a son. That is what they called Manuel Acosta, my grandmother's best friend, under her parents' roof. Shortly after that he escaped the Depression, the taunts and the beatings in Van Nuys with Santiago Chago and Johnny Melendez in a stolen car."

Gutierrez continues, "Many lesbians and gays are familiar with the conflict of having to leave their families, communities and churches in order to find home. The absurdity and pain of making such a choice is even more complicated for lesbians and gays of color for whom few roles exist other than the extremes of insider or outcast." Gutierrez is here speaking to both the rigidity within the Latino male culture and the position of Latinos in general as a minority in American society.

But Latinos are not alone. Today gays, lesbians, and bisexuals make up 30 percent of all youth living in the streets of this country; 26 percent of young gays and lesbians are forced to leave home because of conflicts over their sexual identity; and approximately 30 percent of gay youth have alcohol and drug problems (figures taken from P-FLAG). These figures should make us all aware of the dangers that stem directly from homophobia. Again, once we begin to redefine what it means to be homosexual, and society and our families don't respond to the outdated, inaccurate definitions, young people will not be forced to run away and endanger their lives.

Getting Acquainted

In recent years, as the gay community has developed local outreach programs for all gays and lesbians, including teenagers, it has become safer and easier for those struggling to come out to find a supportive environment in which to do so. This is essential to being able to come out in a healthy way. Coming out is a process that happens gradually, not all at once. Having access to other gays and lesbians willing to share their experience can help demystify what being gay is all about: sexual orientation, not a fatal flaw or a contagious disease.

Many of us first ventured into gay lives through our participation in certain activities, going to gay bars, or finding ourselves suddenly in a sexual encounter. As if by accident, we found ourselves attracted to our best friends, having crushes on our teachers, or being seduced by others. Whether our first sexual experience with someone of the same sex is at fifteen or thirty-two, the beginning stage of processing these feelings is intense and can be overwhelming. When we finally explore the urge and have it fulfilled, most of us feel a tremendous sense of connection to ourselves — because it feels so right, so natural — but the residual feelings can be confusing. Again, we are confronted with internalized homophobia: What will people think? Am I the same person? Will people still love me? Will I ever meet someone?

Some of us test this new aspect of our identity by comparing ourselves to straight people. Others are not so much uncertain about our identity as curious about acting on our desires. Having sex — whether it's merely kissing or sexual intercourse — becomes at one point or another an important step for anyone trying to live a full life.

After I realized I was a lesbian, I began to wonder what this meant, where these feelings might take me. Like any teenager, I wanted to see what it felt like to kiss someone I was attracted to. In the middle of my junior year in high school, my mom moved to New York to do several films. She got an apartment downtown in the Village, and I moved in with her. While it was nice to live with my mom and have a real home again, I was forced to hide a big part of myself and my life from her on a daily basis. I became extremely self-conscious around her, but I was still afraid to tell either of my parents.

My mom and I began to have even more separate lives, even under the same roof. In some ways, I had become used to her not being around or involved in my daily life. I tried to keep my distance from her, telling her very little that was going on in my life. But I was aware that I was living a split life, and I felt deceitful and anxious about having to hide what I was up to, whom I was seeing.

At the time I rationalized my not telling her by telling myself that she was too busy and distracted by her work, that she didn't want to know anyway, that it didn't make a difference if she knew or not. I told myself I needed time to digest my feelings in my own way. But the truth was I was terrified to tell her.

Now that we lived in the same apartment, she saw much more of me. As always, I was very sensitive to her criticism of how I looked and dressed, and at sixteen I really wanted her approval. When my mother didn't like an outfit, she would say something that would make me feel completely insecure and bad about myself. I became totally intimidated by her. In my mind her criticism was directly related to my being gay. With her already seeming so critical of me, how could I tell her I was gay?

Many gays and lesbians harbor the knowledge that they're gay from those closest to us, especially our parents. As we try to get used to the idea ourselves, we usually come out to those with whom we feel most safe or those we are not at risk of losing. I think it's a good idea to tell someone — a counselor, a friend whom you can trust, before telling your parents. It's also important to reach out to the gay community. Nowadays there are gay and lesbian community centers in most cities and large towns. There are also on-line chat rooms, magazines, and numerous books that help you explore your sexual orientation in a safe, private way before you take the step of coming out to people you know.

Many of the negative coming-out experiences had by people I spoke with occurred as a result of ignorance — people just didn't know any better. As knowledge about homosexuality increases and lesbians and gays become less marginalized in our society, coming out will become easier and less threatening.

During the summer between my junior and senior years of high school, I stayed in New York. I was living downtown and would ride my bike all the way up to Central Park for fun. One beautiful Sunday in June, just after school let out, I was finishing my ride, exiting the park on upper Fifth Avenue, and ran right into a parade.

As I got closer, I realized that everyone in the parade was gay — it was a gay parade. I was shocked, amazed, and finally excited. I had never known there was such a thing! I joined the parade and kept riding with it down to Washington Square.

Up to that point, I had never heard of a gay pride parade. I was still under the impression that the only outlet for gay people was bars. The mere fact of seeing hundreds of gay people celebrating felt exhilarating. This was my first sense of belonging to a community larger than one — me.

Chapter 4
Parents
The Time Bomb

*"It was near the end of the day, the time of day I
don't like talking about, that nameless hour when
the sounds of evening would rise up from every
floor of the prison in a cortege of silence."*

ALBERT CAMUS,
from *The Stranger*

Busted

Living a double life can feel like suspended animation. Although I was still madly in love with Julie, my mother's renewed presence in my life kept me constantly in fear of some impending doom. She and I had moved into Tom Cruise's loft on West Fourteenth Street in the Village, which he was in the process of renovating. Elijah was almost ten years old and away at boarding school on the East Coast.

The loft was actually made up of two apartments, and Tom was in the middle of knocking down a wall to create one large space. In the meantime, my mom and I lived in the smaller apartment — she slept in the bedroom, and I slept on a pull-out sofa bed in the living room–kitchen area.

One night, when Julie and I were on particularly good terms, we went out to the China club dancing. Julie was an incredibly good and very sexy dancer, and we moved well together. Dancing had become something we both enjoyed doing together, and it usually acted as foreplay, leading to something more later in the evening. This night was no exception. When we left the club, we were both anxious to go back to my apartment to make love.

Julie and I quietly entered the apartment, making sure the coast was clear and everyone was asleep. Slowly we made our way to the couch, kissing as we threw off the cushions and pulled out the bed. With our clothes still on, Julie and I began making out in a fever. Suddenly the adjoining door opened, and my mom came into the room on her way to the kitchen, probably to get a glass of water.

From the way the couch was positioned, she could not see Julie and me from the doorway. But instead of just stopping kissing and lying there silently without moving, we jumped to our feet, making it obvious that something was going on between us. As soon as my mom saw us, she turned around and walked back to her room.

Julie and I went back to bed, the heat of the moment lost in my fear of being caught by my mother. I lay awake all night, dreading a confrontation with my mother the next morning. What was I going to say? What was she going to say?

In the morning my mom didn't say a word to me about it, though she acted very distant and distracted. Julie told me later that while I was showering, my mom had approached her and asked what had happened last night. Julie responded with a halting explanation of how she and I had fallen asleep and were startled awake when my mom walked in. My mother never said anything to me about the incident but began to actively hate Julie.

My seventeenth birthday was two weeks later. I had

planned on a party at a downtown restaurant. The day of the party, my mom picked a fight with me — probably about the way I was dressed — and then told me she wasn't going to the party. Frankly, I was relieved. Without my mother at the party, I knew I'd have a better time with my friends.

It wasn't until years later that my mom finally admitted to me her real reason for not coming to my birthday party: she was devastated after walking in on me and Julie.

From that moment on, my mother made it abundantly clear to me that she couldn't deal with my sexual orientation, or me in general; this made me more terrified of her. Her disapproval felt like an immutable fact, and it seemed as if telling her outright would only increase the distance between us and potentially destroy the entire relationship. As a result, we avoided the issue entirely. We very self-consciously chose conversational topics that had nothing to do with my personal life: her work, my college plans, how my aunt Georgeann and Elijah were doing.

She still had a problem with how I dressed: she didn't like my short hair, my Doc Martens, my baggy pants. Looking back, I think her comments on how I looked seemed to be the only way she could express her anxiety about my being gay. The more clear it became that I was gay, the more anxious she became. At the time, I was oblivious to the fact that my mom was struggling with fears and worries about me, as well as disappointment. I could only see and feel the distance between us and the unspoken criticism of who I was. Needless to say, this was an extremely painful period of my life.

During my senior year my mother became busier than usual. She was doing three movies, including *Moonstruck* and *Witches of Eastwick*, and I took advantage of her distractedness to avoid her as much as possible. I was absorbed in my own life in any case: where to go to college, whether I was going to be a film student or a drama student. I allowed my preoccupation with my plans for the future to divert my mind from the tension between me and my mother.

The more turbulent my relationship with Julie grew, the more I needed to talk to someone about it. In her ambivalence about being involved with me and her confusion about her sexual orientation, Julie constantly pulled me toward her and then pushed me away. Our relationship was an emotional roller coaster, and I was feeling isolated: I needed the comfort of someone who could help explain what was going on, and obviously my mother was not that person. I turned to my aunt, my mother's sister. Georgeann, or Gee, as I grew up calling her, had always been very close to me. Throughout my childhood I had gone to her for support and comfort. And since she and my mother were best friends, Gee spent a lot of time with us, often traveling with us and always living nearby. Because she was my aunt and not my mother, I felt less afraid to be open with her, and she in turn didn't have the same issues with me that my mother did.

I never formally came out to Gee, but there was an understanding between us: she knew and tacitly acknowledged that I was gay. Gee told me recently: "It was an unspoken thing. I remember a conversation you and I had at the Morgan Hotel in New York. We were going to a function, and somebody said something to you about wearing a black velvet dress, and we looked at each other and gave a face. From that moment on it was understood." When I turned to Gee about my heartaches over Julie, she was comforting and gave me advice without mentioning the fact that I was in a relationship with a woman. I also knew that I could count on Gee not to tell my mother about my being gay. But it's not Gee's style to be secretive, and she has since told me that although she understood my fear of telling my mom, concealing anything from her sister made her very uncomfortable.

During this period I was also very close to my dad. He still seemed to accept me for who I was, much as he had when I was a child; he did not judge the way I dressed or carried myself. But because we were so close, it was becoming harder and harder to keep from telling him what was going on with me. Because of my mother's distance, his love and closeness meant that much more to me, and I was afraid of jeopardizing my relationship with him by telling him I was gay.

I continued to censor my sexual orientation from him. I would seek out his advice about my relationship, but I'd use "Johnny" instead of "Julie" and change my pronouns from she's to he's. I now know this is a common tactic used by closeted gays and lesbians. For the time being, it satisfied my needs, but as time went on, it became harder and harder to deceive my dad.

By the end of my senior year, Julie and I had finally, inevitably split up. In one way I was completely heartbroken, but I was also relieved not to be tortured by my feelings for her and her ambivalent behavior toward me. I tried my best to put that relationship behind me and focus on my future. After school let out I went to Europe for a month with a friend, then spent the rest of the summer working in L.A. at my dad's restaurant and spending time with him in Palm Springs, where he taught me to drive. That summer, I began taking baby steps toward coming out to him. I would ask him questions such as "Is there anything I could do that would make you not love me?" I also brought up gay current events in a casual way, testing how he would respond. I strategically left a lesbian romance novel on my nightstand, hoping he'd find it. Finally all my not-so-subtle hints paid off.

In the fall of 1987, when I returned to New York University, my dad and his wife, Mary, came for a visit. Their first night in town, we all went out to dinner at Smith & Wollensky's, our family's favorite New York restaurant. After a much-enjoyed meal, we returned to my dad's hotel. As we entered the lobby, my dad turned to Mary and asked her to leave us alone for a few minutes. My dad and I then went into the lounge for coffee.

After a few minutes of small talk, my dad looked at me and said, "Chas, I've been feeling that you want to talk to me about something. I want you to know that you can tell me anything."

Of course I knew exactly what he was getting at.

After hemming and hawing, I finally got up my courage and blurted, "I'm gay."

I quickly explained that I had wanted to tell him for a long time, but I was afraid, afraid that it would affect our close relationship.

"Well, I've got to confess that I've suspected for a while, but I was waiting for you to tell me. When you didn't, I figured that you needed me to help you out." He paused and then said, "I love you no matter what, and nothing can affect our relationship."

Telling my dad lifted a huge weight from my shoulders. Now I could finally be myself around him. I can't express how grateful I feel to my dad for his willingness to raise the subject. His support helped me feel more positive about myself and brought us closer.

It's hard to describe or capture exactly how censoring information about ourselves affects our relationships. It's often only in hindsight that we are able to see the difference between before and after: before telling my dad that I was gay, we were close. But after I told him, the quality of that closeness became much more trusting. I felt more relaxed around him, and as a result the quality of our intimacy increased.

When I came out to him at seventeen, my father was there for me when I really needed him. In the several years before his death, my father and I had grown apart as a result of his being elected to the House of Representatives in 1994 and getting more involved in his fourth marriage and new family (he had two children with Mary — kids I absolutely adore). Also, as I became more politically active, I became more clearly at odds with his politics. On the one hand, he was always personally supportive of me as a gay person; on the other hand, he not only supported but sponsored the 1996 Defense of Marriage Act. Unfortunately, our differing views got in the way of our closeness, but not our love for one another.

Though I was walking on air after coming out to my father, I was still terrified of telling my mom. Gee encouraged me to tell my mom; I dreaded it. With my dad, I was scared, but wanted to tell him because I thought it would make us closer; I had more trust in our relationship. But I thought telling my mom would have the opposite effect, that it would drive us further apart. I just didn't want her to know and felt compelled to hide it from her. We avoided the subject by mutual consent: I didn't want to deal, and she didn't want to deal.

No Turning Back

During the first semester of my freshman year at NYU, I was walking out of a "History of Comedy" class, a big survey class with a huge reading list, when a woman about my age approached me. Explaining that her roommate, who was in my class, was home sick, she asked if she could borrow my notes. I said, "Sure, but I don't know if I'm the best person to borrow from — my handwriting is atrocious." The woman introduced herself as Ann*. We started talking and then decided to get something to eat at the Waverly Coffee Shop, an NYU hang-out. Once we sat down, we soon came out to each other. She was one of the first gay people my age I had met, and I was thrilled. We soon became friends, and I began to suspect that she had a romantic interest in me, which I did not have in her.

One day she brought me back to her apartment. Now, I'm not the neatest person in the world, but this apartment was be-yond the pale: Coke bottles were scattered, half-eaten sand-wiches had been left on couches and tables, and clothes were strewn all around. Ann's roommate, Heidi, was upstairs suf-fering from a week-long migraine. When I went up to meet her, it was obvious that she felt terrible. But it was also ob-vious that there was an immediate energy between the two of us.

When Ann mentioned that they were having a plumbing problem, I transformed into Ms. Fix-it and went to work. Then Heidi came downstairs and asked me if I wanted to watch a movie that night.

When I returned later, Heidi's girlfriend, Nora*, was there. Ann had already told me that Heidi and Nora were on the skids, so I felt comfortable. They had rented the lesbian classic *Lianna*, a film by John Sayles, which I hadn't seen. Dur-ing the movie, there was obvious tension between Heidi and me. We started teasing and throwing gummy bears at each other — stupid stuff that revealed our growing attraction to one another.

Ann and Nora went to bed, and Heidi and I stayed up until five in the morning, talking and talking, sharing our life stories.

It was almost Christmas, and Heidi had plans to go out to San Francisco with her friend Jane to see the New Year's Grateful Dead show — she was a total Deadhead. I had plans to visit my father in Palm Springs and spend New Year's with his family. Before I even left New York, I decided to hook up with Heidi and Jane in California after the holidays.

I got my own room across the hall from where Heidi and Jane were staying. By this time, I was already smitten with Heidi. The chemistry between us picked up where it had left off in New York. We three spent the next two days exploring San Francisco. Heidi and I spent the nights together, talking into the wee hours, finally falling asleep in each other's arms.

The last day, when we were getting ready to fly back to New York, Jane had a panic attack about flying and decided to stay. Heidi and I flew back to New York on the red-eye. The flight was the shortest trip of my life. We stretched out in the back row of seats, cuddling and talking the entire time. We arrived at about six in the morning, and before going back to Heidi's apartment, headed to the Waverly Coffee Shop.

And who was there when we arrived but Ann. In our excitement, we told her about our newfound romance. Ann took it on the chin, so to speak, and that night I spent the night with Heidi. After that we were pretty much inseparable.

All of a sudden there was this new person in my life. As I spent more and more time with Heidi, I spent less and less time at home. I was still living at Tom's apartment, with my mother's boyfriend, Rob, even though my mother had returned to L.A. for work. Looking back, I'm sure that my whole demeanor changed: I went from being a chronic mope (after my breakup with Julie) to being animated and enthusiastic about life again. Even though I didn't see my mother regularly, I'm sure she noticed how happy I'd become. It didn't take a genius to figure out something was up. Also, I think Rob probably told her that I was not sleeping at home every night.

I told my aunt about my new love, and after saying how happy she was for me, she again told me that I should tell my mom that I was gay. Gee felt really bad about keeping secrets from my mom. And although she probably had some idea of how my mom would react, she thought it was better to be honest with her. I knew Gee was right, but I was still terrified of confronting my mother, and since I was so blissfully happy with Heidi, and my mother seemed so far away, I kept procrastinating.

Then, one morning after Heidi had spent the night at the apartment, we woke up to Rob, knocking on the door.

"Chas, you've got to call your mom. She talked to your dad and she knows what's going on. She's expecting you to call her." It was very early in the morning, and Rob looked exhausted. I got the impression that he and my mom had been talking on the phone the entire night.

Absolute terror set in.

My hands went clammy, my heart started to pound in my chest. I thought I was going to throw up.

My worst nightmare had come true. The moment I'd been avoiding for years had arrived.

So I called her.

"Mom, it's me."

"Chas, why didn't you tell me what was going on? How could you do this to me! I had to find out from your father of all people!"

She was furious. I was trembling from head to toe, trying to explain why I hadn't told her.

Then she launched into a tirade about how everyone had known except her and consequently she felt like an idiot. She said that my father had told her that I had gone to a gay bar over Christmas with Joan and her friend Scottie while I was visiting him in Palm Springs; this, of course, was a complete lie. It was becoming clear to me that my dad had taken advantage of the situation in order to really stick it to my mother, exaggerating and even lying outright.

My parents' relationship had always been complicated, dramatic, and full of contradictions. This was right around the time they appeared on David Letterman's show and sang "I've Got You Babe"! Like most divorced couples, they were still very attached, but the tension between them sometimes escalated. In some ways, I think ever since their show ended, my father had felt competitive with my mom, and he used the fact that he knew about me before her to aggravate her.

Meanwhile, my mother was now fuming. She rarely became angry or lost her temper, but in this instance I had never heard such rage from her.

I tried to get a few words in. "Mom, maybe this will make our relationship closer."

After a few minutes, she simply said, "No, this only makes it worse and will push us further apart. I want you to leave that apartment right now."

And she hung up.

I was devastated. Then there was a minute of relief: the worst was finally over. I packed some of my things and calmly left the loft with Heidi.

Needless to say, I was in shock. I followed Heidi back to her apartment, walking numbly through the day — eating, brushing my teeth, going to bed. I kept hearing my mom's voice ringing in my ear. But somewhere deep inside me, I knew that my mom still loved me, that her fury was going to pass. I also began to feel relieved: my secret was finally out.

Within a couple of days, after my mom had a chance to calm down, she called and told me she wanted me to come out to L.A. so we could talk about everything. I was so relieved to hear her voice, I would have promised her anything. She said that she wanted us to go to her therapist together and try to find a way to deal with this as a family. And she wanted to meet Heidi. So we arranged that; I was to fly out, and then Heidi would follow in a couple of days.

This was the beginning of a long process during which my mother and I tried to learn about each other's feelings and teach each other about what being gay is all about. And in our mutual desire to save our relationship, we would draw closer as we struggled to find some way of dealing with both her disappointment in me and my fear of her.

Dealing with the Fear

As I have listened to hundreds of coming-out stories in my travels around the country these past few years, the most consistent feeling gays and lesbians spoke of when describing the initial confrontation with their parents, however it came about, was fear: fear of disappointing their parents, of being rejected by them, of hating themselves.

Fear was what kept me from telling my mom. Because we had already grown so far apart, I believed that losing my relationship with my mother was a real possibility. In my heart I knew that my mother didn't want me to be gay.

Looking back, my unshakable fear and avoidance of telling my mother is a clear reflection of the intense significance all lesbians and gays give to the process of coming out to their parents. The sense of difference we first experienced as children comes to a head in the act of telling our parents that we are gay: it is the most concrete sign of our difference from them. One story that struck me as particularly significant was Bruce's. His fear of telling his parents was so intense that days before his mother finally confronted him, he had planned to kill himself.

BRUCE

Bruce was only fourteen when his mother approached him with a news article in her hand. "Bruce, here's an article about a gay and lesbian youth group an hour away from here.

Isn't that great? They have a gay support group for teens," she said to him, smiling. "If you know anyone who could benefit from this, why don't you pass it on."

He remembers shaking like a leaf. He took the article from his mother and retreated to his bedroom. "I was scared. Oh, my God, she knows. But I still couldn't say anything. I was a nervous wreck when I went to school the next day. In the preceding days, all I had been thinking about was what would be easier for my mom: if I killed myself or if she discovered she had a gay son. I'd basically come to the conclusion that it was better to commit suicide than tell her I was gay.

"When I got home that next evening, I took a really long shower. When I got out, my mom said, 'Why don't you come here and talk to me.'

"I went into her bedroom and started telling her how my day went. I told her how I was being called fag and being harassed. By that time, she'd been aware of what was going on at school and she knew I was depressed. Finally, she wrapped her arms around me and said, 'Bruce, are you gay?'

"I whimpered and then started crying.

"Then I started blabbering, saying how I was sorry to disappoint her, that I knew it was unfair to her.

"She just held me tight and said, 'You could never be a disappointment to me. I love you no matter what.'

"I felt relieved, though I was still convinced my being gay was unfair to my mom. I still felt I was disappointing to her."

Before she handed him that article, it didn't occur to Bruce that his mother already suspected that he was gay, despite the fact that for the past several months he'd been coming home with stories of students ridiculing him in front of other classmates by calling him "faggot" and "queer," by defacing his locker, by following him home and taunting him. Similar to me, he was locked in his own world. But the fear of rejection can run so deep that even when people say it's okay, we may not believe it.

Bruce continues, "I told my mom not to tell my dad. I was afraid of his reaction too. I thought he might be hostile. The next day my dad picked me up at school like he always did. He acted totally normally, talking to me about this and that like always. I remember feeling relieved that my mom didn't tell him. I went into the house, and my mom asked me how things went with my dad.

"I looked at her in confusion and then said, 'What do you mean? Everything was fine.'

"She looked at me, smiled, and said, 'Well, he knows.'

"My mouth just about hit the floor, and the next thing I know, there are these two big, hairy, muscular arms wrapped around me. And my dad said, 'You're my son and I love you.'"

When I asked Bruce why he had anticipated a negative reaction from his father, he said that he and his father were dissimilar. "Although my dad and I are very different, we respect each other. He is very masculine and enjoys doing masculine things like fixing cars. I may like to drive cars, but I don't like to get dirty. He has a green thumb, but I can kill a fake plant if I touch it." Bruce sees the fact that he and his father are different as adding to his fear that his father could reject him.

I think this was true for me too. My mother and I now have some things in common — our interest in film and books, for instance. But on the exterior, we couldn't be more different. I think that this external difference exacerbated the tension between us and made me feel less secure about telling her that I was gay. She has since told me that seeing me grow up and become so different from her made it difficult for her to relate to me.

Despite Bruce's parents' strict religious background (they belonged to a Pentecostal Christian church at the time), they were able to reach out to their son and help him. Bruce's parents immediately helped by driving him to the gay and lesbian youth group, which was over an hour away from their home. Bruce was only fourteen and scared about taking this first step. "I didn't know what to expect; these were the first gay people I ever met in my life. It was a freeing moment. I realized that there were all these different types of people who were gay. Most of the others were teenagers, so they pampered me because I was the youngest. They had two facilitators who monitored and kept meetings intact, and the rest was up to the youth. After the first meeting, I came back to the car, and my mom asked how it was. I smiled — it was probably the most warm and positive I felt in years. I knew for the first time in my life that I could have a positive life. Before that moment I didn't think there would be much of a life for me. I had thought gay people were mentally ill or sex fiends. I knew I didn't fit those stereotypes. I had a really strong Christian background, and I thought I was going to burn in hell."

At the same time, Bruce recalls, "When I first came out to my mom, I felt like it was twenty questions. She'd say, 'Now in fifth grade I remember you had a crush on this girl.' And I'd say, 'Well, I lied.' Then she'd ask me if she was too overbearing as a mother, and I'd tell her, 'No, you've been a good mother.' Then she'd say, 'Well, your dad wasn't absent in your life.'"

Bruce is pointing to the erroneous, stereotypical, and very limiting definitions of homosexuality that are still rooted in our society. His mother assumed that there was a "cause" for Bruce's homosexuality. She also assumed it could have been her *fault* that he was gay. Her ignorance was in part due to her limited knowledge of homosexuals, but it was also due to her exposure to very prejudiced, inaccurate views of homosexuals through her church.

Bruce continues, "She just wanted to make sure it wasn't

anything she did. A few months after she found out, we were taking a walk in the forestry, and she put her hand on my shoulder, and she said, 'I finally figured out why you are gay.' I rolled my eyes and said 'What?' and she said, 'I chewed Juicy Fruit gum while I was pregnant with you.' We started laughing, and from that moment on we've had a sense of humor about it. All communication has been really open and honest."

Though in some cases a gay person's expectation of anger or rejection can be realistic, and it may actually be dangerous for a gay person to come out to his or her parents, more often than not the reaction we fear is worse than the reality. In my case, my mother's response hurt me deeply, but her quick recovery and commitment to me helped begin our mutual acceptance. It was a hard lesson, for my mother's reaction made me acutely aware that I was not the only one going through a process: so was she.

Real vs. Irrational Fear

PAUL

Some parents take longer to get to the point of being ready to accept their child's being gay. When Paul's parents discovered one of the notes he had written when he was eleven, they confronted him, and it took a long time for their anger and shock to subside. Paul was fourteen at the time and remembers the day clearly: "We had just finished lunch [at school], and they buzzed over the intercom summoning me to the office. On account of my good grades, I was used to being buzzed to do an interview or talk about my grades. When I got to the principal's office, my mom was there crying. I immediately thought someone had died. My mom turned to me and said, 'You're coming out of class today.'

"Both my parents were in the front seat and I was in the backseat. No one said a word. I still wasn't sure what was going on, and then all of a sudden my dad started crying. That's when I knew. Then my mom handed me the note over the back of the seat, saying, 'I found this today cleaning.' And she started to cry again, then I started to cry as well. I apologized over and over. They said they didn't know what they were going to do. They had already spoken to the preacher before they had taken me out of school.

"Things began to get really bad around the house. Everyone was fighting. There was continuous screaming and an increase in punishments. My parents had always 'ruled by the rod and belt,' so to speak. But we had only been spanked if we had not done what we were supposed to. Now it seemed that I was being punished for the most inane things. My parents could barely speak to me. All my father could do was yell at me; my mother just cried. My sister and brother just stared at me, angry that I was causing so much trouble for the family. My parents were talking about sending me to a military academy. After a few weeks, I ran away from home for about an hour. My father and I had yet another fight, and I went and hid under a windowsill. I came back when everyone sat down for dinner.

"But home had begun to feel like an unsafe place for me. The next time I ran away for a day; that's when I found out there was a gay club in town. I wrote a long letter to this club, begging for someone to help me. Of course, because I was a minor, they ignored me. This was in 1980, and there was no outreach then. I felt there was nowhere I could turn. At the restaurant where I was a busboy, I had met one friend, a woman in her thirties, who talked to me a lot. But there was only so much she could do. She assured me that when I became an adult, things would go smoother for me. But she was the only one who gave me any sense of self-worth and some hope for the future.

"Then my parents decided to take me to a psychiatrist; the preacher had recommended someone who was into aversion therapy. I went once and told my parents I wasn't going to go again. Then they took me to a second psychiatrist, who was interested in all my fantasies. But I was only fourteen, and at that point I wasn't even fantasizing. He was so intent about my fantasies that I began making them up so that he would stop bothering me. I had read a lot of Anais Nin, so I told him about fantasies I had read about in books.

"He wanted to force a confrontation with my parents, and that's when I started shouting, 'I hate you, I hate you.' I didn't really want to do that, but he forced me to do it; my parents wanted him to convince me that I wasn't gay. The whole thing felt like a farce to me. He wasn't helpful, and I didn't trust that he would make things any better for me in terms of my parents. I became even more desolate. That night I ran away from home and hitchhiked to a gay club. I stood outside for a couple of hours until a man drove by in his car and took me home to his house. This was my first adult sexual experience. The man was really sweet when I told him about the problems that were going on, and he told me he couldn't help me. Not only was he a lot older than me, he was also black. I asked him if I could stay with him, and he said no. At the time, I didn't understand why he wouldn't help me. Now I do: he was a gay black man in South Carolina, trying to help a fourteen-year-old. He would have gotten lynched. The next morning, he dropped me off in front of the club, and I went home.

"The next weekend I ran away to the gay club again. This time I had prepared everything. When we'd gone to church, I complained of an upset stomach and went to the bathroom, stripped off my church clothes and changed into my T-shirt and shorts, and hitchhiked to the gay club. At some point, my parents realized I was gone and went hunting for me.

"I had gone to the gay people out in the parking lot; they asked me if I wanted to smoke a joint. These two gay girls I met were really sympathetic. I was crying. Then this one guy I had met agreed to take me back with him to Asheville, North Carolina. Right before we were about to leave, my parents showed up at the club with the police. I ran from the car and hid in a field. I was lying flat in four feet of weeds, and at one point, my dad walked about five feet from my head. He was yelling my name, and I just lay there — absolutely terrified.

"I just knew there was no way to work it out with them. They were completely unwilling to compromise and look at the situation in any other way. They talked about sending me to a military school. It was either that or them taking me to a psychiatrist who was going to use aversion therapy on me. I wasn't going to a therapist to convince me I wasn't gay. They were so intolerant, it felt like survival to get away. I knew I had to get out of there. I didn't see another escape route."

Paul pauses and then says, "I still experience a lot of trauma around the whole incident; so much so that I've forgotten a lot of it. I do remember later running from car to car and spotting the two women; they called the guy from Asheville, and he came and picked me up and took me to North Carolina.

"It only took me a week in North Carolina to realize that there were a lot of other gay people, people like me. It was my first positive exposure to the gay community. Then I became extremely homesick. I called my parents and told them I wanted to go back home. My father was stationed for that whole summer out on the West Coast and had been gone the month I was away. So when I arrived home, it was only my mom, brother, and sister. The following week we left for a trip to visit my father.

"During that first week, it was real intense. There was a lot of fighting, and to make matters even more dramatic, Mount Saint Helens was blowing up in the background. My sister was the only one remotely sympathetic. When my dad and I got into a fight that afternoon, I ran away again. I went to the highway with two dollars and bought a pack of cigarettes — smoking was a big rebellious thing for me to do. Within twenty minutes, a reporter picked me up and drove me to Portland. He dropped me off in the gay section of the city, where three guys spotted me right away. One guy was Joel, he was a chiropractor at the time. He said I could stay with him."

When I ask Paul if he was ever afraid or hesitant to trust the people he met, he shakes his head and says, "I was charmed. I could have encountered many dangerous situations, not-so-nice people, but I was lucky. I got two jobs right away at two different restaurants. I had to lie about my age — thank God I still had a fake ID. That was my saving grace; I would have been in really bad shape. I was lucky; I kept meeting really nice and generous people. I think at the time, the gay community realized that there was no other place for us to go."

Here again I am reminded of the fact that Paul — a lucky survivor who has a success story to tell — was one of thousands of teenage gay and lesbian runaways who, after being rejected and often abused by their families, leave their homes and turn to the streets. He was lucky enough to avoid being physically hurt, including becoming infected with HIV.

Paul continues, "After work I began hanging out at an underage gay bar called Metropolis. One evening as I was going in, the doorman stopped me and said that two men had come into the bar that afternoon with a picture of me. I realized that detectives were looking for me. I thought that the only way

out was to run again. I went to both my jobs and got my pay-
checks, cashed them, and bought a one-way ticket to NYC for
ninety-nine dollars. From all my reading I knew to go to
Christopher Street. I quickly met other people my age who
were from much worse or similar situations.

"The first couple of nights, I slept on the street; then I
found a flophouse with a couple of prostitutes and a couple of
other guys — we all looked out for each other. There was a
twelve-year-old kid, but the rest of us were around the same
age. A girl named Cindy, who was my age, taught me how to
protect myself. I don't recall being scared; I knew that there
were other kids like me, and they taught me how to avoid
cops."

When I ask him how he survived, he says, "Well, I did
turn a few tricks at first. Yeah, that's a really long, interesting
part of my NYC experience. My first attempt to turn a trick
was with a guy in the movie *Fame*. His name was Moose, and
he was a drag queen. He told me that this rich guy wanted both
of us to go up to his apartment. So we went back to this guy's
home, which was a four-story town house in Greenwich Village. The guy turned out to be an editor of *Penthouse* magazine. He brought Moose and me up, and when he started to put
his hand on my leg, I bolted back to the bar. Moose came after
me and gave me the money anyway. The guy had told Moose
to tell me to come see him if I needed any more help.

"After that incident, I turned a couple of tricks by myself.
That was pretty traumatic, but I guess I was lucky — they
could have been worse. I realized that I had to separate from
the kids I had met. I was not going to live as a prostitute. I
knew that I had succeeded getting jobs in other towns. Soon I
met a man in a bar, and he said he had a place available for me
to stay and then said he'd help me get a job. I stayed at his
place for a month for free, then he got me a job at New York,

New York, a restaurant/bar. From there I branched out and made a lot of friends and other contacts.

"I was a fifteen-year-old working as a waiter; I didn't have to turn any more tricks, because I was getting a regular paycheck; I was a regular member of the community."

When I asked Paul how he reconciled with his parents, he sighs and says, "I got my heart broken and called my parents for support. It was my first love, and it didn't work out. I can't really remember what was going through my head. I knew that things at home weren't going to be easy, but I hadn't lost hope that my parents would come around. When you don't have any other area of support, you turn to those closest to you."

Paul's courage and hopefulness were the catalysts for his parents' ultimate acceptance of his homosexuality. But before they were able and ready to truly embrace their son again, they were forced to confront yet other dashed expectations: their second son announced that he too was gay.

No More Regrets

Many of us have stories that reveal the difficulty we experienced when our parents discovered we were gay. As you can imagine, my mother's reaction to finding out I was gay was very traumatic for me. In hindsight, I could have handled things differently. First, I could have tried to understand more about my fear of my mom and thus felt better able to approach her. In many ways, my reluctance and avoidance only exacerbated her anxiety and disappointment. Second, if I had been able to present a more positive perception of being gay, she may not have reacted so negatively. And obviously her having been the last to know and hearing the news from my father only increased her hurt and anger.

Looking back, it's clear to me that had I been more prepared, known more gay people my age, or begun to develop a support system within the gay community, I might not have been so afraid to approach my mom directly. As it was, the years of distance between us had increased my fear of rejection to such a degree that I had no trust in my mom's love for me. Her quick turnaround in the days following that horrible phone call, however, proved to me that she did care about me and wanted to find a way to deal with the situation. She made it clear that she didn't want to lose me or our relationship.

This is when we often begin the healing process. I began to nurture a deep faith in my mother's love for me and on my own determination to maintain our relationship. Together, we began to map out a new way to relate to one another — with honesty and mutual respect.

Chapter 5

Taking Control
Navigating the Reactions

"Mom. Momma. I'm a homosexual, Momma. Boy, did that come out awkward."

TONY KUSHNER,
from *Millennium Approaches*

Going to the therapy session with my mother was a wonderful, healing experience for me. My mother had returned to her very controlled, collected demeanor, and it was clear to me that she wanted to work on our relationship as much as I did. Although over the next few years we would stumble on some potholes, the first time we saw each other after she found out I was gay was a reunion. The healing had begun.

Many other gays and lesbians, usually those who come out later and feel a stronger sense of control over their lives, are able to approach their parents and tell them directly.

When We Do the Telling

Those who tell their parents directly may still fear rejection as well as disapproval, but they've achieved enough self-acceptance to give support to their conviction that they need and want to tell their parents they are gay.

DAVIS

When Paul's brother, Davis, came out to his parents ten years after Paul did, they had a much more positive reaction. In the intervening time, their parents had not only done an enormous amount of reading, they had also begun to reevaluate their ideas about homosexuality. The transformation was by no means immediate, but it was sure and steady. Their hostile and rejecting attitude toward Paul, a result of the culture — both social and religious — that held them in its grips, took a long time to be dislodged.

Davis remembers telling his mother first. "I had just graduated from college, and I went home for about six months. I had made this big move, and I knew it was a good time to make a life change. I had finally gotten out of that total straight environment [at college]. I was working at a restaurant; there were several gay people, and I had met this guy, Daniel*, who I thought was the one. I fell madly in love. Looking back, I see that I was young and immature, but at the time I thought if I was going to spend the rest of my life with this guy, then I had to tell my parents I was gay.

"I was terrified to tell them. I had no other support than Daniel. I talked to him about it, and he cautioned me against it, saying that I would ruin my relationship with them. He said that he'd told his parents, and he'd regretted it ever since. I thought about it twenty-four hours a day; one day I went home and there was this Oprah Winfrey show on coming out — it was for National Coming Out Day in October. Watching the show got me more motivated. I called my brother, who was by that time living out in northern California. I thought he was the safest person to tell, even though we had never been that close. I told him I was gay, and he was surprised. When I asked him if he had suspected, he said he thought maybe I could be, but he wasn't positive. Then he told me he loved me and wished me well. He asked if I had told mom and dad and said he'd keep it a secret if that's what I wanted. He was very kind — it was probably one of the more tender moments between us. But obviously he wasn't totally behind me telling our parents. I'm sure, even ten years after our parents found out about him, he was still hurt from all the trauma.

"But I persevered. I thought my parents would miss out on a lot in my life because I hid so much from them. I was lying to them, which I didn't feel comfortable about. So that night I decided to tell my parents. I was helping my mother make dinner, with my stomach in knots the whole time. I kept waiting for the right moment. Finally it was time to go to bed. My mom always reads before she goes to bed and I went into her room. She looked up and said, 'What?'

"I burst out crying and then said, 'I'm gay.'

"She put her arms around me and told me she loved me. 'It's okay,' she said. She was really cool about it, and she ended up telling my dad.

"I was real hesitant about telling my dad. Since my coming out we've gotten much closer, but before that we were never that close. Ever since I was a kid he would try to push me into his interests instead of letting me have my own. There had always been a lot of tension between us.

"After my mother told him about me being gay, my father wouldn't talk about it for a couple of weeks. Then one day we were in the car, just the two of us, and we were at a red light, and he said, 'Do you think if you had sex with a woman you could change?'

"I immediately said, 'No,' and then he said, 'Okay.' That was it. Of course there was an adjustment period. Every time I went out, they would get worried. They thought I was going to get into trouble like my brother — carousing and smoking dope. They knew I was going out to a gay bar in Greenville. I could tell from my father's classic facial expressions that he was worried. I would have to say, 'Yes, I'm gay, but I'm not Paul.' It was hard.

"Once we got over that barrier, little by little we could talk about things. Having a second gay child made my parents reevaluate homosexuality. There was so much negativity around my brother's coming out." Davis acknowledges that although his homosexuality was also a cause of pain for his parents, they were more sensitive to him than they'd been to Paul; his parents didn't want Davis to go through the same torment his older brother had.

When I ask Davis about measuring the desire to tell his parents against the fear he may still have associated with coming out based on his brother's experience, he says, "It was one of the best things I could have done. It brought our relationship to a new level — there was a lot more openness and honesty."

By the time Davis came out, his parents were much more ready to accept and work with him to integrate his being gay into their lives. Davis still feels the family hasn't healed from Paul's trauma. Paul has forgiven their parents and leads a fully out life. But no one says it's easy. As Davis says, "People need to hear how important it is to be integrated with their parents. The people who haven't told their parents, or who haven't worked it through with their parents, are usually still in the closet in some way or another."

Davis believes above all that "if your parents really love you, they will eventually learn to accept it. It's worth the risk, but it's also important for kids to help their parents along on that journey."

Gonna Sit Right Down and Write Myself a Letter

RICHARD

When Richard, the urban planner, told his mother that he was a homosexual, she was not surprised. Like my mother, she'd always known a lot of gay people, especially gay men, and she did not attach a lot of moral judgment to the idea of homosexuality. Still, it was scary for him to come out to her. Richard remembers: "I was living in Paris, studying architecture, and my mom called me from my sister's house in California. She told me that she'd read the article about Simon Le Vay's study on homosexual men, which supported the idea that homosexuality was biologically based. There was this long pause, and then I said, 'I'm gay, Mom.' Then I burst into tears. She said she loved me and that everything was fine. She asked me why I had waited so long to tell her. I explained that I was afraid. She'd been making all these references to getting a girlfriend and getting married. Two of my sisters had recently gotten married, and another one was already on to her second child. Then my mother said, 'I just want you to be happy.'"

By that time Richard had already told a couple of his sisters, who had continued to be supportive — even Terry, the one who had given him a hard time when they were growing up. However, coming out to his father was another story. Richard waited another five years before telling his father, who had since remarried and was living in Florida.

Although most of Richard's family, himself included, considered themselves Catholic, they did not agree with a lot of church teaching, including the church's harsh stance on homosexuality. His father, however, still maintained a strict religious life as a Catholic, going to daily mass. Up to this point,

Richard had used his father's geographical distance and his lack of involvement in his daily life as an excuse to put off coming out to him, but as his life become more and more gay oriented, Richard became fed up with what he felt was his own deceitfulness.

He decided to write his father a letter.

Dear Sheila* and Dad,
I've just returned from the beach, where I spent Memorial Day weekend with some of my friends. It's just beginning to rain and thunder — summer truly has begun.

This will not be an easy letter to write to you, but life isn't exactly easy, is it? I want to share something with you that I am no longer able to, or perhaps I should say that I no longer wish to keep from you. I am gay.

I can't imagine that this news will come to either one of you as a surprise. I've wanted to say this before, but I never found the right opportunity. Now that you are in Florida, the phone is our only communication link, but I really don't like the phone, so I am writing this letter instead.

I realize that despite any suspicions you may have had, this news will still probably come as a shock. I hope that in time you will learn to accept me regardless of my homosexuality. When you receive this letter, please contact me by phone or mail so I know you have received it. I want to answer any questions that I am sure you will have.

Having written the above words, I can say that this letter is truly difficult for me to write, but also necessary. You are my father and stepmother and have known me my entire life; I cannot continue withholding this part of myself from you. I want to be closer with you, but I haven't been able to. I love you both and I hope that we can be closer now that I have expressed myself to you honestly.

While there is a good deal more that I could write, I believe that I have already written the most important words. Please be in touch soon.

Love,
Richard

A few days passed, and his stepmother called in tears, saying, "It was a wonderful letter. We are so happy that you wrote it. We love you, and here's your father."

After assuring Richard that he loved him, his father brought up the moral questions regarding homosexuality that went along with his Catholicism. Richard remembers his father saying, "I know that God had his own reasons for making people gay, but it's up to you to make the right choice." In other words, Richard inferred, he could choose to do the "right" thing and be celibate. Richard and his father continued to speak, and, signing off, his father said, "Be careful." Richard understood this to be his father's indirect way of telling him to have safe sex and be careful not to contract HIV. "He was worried about my physical and spiritual health."

After this conversation, they didn't have any more dialogue on the subject, and both retreated into their daily lives. For the next couple of years, Richard and his father communicated irregularly. Richard felt awkward, and his conversations with his dad were limited to safe topics: business, his father's golf game, Richard's swimming, his sisters.

Two years passed. Richard's father called, and after all the usual topics were exhausted, he was still pressing Richard for news or information. So Richard took the plunge: he told his father about his boyfriend, Mark*, whom he'd been involved with for over a year. Although he didn't quite admit that he and Mark were discussing moving in together, Richard's mere mention of Mark's existence was a huge step. At first his father replied awkwardly, "Well, are you okay with that?"

"What do you mean, Dad?"

"Well, have you discussed this with any of your priest friends?"

Richard laughed to himself and then said, "No, Dad, I haven't. You know, you'll really like Mark. He's a great guy."

"Well, I'm sure I will." Then a pause. "Is he a college boy?"

"Do you mean did he go to college?"

"Yes."

"Yes, as a matter of fact he went to Yale."

"Well, that's a fine school, fine school."

They talked of other things, and then his father said, "Well, I see we disagree a bit; maybe one of us has to change or come to another understanding of it." To Richard, his father's mere suggestion of the possibility that he may have needed to adjust his point of view was groundbreaking.

This conversation between Richard and his father occurred a couple of weeks after a group of American Catholic bishops sent out a decree to all the American parishes stating that it was the duty of parents *not* to reject a child if he or she was gay. The bishops' letter went on to state that parents needed to embrace their children and love them. This was not condoning the "gay lifestyle," but rather the duty of parents to continue to love their children no matter what. Richard wondered if his father's suggestion that he might need to adjust his point of view was a result of this decree.

I see this action of the Catholic Church as a significant step toward redefining its stance on homosexuality. It's important because it holds parents responsible for their children's well-being. Richard hoped that there was the possibility of change in his father's attitude toward homosexuality, which in turn could promise more closeness between them. In this way, Richard and his father benefited from communication and the willingness to be honest.

For all parents there is an adjustment time; my mom's was relatively short in terms of her willingness to directly confront my being gay. Paul and Davis's parents had a longer, more protracted period of adaptation. And Richard's father is still in the process of accepting his son's homosexuality. But he is moving in the right direction — if only inches at a time.

Taking the Reins

JUDY

Judy came out to her parents in the middle of her divorce. She'd been in therapy, struggling with the crises of realizing she was gay, falling in love with a woman, and needing to tell her husband that she wanted a divorce — and why. "I had fallen in love with Lenore, and I knew I didn't want to be married to my husband. But it was a terrible period of my life. At the time, I was working for the city [in a middle-management job in the Parks and Recreation department]. All the stress and trauma that was going on at home was definitely affecting my job, so one day I felt I needed to explain to my boss what was going on in my life. I told her what was happening, and she seemed to be understanding. She said something like, 'Oh, I understand. I'll keep it in the strictest of confidence.' Well, at the next city council meeting, I saw my boss sitting next to another city councilwoman, and they were talking to one another. I just knew they were talking about me. I went home, and that night I didn't sleep. And I was bombarded by thoughts that I was a terrible mother because I was leaving my children and going into this situation that was wrong and bad. I definitely felt suicidal."

She says, "My parents always taught us that everyone had equal rights and that no one was better than anyone else.

There was no blatant judgment against homosexuality." But when I asked her why she had suicidal thoughts, she admitted that the negative associations with being gay made her feel like a terrible person. "I just couldn't get away from the idea that what I was doing was wrong, and that I should stay married. But I also think that my parents' initial response was neither liberal nor supportive, even though that's the way they were in other situations.

"I remember when I was first going through this and going to counseling and saying to myself, 'What am I going to say to my husband, how am I going to get out of this, and what are these feelings I'm having?' My parents had always been so open and understanding, so I wanted to tell them before I told my husband. The counselor suggested that my folks come down for a family session, which I thought was a great idea.

"So my parents came down from Seattle for a two-hour session. When I told them that I was a lesbian, I started sobbing. The first thing my dad said was 'You just don't want the responsibility of being a mother anymore.' I remember the counselor pointed out that that wasn't a fair statement. The other thing my father said was that I just wanted to play both sides of the fence. He was very angry. Then he surprised me by saying, 'Well, I figured this since the time you were a little kid.' I think that was part of his anger. From that point on, it was a vertical learning curve for all of us."

Judy's story reminds me of my own. Like my mom's first reaction, Judy's parents' response to the news that she was gay was anger. They weren't considering their daughter's situation, her pain and confusion. All they could do was lash out at her. But like my mom's, after a brief spurt of fury, their shock subsided. Her parents were then able to approach the situation more openly and focus on how to help their daughter through a difficult personal crisis.

"A couple of weeks later I brought my husband in. He came into counseling thinking that we were going to save our marriage. The counselor had to remind him, 'You don't understand: your marriage is over. What we need to do now is figure out a way to end it.'"

When I asked her how she dealt with her husband's feelings of rejection, Judy said, "I just kept trying to talk to him. Every time I would try to talk logistics, he'd start sneezing. He told me that I had to tell the kids about the divorce. At the time, my daughter was five and my son was three. When I sat them down and told them that we were splitting up, my daughter said, 'You're not my mom anymore, you're not my mom anymore.' She began hitting me, and my son was just sobbing. It's all kind of a blur; it was a very painful time in my life. I had worked so hard to be a good mother, and I'd worked hard at my job. I'd always tried to be the right kind of person. Then all of a sudden I felt everyone said I was a bad person — the city councilwoman, my kids, my husband — everyone was telling me how awful I was.

"My husband went around announcing to all of our friends, 'My wife left me for a woman.' I could understand his anger; why should I blame him for telling the truth? But I felt lousy. I hated myself but loved this other person. The only thing that kept me going was trusting my love for Lenore."

Dress Rehearsal

SYDNEY

Judy decided to tell her parents first, but some of us "rehearse" by telling other adults first. I told my aunt and Joan. The first person in her family circle that Sydney told was her mother's best friend, a woman and neighbor who was more than twenty years younger than her mother, who had had Sydney when she was forty. Sydney was smart to first tell someone she felt would be supportive and nonjudgmental. In this way, she felt better prepared to tell her parents.

Sydney had begun a relationship with a woman named Chris and felt fairly secure about calling herself a lesbian. At the time, she was a student at SUNY Purchase, a school, according to Sydney's estimate, that was at least 50 percent gay and/or bisexual at the time. Sydney remembers: "The first person I told was my mother's best friend. It wasn't a really conscious choice, but she'd always been a sounding board for me — I think because my mom being older made me feel awkward telling her things. She was from such a different generation. My mom grew up before civil rights.

"My mom's friend lives around the corner from my mother, and one day we were talking on the phone, catching up, and in response to one of those innocuous questions like 'What's new?' I said, 'Well, I have a new crush with a twist.' She didn't really have much of a reaction. I think she thought that I'd already jumped so many fences, this was just another wrong side of the fence to play on. I think my being involved with a woman fit into her image of me as a rebel.

"My parents were the only ones whose reaction I feared. I told my mother that summer after sophomore year. I was twenty at the time. My mom had already met Chris and liked her. She was angry that I waited until they'd already met. She said, 'I can't even hate her.' We were in the kitchen when I told her I thought I was a lesbian. She dropped a knife in the sink and begged me not to tell my father. She seemed more worried about his reaction than her own. She was panicked that I was setting myself up to be in harm's way and that I was destined for a hard life. She was convinced I was going to be endangered. She hadn't had any real exposure to gay people, so just imagined the worst, believing all the stereotypes about how gay people lived on the margins of society. I'm sure she associated this kind of bad treatment with her own experience of racism. After all, my father's life had been endangered for integrating a public swimming pool."

When I ask Sydney whether there was a reaction to the fact that Chris is white, she said, "Once you cross the gender line, the racial line is rather moot. Put it this way: I don't think I would have gotten any points if I had been involved with a black woman."

Sydney's father was a deeply religious man with unshakable morals. Her mother was afraid that the news of his daughter's being gay would shatter him. But that wasn't the case. "I told my dad two years later. I had made a deal with my mother that I would not volunteer the information, but if he asked me I wouldn't lie, and that's how it happened. But it's not like I went out of my way to hide it. I had an eight-by-ten photo of Chris that traveled with me. Chris graduated before me, and we moved to Albany. My dad was driving me up there, helping me move, and he finally asked me, 'So is this some kind of lesbian relationship?' I grabbed the 'Oh Jesus' candle in the car and said, 'Yes.' And he said, 'Well, I guess we can stop worrying about you getting pregnant.' I knew he was happy about it, though I'm sure he was a bit disappointed, but he hid those feelings from me, and in the end he was very good-natured about it.

"I never doubted my dad's love for me, but there was some adjusting to do. For the first six months or so we went through bouts of intense arguing like we'd never done before, but ultimately we became much closer. It put us in the position of saying things we otherwise wouldn't have said. He told me that he'd come to realize, no matter what his feelings about the relationship were, there was no way to support me without therefore supporting the relationship, and no matter what, I was still his kid and nothing was going to change that.

"After he died two years later, I learned from my uncle and mother that it was much harder for my dad to deal with than he ever let me know. My mother said he had a lot of trouble with where to put the idea of homosexuality in the context of his religious beliefs."

Sydney feels enormous gratitude that she had the opportunity to be honest about herself before her father died. She is frank about how well loved and cherished she'd always been by her parents, how spoiled she was. Talking to her, I was struck by her sense of joy and pleasure in being gay. For Sydney, discovering her love of women, especially Chris, her lover now for over seventeen years, was a gift.

KARI

Like Richard, Kari came out to her parent in a letter, and like Sydney, she turned to another adult, her mother's close friend, for a kind of rehearsal. "I had told a couple of my straight friends — I wrote letters to them. Two of them were like, 'We've known for a while.' But the third one remembered asking me a couple of years before if I was gay and I had said no. She said to me, 'I love you; you're my friend. I just need time to adjust.'

"By that time, I was twenty-three. My dad had passed away when I was nineteen. I had recently met this woman, Jane, at a bar and had been seeing her. The more important Jane was becoming to me, the more I needed to tell Mom about my new relationship. But it was scared shitless." So Kari decided to write another letter. "I felt like I could say what I wanted more concisely and clearly. I was afraid I would chicken out. I left the letter at home. I was going away for the weekend with Jane. I told my mom's friend Barb that I had written the letter and asked her to be there for my mom. I learned later that she called my mom and they went out for a drink. Basically, Barb came out to my mom for me."

Kari was afraid of losing her mom, just as I was. "I had already lost my dad, and the thought of losing her, of having her reject me, was overwhelming. I'd heard so many horror stories about lesbians and gays not talking to their families, of their families basically shunning them. I didn't want that to happen. In one part of my mind, I was ninety-nine percent sure that everything was going to be fine with my mom, but that one percent was what made me afraid of confronting her directly."

Again, it was Kari's limited exposure to the gay and lesbian community that reinforced her fear. Her contact before this point was mainly limited to the women she had met in her band. When Kari came home two days later, her mother simply embraced her. "I was in my room, and my mom came in and started hugging me. She told me that she loved me. She was a psychologist, so the only thing she was afraid of was societal pressure and other people being mean to me. She loved me to death and has been incredibly supportive from day one. Not too long after that, she got involved with P-FLAG."

NINA

Nina's parents also responded to her homosexuality with love. During her senior year of college, Nina returned home to Houston for the holidays. She'd decided to tell her parents, but she let the entire Christmas vacation pass without summoning her courage to come out and disclose that she had been involved in a relationship with a woman for several years. When her parents took her to the airport, she asked her mother to walk her in while her dad stayed in the car. "I wanted my mom to know. She was president of NOW and had always been supportive of women's rights. At times, she had even called herself a radical feminist. But I didn't know how to talk to her. I decided to give her a hint and sent her some pictures of me and my lover dressed in tuxedos for New Year's Eve. So as we waited for my plane to board, she grabbed me and said, 'I just want you to know that I know about you and your friend, and I love you.' We both started crying — it was a pretty powerful moment. I gave her a big hug and told her I loved her.

"It was such a huge relief to know that my mother accepted me for who I am. One of my first questions was whether my dad knew. He was equally as accepting. He was a bit worried but only wanted me to be happy. Later my mom revealed that she'd been suspicious but wanted me to learn about myself at my own pace. But when she got the pictures, she knew it was true."

Nina's extended family, specifically one uncle, was not as accepting. "My mom was so proud of her lesbian daughter that she thought it would be okay to share the news of my coming out with her sisters and brothers. The next thing I know, she is telling everyone in my family. One of my uncles turned out to be arrogant and not accepting. This was a surprise because we'd gotten along for many years and had been pretty close. Once he found out that I was gay, he treated me totally differently. He made a lot of negative comments, questioning what I was doing with my life and telling me my 'lifestyle' was totally unacceptable. I remember him telling me, 'You're never going to get anywhere with your life.' Finally my mom told him to lay off. She encouraged him to be more loving, saying that I was family. We are cordial on the surface, but I haven't talked to him since."

Nina admits that if her parents had not been so loving, accepting, and supportive, her uncle's criticisms would have stung more. "It's hurtful knowing that someone you love can't get past a certain aspect of your self. But ultimately I think it's his loss."

The reality is that some people in our lives will have a more difficult time seeing past their prejudiced, judgmental views of homosexuality. But in the cases where we may grow apart from a friend or a family member because of his or her difficulty accepting our homosexuality, we are better off living true to ourselves. The friends and family who stick by us, perhaps struggling to overcome their fears, will only become more worthwhile and meaningful to us.

Parents Redux

Telling our parents is the single most important and often most frightening part of coming out. Most of us grow up wanting to please our parents. We want our parents to love us, and we fear disappointing them. No matter what kind of family we come from — whether it's a traditional nuclear family with a mother and father as heads of the household, or we have divorced parents, or we live in a tightly knit extended family — as soon as we realize we are gay we are presented with a conflict: we want to tell our family so that they know "who we really are," but we are also afraid to tell them for fear of rejection. Since we are a family-oriented culture in which there is a prolonged period of dependency, we are trained to need our families. We take on their values and experience any difference from them as a conflict.

Deciding on the best time to come out to our parents is difficult. Events such as a parent's death or a divorce can often make us delay the confrontation. Although I didn't know it at the time, I could have done more preparation and probably avoided some of the pain I caused both myself and my mother. Davis felt similarly. When he came out to his parents, he still hadn't taken many steps to prepare — either for himself or for his parents. Although Davis was older and more mature than his brother Paul was when he came out to their parents, he regrets not having spent more time accessing support and information from the lesbian and gay community. His parents may have done a lot of reading, but it was up to him to act as their guide.

By first sharing the news with other gay people, friends, or a counselor, you will begin to process how you feel about being gay. I cannot overemphasize the importance of researching and accessing information — at the library, the nearest gay and lesbian community center, in gay and lesbian publications, or over the Internet. The more knowledge you have, the more understanding you will have of your own identity. Then you will feel more capable of handling and anticipating your parents' reactions and questions. This will help them navigate their own coming-out process.

What's clear to me in hindsight is that the more support we get from other gay people and the more we understand our homosexuality, the better we can present this information to our parents in a positive way. Our ability to reassure them that we are the same people they have always known and loved will help to deflect some of their worries, fears, and possible anger. It's important to be as positive about yourself as possible. I know that if I had told my mom directly she would not have felt so betrayed. She has also admitted to me that if I had not seemed so afraid to tell her she may not have been so worried. You're sharing something about yourself that is not bad, shaming, or damning. If the people you are telling pick up any negative feelings from you, they will immediately question what you are saying. Of course, there are situations in which people's values are so absolute that they will require a much longer, more complicated process to get to acceptance; this is often the case in orthodox or fundamentalist religious families.

Some parents will always be shocked by the news that their son or daughter is gay. But reaching out, learning about what being gay is about, and starting to build a safety net of other gay people, whether friends or through a community outreach program and other such vehicles, will help offset some of the natural anxiety we all feel when we come out to our parents.

Chapter 6

Unearthing Homophobia
Beneath the Surface

"By transforming our lives through coming out of shame, we transform the culture's perception and understanding of our lives, finally breaking the equation that gay=shame."

GERSHEN KAUFMAN, PH.D., AND LEV RAPHAEL, PH.D., from *Coming Out of Shame*

My Tabloid Nightmare

After the trip to Los Angeles in 1988 to meet with my mom and her therapist, Heidi and I returned to New York. We were in our so-called radical phase, wearing pink triangles, going to marches, and dressing in a military style. Heidi had been out only three years, and we both were responding to the gay culture of the time. It was important to us to identify ourselves as lesbians, and at the time that meant adopting a certain look. We wanted to fit in with our newfound community as a way to solidify our identities as lesbians.

I pretty much blew off school the last semester of freshman year and didn't know whether I wanted to go back. I just couldn't find my niche at college. I was thinking of starting a musical career. Heidi and I were living together, and she and I talked about moving to L.A. She was thinking of going into film production.

In the aftermath of my mother's finding out about me, the tension between us had lessened dramatically. So after Heidi graduated that spring, my mom invited us both to join the family on a trip to Europe. My mom had just won the Academy Award for *Moonstruck* and wanted to go away to relax in Saint Tropez with my aunt and brother. On the trip, my mother seemed to feel fine around me and Heidi.

Heidi had never been to Europe, so after ten days with my family, we decided to take the grand tour: we went to Paris, Amsterdam, and London. We thought of it as an explorational trip, and we kept testing out ideas about what we would do with our lives after the summer. By that point, I had decided not to go back to school. We began seriously thinking about forming a band. In high school I had written songs and sung, and Heidi was into music too. We both played guitar, and we'd fooled around working out harmonies together. Every new city or town we'd visit, we'd have a new idea.

In Paris we crossed the Pont Neuf and stopped to watch the sunset. In the last glimmers of the August sunlight, I blurted out the idea that Heidi and I should form a band. It was decided.

We returned to New York and started to put together our band, which we named Ceremony. We both sang; I played drums, and Heidi played guitar. I had some money from my residuals from appearances on *The Sonny and Cher Show*, and we used that to buy all the necessary equipment. We began writing songs and making home demos. After almost a year and a half of practicing, we hired four guys to round out our band and made a demo. Then we started shopping for a deal. Two months later, around Thanksgiving, we were offered a development deal by Geffen Records. We were thrilled.

Our euphoria didn't last long. Right before Christmas, I got a call from my mom's publicist informing me that the *Star* was going to publish an article outing me. I panicked. "Is there anything we can do to stop them?" I asked.

I called my mom immediately. I was expecting a big "I told you so," because she had warned me that something like this might happen. But she felt terrible for me.

Heidi and I were terrified that we would lose our record deal if the public had proof that we were gay. After consulting with a publicist and the executives at Geffen, we immediately pulled out of the gay community and retreated into the closet. We didn't go out nearly as much, and when we did we never went to gay clubs. We began to make a list of things to do: "Find boyfriends" was on the top. Anytime we left the apartment, we were afraid someone would break in while we were gone. We got rid of all incriminating pictures of us — any picture that showed us being the least affectionate. This sounds a bit paranoid, but we were constantly hounded by the tabloids: they called our apartment constantly and followed us when we went out. Heidi and I devised ways of leaving to trick them — she'd go out the back entrance of the building, and I'd depart from the front.

They also harassed Heidi's parents, calling and hanging up, and staking out their house on Long Island. Her parents were still not all that comfortable with Heidi's homosexuality, so for them, the tabloids' intrusion was especially hurtful.

It was now 1990, and militant gay groups such as Queer Nation and Act Up were pushing a radical gay agenda. Up to that point, Heidi and I had identified with queer politics, wanting to feel included in the gay community. But after I was outed in the tabloids, I felt that the gay community turned on me. My mother's publicist had decided I should be seen in public with a man. The publicist had arranged for a beard to escort me to a movie premiere she knew the press would attend.

When I went to her office to pick up the tickets and meet my escort, I realized my date was gay. I told the publicist that I didn't think it made sense for me to attend the premiere with an obviously gay man — it would defeat the purpose. I ended up taking a member of our band with me.

A couple of weeks later gay activist and author Michelangelo Signorile wrote an article in *Outweek* questioning why I was reluctant to be out and why I was pretending to not be gay. I discovered that the guy who was supposed to be my beard at the movie premiere was insulted that I hadn't taken him and told Mike Signorile at *Outweek*. I was furious. I felt completely betrayed by the gay community. The article wasn't a total put-down; Signorile did portray me as a victim, but the fact that the gay press published anything reinforced my paranoia. I wanted to stay in the closet; they were forcing me out.

This was the height of outing both inside and outside the gay community, with such people as David Geffen and Malcolm Forbes being outed. Outing was very controversial in the gay community; people had strong opinions for and against it. Queer Nation was putting up posters outing people around NYC, a practice about which there was a huge debate. And as it turned out, the issue of the *Star* that featured me on the cover was the top-selling cover at that time.

Many of the articles published about me were filled with false statements, and I felt ashamed and humiliated. One article said that I made lesbian porno films while I was at NYU. I was completely embarrassed. When personal information — true or false — is printed in public without your permission, you feel absolutely vulnerable and exposed; the experience began to affect my self-esteem. I became extremely self-conscious and hated going out, even to the supermarket. And I constantly worried about my career, always wondering if there was a picture out there that we didn't know about. Occasionally an article would be published that was very accurate, making me wonder which of my so-called friends had spoken to the press. I remember one article that mentioned that I liked spending time bowling and playing miniature golf. I used to bowl a lot, but I had only played miniature golf once. I knew someone who knew me had talked to the tabloids.

Back in the Closet

The ultimate effect of the tabloid outing was that I went back into the closet. I was twenty. At a time when I was beginning to launch my life as an adult after years of living in fear, I was ricocheted backward. Before this point, I had thought of myself as safe and secure in my homosexuality. I considered myself well-adjusted and out. After all, I had come out to my parents. But instead of standing tall and feeling proud of who I was, I made the decision to hide from the media, pretend that I was not gay, and then became a virtual recluse without so much as questioning my actions.

I immediately and unconsciously took on the general public's perception and fear of homosexuality. In emotional terms this meant that I had internalized the homophobia of others and become steeped in shame. Those closest to me — Heidi, my mother, my father, and Georgeann — all supported my decision to hide my sexual orientation. All of them were afraid that I would hurt my budding music career if I were honest. But it was my own homophobia that pushed me back into the closet.

My anger toward the gay community fueled my homophobia. I began to hate all gay people and resent the fact that I was gay. I didn't want to be associated with images of gay people because I felt that they were the ones who had exposed me, or at least made it worse. Looking back, I understand that this is classic projection: I hated them because I hated myself.

At that point in my life if I could have done something to

be straight — taken a pill, whatever — I probably would have. My dad had been elected mayor of Palm Springs, and one day he was telling me about a city ordinance for some type of antidiscrimination in housing or the workplace. He made it sound as if gays were trying to get special status. I remember being angry, thinking that gays didn't deserve any special favors. With the exception of being in a relationship with a woman, I had completely cut myself off from the gay world and its community.

The tabloid hysteria went on for almost a year. Heidi and I decided to move to L.A. — we'd gotten the record deal with Geffen and felt that we might finish the production better if we were there. The tabloids and paranoia followed us out west. When we arrived we were short one box. We thought it might be the one in which Heidi had put her diary and were absolutely panicked that the movers had sold the diary to the tabloids. To our relief, the box turned up.

In some ways it was almost easier for the press to gain access to us in L.A. I remember someone coming right to the door once. Our ultimate fear was that someone was going to get concrete proof that we were gay; then our careers would be over. That fear of loss was my main emotion; it would take years before I realized I was actually missing out on an enormous dimension of my life by remaining in the closet.

Coming out to ourselves, exploring who we are, and then telling our parents are all momentous steps in the coming-out process. But often in the wake of such events we begin to deal with ourselves at a deeper, more challenging level. As individual people (or, as in my case, the media) respond to us and we confront direct homophobia or attacks about being homosexual, we can internalize the attacks rather than question them. My knee-jerk reaction to being outed was an indication of my own subtle yet entrenched homophobia. Being outed was a blatant violation of my privacy, and it was especially hard to have it happen in a mendacious newspaper, but my reaction still revealed my homophobia. Looking back, it's clear to me that some of my anger toward the gay community was a direct projection of my anger about and fear of being gay in a hostile world.

For the next three years, I denied to the public that I was gay. I lived behind closed doors and windows. This was tantamount to being in a straitjacket and reinforced my negative feelings about myself, increased my insecurity about who I was, and made me feel afraid of being gay.

It's been eight years since my tabloid nightmare. It's only been in the last four years that I finally unearthed my own homophobia and left the closet for good. This latter part of the coming-out process is in my opinion the most trying, because it can be the most vague and difficult to see.

Internalized Homophobia

DAVE

After Dave, the insurance manager from Seattle, came out to his parents, he realized that for him there were two stages of coming out: in theory and in practice. "The theory is when you tell your parents; the practice is when you confront them with the concrete reality of being gay. I told them my second year in college. I sat them down in the living room, and they were not at all surprised. My mom said, 'Oh, we've always known.' Dad was pretty cool as well. He was emotional, which was a change, because he's usually so stoic. That was Part One.

"A few months later I was dating this guy, and it was

New Year's Eve. I still had an AmEx card that my parents had given me for a semester abroad. Phil and I had gone to a party, and we were having a great time. We'd snuck into the bathroom and kissed. I didn't want the night to end, so we drove up to the Silver Cloud Motel and got this big room. I had never done anything like this before — to me it was like committing grand larceny. We spent the night and had a fantastic time. I thought I was madly in love. We ended up breaking up two months later — so much for that!

"Two months later I got a call from my parents, who said there was a charge from the Silver Cloud Motel on the AmEx bill. I was completely humiliated. I ended up writing them a letter about the AmEx card because I couldn't talk to them about it over the phone. When they received the letter, they called me in tears. But they were totally fine. But when I first started bringing guys home with me — I was living with them over the summer — I'd say, 'Oh, no, we're just friends.' I didn't want them to have to conjure up the image of me having sex with a guy.

"Whereas the theory part of my coming out was harder for them than me, the practice part was harder on me. Actually introducing someone to them terrified me. It was taking all these vague ideas and funneling them into this one person. I thought that now my parents were able to visualize and imagine all the things that go on — two guys kissing, having sex. Then all of a sudden I was getting all these images back from the media; I was sick at the thought of my parents reading *The Joy of Gay Sex*. I became kind of obsessed with the idea that they'd go to the bookstore, look at it, be repulsed, and then be repulsed by me. Like some other gay people, my fear wasn't about them disowning me; I think I could do just about anything and I'd be in good with them."

It's clear that Dave projected his own homophobic feelings (e.g., being disgusted by homosexual sex) onto his parents.

He had not yet separated externalized homophobia from his view of himself and his identity.

I asked Dave how long it took until he was comfortable with himself and no longer afraid of that part of his identity. He said, "I guess to a certain degree I'm still not fully comfortable with myself. Gay relationships are not known for their length of time; they tend to be sort of flaky, not long lasting. I know that I don't bring someone home because I don't want my parents to get their hopes up that this is the one and then two months later bring someone else home and start living their worst fears about what homosexuals do."

He continues, "My parents have been married for almost forty-five years, so they hold on to the idea that I will find someone to grow old with — not that it isn't my hope too. I guess I'm a bit more realistic. My brothers and sisters have all been divorced. I'm now in a committed relationship with Martin* after breaking up with my first boyfriend over a year ago. My parents still have a picture of Sam* and me up. When I ask them why they don't have photos of my sisters and brothers and their divorced spouses, they don't know how to answer. I think they hope that I'll get back with Sam, and that since there is no divorce [because gays can't legally marry], my parents don't see the end of our relationship as final. There's something ambiguous about it. Sam and I were together for three and a half years — a little over twenty-one years in gay years," jokes Dave.

Dave's comments here point to his lack of trust in his ability to be both gay and happy. His jokes about the lack of longevity in gay relationships not only perpetuate the negative stereotype but also reinforce his own homophobia. Dave's process is still under way. As Michelangelo Signorile says in his book *Outing Yourself,* "We never fully complete this last and final step — because we will continue to come out every day for the rest of our lives."

Once you have distinguished the difference between how you feel about being gay and how others feel about your being gay, then you can begin to heal any perception you may have of homosexuality as bad or shameful.

ROBIN

Robin also thought she was fully out and totally comfortable with being gay. She'd been in therapy and told all those close to her. But there was one person she hadn't revealed her sexual orientation to: her father. He lived far away, and they had become somewhat estranged. In her anger toward him, she rationalized not coming out to him with a "He doesn't deserve to know."

Similar to me with my mom, Robin was insecure about her relationship with her father and didn't want to increase the distance between them. After several years, she wrote him a letter to tell him she was gay. He called the day he received it, saying he wasn't that surprised, that he still loved her — but also: "Don't throw in the towel yet" and "You may not be certain for a long time — maybe not until the end of your life." Robin had been prepared to lose him entirely; she had even looked forward to the opportunity to tell him how angry she was at his walking out of her life, dropping the ball on being a father to her. But her father was sympathetic: he said he didn't really understand it, but he still loved her. Robin felt better after telling him the truth about herself, but in the aftermath she realized that she had been expecting him to react in a huge way, and when he didn't, the moment was anticlimactic. At first she actually felt disappointed; she thought that when she told him the whole truth, they'd become closer and bridge the gap that had become so painful.

He continued to call her in his same infrequent manner, and in the end his knowing "all about" her hasn't brought them closer. One fantasy was that her coming out would put a final wedge between them; the other fantasy, the one that was even less articulated, was that once he knew her completely he would find it in his power to get closer to her. Neither happened, leaving her alone with her feelings about being gay — which were ambivalent. She realized that her fear of his reaction was in part fueled by her own anxiety about being gay.

She said to me, "Now I realize I'm the one who has to feel okay about it; I'm no longer waiting for his approval or disapproval." At times her fears manifest themselves in the form of fantasies about "going back to men," but when she gets close to that reality she knows she doesn't want to be with a man.

It's difficult to harness this ambivalence, which often feels like a blanket of free-floating anxiety not tethered to any one thing. Sexuality often resists being described or defined completely in words. Part of the challenge for lesbians and gays coming out to their parents is learning to distinguish between real and irrational fears. Caroline is a good example of how an unexamined fear snowballed into an irrational aversion that kept her in the closet for seventeen years.

CAROLINE

Caroline, the sports marketing executive, has been a lesbian for over seventeen years, and during that time she's been in several long-term, important relationships with women whom her family has never met. It wasn't until recently that she had the courage to examine her fears about coming out to her parents. Through therapy she began to enumerate and describe her fears; she discovered very little concrete evidence that her family would reject her: they are not judgmental; they know other gay people and don't demonstrate antigay attitudes; she knows how much they love her. Her fears of being rejected or irreparably disappointing her parents began to seem irrational [to her].

One of the factors pushing her to resolve these issues and

take the step to come out was her involvement with a woman to whom she now felt deeply committed. Her partner, Helen*, was pressuring her to come out; Helen felt that Caroline might deny her in certain situations and wanted to eradicate this seed of distrust in their relationship. Helen pointed out how Caroline censored details of her life — from family and from coworkers.

When Caroline finally came out to her father in a letter, his response was short and to the point: "I love you dearly, and my philosophy is if you're happy, I'm happy."

Like Robin, Caroline is still in the process of integrating her own definition of being gay so that she will no longer respond to either society's negative value judgments or her own irrational fears.

External Homophobia

BRUCE

After Bruce, the Indianian, came out to his parents, he thought for a while that his worst troubles were over. He was wrong. His life would get worse before it got better. He describes the aftermath of telling his parents. "Finally, there was a word for what I was feeling. But by my freshman year in high school, the verbal abuse at school had gotten worse. I was harassed on a daily basis, and teachers wouldn't do or say anything about it. This was a medium-sized public school with about two hundred students in a grade. I was physically attacked several times and received three death threats. I would report these incidents to the school, and nothing would ever be done.

"My parents were fuming. They went in to the principal's office and asked for a meeting to be called, but the school wouldn't do anything about it. I would have names and grades of the students who were attacking me, but nothing was ever done. I finally got to the point where I asked Mom to stop calling, because any time she'd call the threats would just escalate.

"There was one teacher who pulled me aside and said, 'Bruce, I know you're in hell, I know everything you're going through is making you miserable, and I wish there was something I could do to help you, but as a teacher, my hands are tied.' That didn't really help me, it just added to my fears.

"There was this one guy, Tommy*, who from the first day of school would harass me. I was five eleven, but Tommy was a jock and kind of a badass. Every day on my way to PE class, he would push me and knock my books out of my hands and call me a faggot. I would try to take several routes to PE class; I tried everything in my power to avoid him.

"I turned him in to a counselor, who didn't do anything to stop him. Finally one day I had had enough, and when he called me a fag, I turned around and said, 'Shut the fuck up, you nigger.' The word just slipped out, and then he punched me, and I punched him back. We got into this brawl. I have martial arts experience, and I think he was surprised at how tough I was, but I just hate fighting. I was so angry — not because of what they would do to me, but what I would do to them.

"After the fight, I went right to the principal's office and told him everything. I felt awful for it, the lowest dirty person in the world. I hated myself for calling him 'nigger'— at the time, one of my best friends at the youth center was black. I knew that what I had done didn't make me any better. But still the principal didn't do anything.

"That's when my mom knew she had to get me out of there. She'd been researching home school, and when she first told a counselor about sending me to home school, the counselor had said, 'Well, the principal is going to fight you on this;

he's completely against home school.' My mom said, 'Well, just set up a meeting.'

"So she went into his office and pointed to a poster in his office that said, 'School should be a safe harbor for our kids.' 'Well,' she said, 'this place is not a place of safety for my son. He's being harassed and beat up.' 'Why are they doing that?' My mother looked at him point blank and said, 'They're calling him a fag and queer, and to be honest, he is gay.' Then the principal said, 'Where are those papers, I'll sign them right away.'

"He didn't offer any alternatives; he just wanted me out of there so he wouldn't have to deal with the problem. As my mom was leaving his office, he said to her, 'Well, I hope you know that a lot of doors of opportunity will be closed to your son.' I think that planted the seed of an activist in my mom. From that moment on she wanted to prove him wrong. She knew there was more to life than Seymour, Indiana. She believed in me and knew that I had the potential to be a good student and to succeed."

Bruce knew instinctively that it was wrong and unacceptable to use a racial epithet — even against someone who had been so cruel to him — and the authorities at the school also recognized and condemned his behavior. However, the school's not responding to the constant harassment of Bruce demonstrates how, even so, it tolerated the antigay abuse.

Bruce's case underscores a common misconception that is held by both heterosexuals and homosexuals themselves: that gay people are cursed and will not be able to succeed. This myth is often reinforced and perpetuated by gay people who are afraid to be out of the closet. They convince themselves that they will lose everything if they are honest about who they are. But, as the highly esteemed gay activist Torie Osborn has said,

> Coming out to ourselves, and to our friends, family, and co-workers, is always empowering to our identify, self-

worth, and potential. In addition, our individual act of coming out reverberates into the world around us, setting in motion a dramatic chain reaction in the lives of people we know and the organizations we affect. In the wake of our personal honesty and courage, powerful, positive, and often permanent changes ripple their way through people's lives and the various arenas in which we travel.

WILLIAM

In Bruce's case, his parents' decision to home school him prevented him from experiencing any more physical harm. But sometimes when external homophobia goes unchecked, the result is quite serious, as was the case with William. William also suffered from explicit, uncontained homophobia growing up in a small town in Arkansas. As he said, "I knew from the beginning that I was gay." He describes his family background as "All-American mutt"— his mother's family was Catholic, his father's family Methodist. "When I was growing up, I didn't have too much trouble coming to terms with the fact that I was gay. I remember feeling a bit different from the other boys, but it didn't bother me. I knew it was a bit odd when I had a crush on a friend in the first grade. But I naturally identified more with boys, and I was never athletic. As time went on, I finally realized what was going on. It wasn't like a light bulb went on."

William didn't experience the realization of his being gay in a traumatic way. "I remember my grandfather would use the word *fag*; I didn't even know what it meant. But other than that, my family didn't seem to have a negative view of homosexuality. I never really thought about being closeted or hiding it. I was kind of worried about what my parents would think about it, and I was completely sure; I just needed to find the words for it."

By this time, he'd explored his identity in a sexual way. "That first happened when I was twelve, and it was with one of my friends. We were friends for about three years. I told him that I was gay, and then later that night he came out to me. It was actually kind of odd. I didn't suspect that he was gay at all. Later that night we had sex. I would describe our relationship as a cute little experiment, which lasted about two years. But he was the first person I told I was gay."

But William was obviously suffering from some sort of crisis, which led to his entering an inpatient mental health facility at age fourteen. "Right before I came out to my parents, I was in Charter for trying to kill myself. A lot of shit was going on. I lived in a town where I had no friends, and I felt extremely isolated. There were a lot of rednecks, some of whom were so gay there's not a closet big enough for them to hide in. But still they never say anything about it. The thing about me was that I didn't really give a fuck; I didn't act any differently, I didn't try to change who I was or how I acted. But as a result I was ostracized. I was also overweight, and I didn't make the best grades. This was a pure little Southern Baptist town. Being gay was a component, but it wasn't the only one.

"So when I came out to my parents, I had been in Charter for four months. I'd been doing a lot of group and individual therapy. It was a nice, supportive place for me. Charter didn't take a stand on me telling my parents; they treated it like any other issue. The staff was really nice about it. I decided to tell my parents, but I wasn't exactly sure how they were going to take it." William was lucky. His parents' response was "Is that all?"

"I was getting nervous, and they thought I was going to tell them something horrible." He continues, "It felt really good to tell them. Afterward, my parents were totally and completely supportive of me. I had already told my older sister. She had always been nice to me and cares about me as a brother. After I got out of Charter, my parents decided that being in that city was a bad deal for me, so we moved to Fayetteville, a larger city. What I didn't realize at the time was that a month before, my uncle (my father's twin brother) had come out to my parents.

"One day I called down to my old friend Trevor's* house, and his mother answered, and I asked to speak to him. She said no, and then she said, 'It's better this way.' I hung up; I knew what she meant. My mom overheard the whole thing and she called Trevor's mom. Apparently he had told his mom that I'd been getting him drunk and taking advantage of him, and that made me decide never to go back to that small town.

"I was happy in Fayetteville, and after a while I found new friends. I started in the eighth grade, and by ninth I had come out to some people at the school. One day I was telling a friend that I was gay, and this girl was eavesdropping. The girl turned and said, 'I didn't know you were gay — how interesting.' By seventh period the entire school knew. I was furious. After a while the shock began to wear off for everybody, but they still made fun of me. There was this rumor going around that I had raped and killed my dog, or that I was hitting on certain kids. It was really juvenile, petty shit from five-year-olds.

"For the most part, the teachers were aware that I was being harassed, but they weren't aware why it was going on. And I didn't tell my parents. I didn't want them to think I was in trouble again. In one of the classes I had made enemies with this kid named Brian*. He really hated me; he'd go on and on about how he was going to kick my faggot asshole. I knew he was spineless; he's fat, he's tall. He was fifteen. Everyone heard him go on and on about how much he hates faggots. One day I heard these rumors that he and his friends were going to beat me up at lunch, even try to kill me.

"That day I went to lunch as usual — it seemed like it was going to happen the next day. My friends and I walked to this BBQ place for lunch. On the way to the restaurant, this blue truck pulls up, and eight guys filed out. Though some of my friends were bisexual, they weren't out; but they were being targeted because of me. 'Hey, you fuckin' faggot,' and I didn't respond. I just started punching. The rest is all a haze. Three people actually did the attacking. None of my friends got hurt; they couldn't really do anything about it. They didn't help me out. One friend called the police, and someone else called my father. My nose was broken twice. I had bruises and hematomas all over my head, badly bruised kidneys, scrapes, and bruises.

"The police came by and said they'd meet us at the hospital after going after the guys in the blue truck. At the hospital we had to wait for two hours. All the pain was in my head, but my nose wouldn't stop bleeding.

"Since then we've only found two of the eight guys. The charges were dropped [against six of them] because there were no lasting injuries or major-league deforming." The criminal trial against two of them was set for four months from then.

"I went back to school, and within a week the school's bullshit got to me again. Then one of my friends was attacked by a group of girls. They were taunting her, saying how gay people should be shot. She told them off, and they attacked her. A teacher held my friend down while she was getting the shit beaten out of her. Afterward the teacher wasn't even reprimanded, and the office didn't do anything. My friend was punished for threatening the other girls. That was the day I truly realized they weren't going to do anything, so why even bother. I dropped out and decided to get my G.E.D."

It's been two years since William was gay bashed. The trial ended with two of the eight young men found guilty of assault. He is now finishing his G.E.D. and applying to college; he wants to study anthropology. He doesn't regret for a minute coming out. When I asked him about the emotional effect of the attack, he was nonchalant, almost dismissive. "My mom was really worried about me, but for me it wasn't anything new. I know it's sad to say, but I knew that sooner or later someone was going to attack me. I didn't know whether I would win or lose, and I didn't know how many of them there'd be, or whether or not I was going to die. But I kind of resigned myself that if they were going to attack me for being myself, then it was worth dying for. It's the price of freedom."

I think one of the most moving aspects of William's story is his sense of inevitability about one day being hurt, even killed. The fact that his school took no responsibility for the abusive behavior of the students, forcing William to drop out, is outrageous. This blatant display of homophobia in the form of gay bashing is why some of us fear coming out. This kind of violence continues to occur in schools around the country, reinforcing the sense of fear and shame surrounding being gay. But William is right; it is worth it.

For William, his parents' love and support helped him make the right decision to leave school. He was able to begin to heal and realize that the attitudes and behaviors of those who beat him were contemptible — not his own. In the face of such violence, it's a challenge to separate the two, but they did it.

The tabloids said hideous things about me, and no matter how accustomed I may have been to the press, having grown up with parents who were in the public eye, the articles still affected me. And instead of being able to separate their attack on me from who I really was, I internalized the shame and went back into the closet.

This is one reason reaching out to the gay community is so important. We all need the support of people who will assure us that we are okay, that there is nothing wrong, bad, or shameful about being gay. With the love and support of the gay community, our friends, and family, we will begin to taste the tremendous wonder of finally being open about who we are.

The Bold and the Beautiful

ERIK

Erik, who is now a gay activist living in Washington, D.C., is a good example of how some of us experience the coming-out process as a combination of steps forward and steps backward. "It all started when I came out to my mother; that was the first step, and it was like taking a load off my back. From that point on it just got easier and easier to tell people. After I had gotten out of the hospital [from Crohn's disease], I had the opportunity to go across country with my cousin, who was gay. He was the one who took me into my first gay bar. I can remember how freeing that felt: you walk into this place, and you know everyone else is the same as you. I felt a strong sense of community, but at the same time there was a strong sense of fear. I was just entering this community, and I didn't know what to expect or what was going to happen."

Erik tested his homosexuality, something we have seen with others: "For my first year of college, I decided to go to St. Louis because it was a big city and had a gay life. No one knew me, so I felt there were a lot of possibilities and good things that could happen. I began to come out to people on campus, but I was still a little bit shaky. I was not a hundred percent sure and thought if I had a girlfriend or a sexual relationship with a girl that it might make me straight. But I still felt more comfortable with men than with women. I was a theater major at the time and heavily involved in theater projects with women and developed a really close relationship with one that soon developed into a sexual relationship. It was nice, but that special feeling just wasn't there. This went on and off for a year; at the same time I was dating a guy on campus. She knew about it, so it was an awkward situation between the two of them.

"Meanwhile, I was learning more and more about homosexuality, but I was still involved with a woman, and we were becoming more and more involved emotionally. We had a nice relationship, and then she found God and became a born again. I'm Jewish, so her religious views, especially about homosexuality, became a real point of tension between us. She hoped to convert me and make me straight; at times I would hope for the same thing, but it just didn't work out that way.

"At the time, my sister helped console my mother. My sister was in college and had a lot of gay friends. She was helpful then and has been supportive ever since. I had asked my mother to go to a P-FLAG meeting; she was living in Des Moines at the time, and she refused. Her reasoning was that she was a Jewish woman living in Des Moines, and the P-FLAG meetings were in the basement of a church on a Sunday afternoon. She thought she'd have to explain to her friends why she was going to this church, so she just didn't want to do that, even though she had friends who were gay in Des Moines. I suggested that she talk to some of her friends, and she'd say she just couldn't, that she wasn't ready. Then it all came to a head.

"I went to visit her one summer, and we were getting ready to go to a benefit concert. I had started wearing a pink triangle earring, which had been a point of contention between us. As we were walking into the concert, she asked me to take the earring out.

"I said, 'No, I can't.'

"She said, 'Why?'

"I said, 'It's a sign of who I am. It's something that I'm

proud of and it opens a dialogue for people. If someone sees it they can feel comfortable coming up to me and talking about gay issues. Or maybe they're thinking that they may be gay, and they know it's a sign, which means I could make them feel better or provide support for them.'

"And she said, 'You're just going to embarrass me, and people will think that I have a gay son, and I need you to take it out.'

"I said, 'If you take off your wedding ring, I will take my earring out.'

"And she said, 'No, I can't take my ring off.'

"I said, 'Why?'

"She said, 'Because it's my wedding ring.'

"And I said, 'See, it's a sign that you're married. It's a symbol of your commitment to your husband, just as my pink triangle is a symbol of me being gay and is a part of who I am, just as the wedding ring is for you.'

" 'No, no, you don't understand.'

"And I said, 'No, no, *you* don't understand.'

"And I didn't take the earring out. My stepfather was upset with me, and she was upset with me, but at that point I was really adamant about telling her that I was proud of who I was.

"She said, 'Well, I'm proud of you too. I'm just not ready to let other people know.'

"At the time, she didn't understand the connection between her ring and my earring. It wasn't until she moved to Baltimore about three or four years ago that she made a promise to me that she would go to a P-FLAG meeting. She became more and more involved, got elected to the board, and then asked to be a regional director, which she's been doing for a year and a half."

Erik's strong belief in himself enabled his mother to accept his homosexuality. Again, the connection is clear: the more we as gay people understand and accept ourselves, the more likely it is that those around us — parents, family, friends — will accept us as well.

Sydney and Kari are also good examples of how once gay people accept their homosexuality, negative criticism doesn't affect them so deeply, and instead pushes them to embrace their lives and potential in a positive, truly awe-inspiring way.

SYDNEY

Sydney thought her biggest obstacle in coming out was her father. After he died, she realized that her mother had an even more subtle homophobia, but a kind laced with support. This is typical of how many of us and our parents react with mixed emotions. When I asked her to describe her mother's attitude now, she said, "My mother likes Chris a lot, but I don't think she thinks of us as a couple. If the three of us go somewhere in public, and Chris and I hold hands, it would still make my mom uncomfortable. By the same token, my mom is my most reliable source of gay programming. She tells me what's going on; she knows more about what's happening in the gay community than most people I know."

Sydney lives a fully out life and doesn't actively censor herself. She explains, "Most places I go, people who meet me assume that I'm straight, and I don't always say something to alter that perception. But I'm out at work; I outed myself during my interview," she says, laughing.

Again, it is Sydney's sense of freedom and fun that is so inspiring. The conflicts of others, notably her mother, don't get in the way of Sydney's own lust for life.

KARI

When Kari and her first partner decided to have a commitment ceremony, they wanted to invite all of her relatives. She knew it would be easier not to invite those relatives she knew would be uncomfortable, but on principle she sent them invitations anyway. "The response was amazing. We invited two hundred fifty people and received so many wonderful responses — a gift or a card with 'Good Luck.' The worst response came from my paternal great-aunt. She'd been a Christian missionary, a wonderful, sweet woman. She wrote me a letter and included a couple of Bible tracts, saying that she was concerned about my soul and asking me if I wanted to spend eternity away from my family. She was very clear that she thought my being a lesbian was wrong in the eyes of God. I asked my grandmother how to respond, and both my grandmother and great-grandmother were like, 'Oh, Dottie, keep your religion to yourself.'

"In my response to my great-aunt I told her that one of the great things about our country was the freedom to have different religious views. I told her that although I respected her views, I didn't agree with them. I went on to tell her that if she felt the need to pray for me, to please pray for my health and happiness. The rest is up to me. It's between me and God, and no one else can tackle that for me."

I asked her if she was hurt by her great-aunt's views of her. Kari explained her feelings in this way, "In my heart I know I'm a good person, and I don't believe any supreme being who created people in his own image would condemn someone for loving someone else. The reactions of the majority of the people made me realize how lucky I am.

"I've been lucky that I've never had a negative experience coming out. The worst was my great-aunt, and she still loves me. I still get Christmas cards from her, and she includes my partner when she addresses them. As the saying goes, we've agreed to disagree. As far as coming out to my coworkers, I work at Ticketmaster, where half the staff is gay or bisexual. I don't announce it, but if someone asks me, I am not going to lie. Most of the time I find the people that I am most comfortable with are usually astute enough to figure it out anyway. Then I say, 'Oh, by the way . . . I'm gay.' I've never really surprised anyone."

Breaking the Mirror

When I was outed in the tabloids and lost control over my life, I panicked, regressing into the closet. This exposed my internalized homophobia; I thought that I was okay with being gay, but it was only when I was safe in my own world. At the time, I was ignorant of the power of internalized homophobia. Before the tabloid incident, I was convinced I had fully accepted my homosexuality. But that illusion was soon shattered.

The outing was a shock that brought me to a place that I'd never been: I suddenly became aware that at some deep level I was ashamed of who I was.

I lived in fear for a few years; then I started to watch other people coming out and felt envious. But I still couldn't come out. I remember Heidi and I wrote a song for our album called "Our Love." It was a non–gender specific song, which most of ours were. But our producer convinced us that it sounded like a dyke song, so we changed the lyrics. We made the "you's" to "he's." And once again, I didn't question his opinion. We were in defense mode; all we could do was protect ourselves. We weren't thinking about what we were losing by living that way. We were still irrationally afraid of what would happen if the truth came out.

It was only in hindsight that I recognized that my retreating into the closet not only damaged my career but also got in the way of living a full and happy life. As my mom has since said to me, I made decisions from a place of weakness rather than strength. Although it's easy to say and not so easy to believe, many of our fears are worse than the reality. However, if you prepare before coming out to family and friends, you can lessen some of the anxiety. By preparing how to deliver information to your parents in a way that allows them to begin to process, you can avoid angry, impulsive reactions, such as occurred with my mother.

Telling our parents is one of the hardest, most frightening aspects of the coming-out process, and dealing with your own reaction as well as the reactions of others can be quite difficult and stressful. Most parents go through a period of adjustment. My mom's initial anger passed, and she became disappointed, sad, even felt guilty. She wondered what she could have done to "prevent" me from being gay — as if my being a lesbian were tied to her parenting skills. My mother also withdrew from me, and as I've mentioned throughout the book, her emotional distance was always a cause for alarm on my part. Thankfully, my mother is familiar with processing her thoughts and feelings, and it didn't take her long to deal with me in a supportive manner.

As gays and lesbians, we are responsible not only for helping to guide our parents through the process, but also for doing our own emotional homework. I wasn't aware that I had my own issues with being gay; I thought I was well-adjusted — until I was outed by the tabloids. It wasn't until several years later in therapy that I began to examine closely the more subtle issues of my coming out and define for myself what being gay meant.

It is still true that people exist who will try to hurt you because you are gay; in some cases, notably those of Bruce and William, people strike out in violence. Hate crimes exist, but those subjected to such violence are in the minority. Indeed, not only is violence becoming less tolerated, but the consequences for such hate crimes are being enforced.

When we first come out to ourselves, we must realize that

just because others may define homosexuality in certain inaccurate terms, we don't have to. Indeed, it is our responsibility to ourselves to redefine those terms once and for all in positive, life-affirming ways. In his scholarly study *Gay and Lesbian Politics*, Mark Blasius points out, "While there has been homoerotic behavior of individuals throughout history and in most cultures, as well as people who have self-identified on the basis of primary or exclusive homosexuality, it was not until the middle of the nineteenth century that physicians and psychiatrists conceptualized a homosexual type of person." This implies that the definition of homosexuality as perverse, immoral, or unnatural did not come into being until homosexuals were labeled as a group, which did not occur until the mid-nineteenth century. As Blasius underscores, "What is not disputed is that the invention of the term 'homosexual' was preceded by, and was an attempt to label scientifically and hence govern, individuals who participated in a distinctive way of life."

It is the responsibility of the gay community to help demystify homosexuality — for gay people as well as straight people. We need to be aware of the deep impact that negative portrayals of gay people in the media can have. The first step to preventing the internalization of homophobia is to eradicate external homophobia. We need to demonstrate that it cannot be tolerated. The more gays and lesbians come out, the more accurately we will be represented — in the media and to the world.

Chapter 7

The Ongoing Process
Three Steps Forward, One Step Back

*"Forty-six and dying by inches, I finally see how
our lives align at the core, if not in the sorry details.
I still shiver with a kind of astonished delight
when a gay brother or sister tells of that narrow
escape from the coffin world of the closet. Yes, yes,
yes, goes a voice in my head, it was just like that
for me. When we laugh together then and dance in
the giddy circle of freedom, we are children for real
at last, because we have finally grown up."*

PAUL MONETTE,
from *Becoming a Man*

A Blast from My Past

Like many processes we encounter or embark on during our
lives, coming out does not happen all at once. After retreating
into the closet for several years, I began to realize what I had
given up and missed out on by living a secretive, dual life. At
the same time, between 1990 and 1993, there were significant
advances made by the gay community: several notable people
in politics, entertainment, and other areas of society came out.

The importance of their contribution is inestimable. They became instant role models, helping to break the negative stereotypes of gays and lesbians, showing the gay community as well as the heterosexual majority that being homosexual did not prevent one from achieving great success and that our community was as diverse as any other segment of the population.

Recording artists such as k. d. lang and Melissa Etheridge came out and were received well. Pronouncing their sexual orientation did nothing to detract from their commercial success or popularity; in fact, it seemed to add to their appeal. Olympic athlete Greg Louganis, Congressman Barney Frank, Elton John, Martina Navratilova, and Colonel Margaret Cammermeyer also came out, showing the world that being gay is nothing to be fearful of, that it is, rather, something to be proud of. This array of individuals also points to the diversity of the lesbian and gay population.

But I was still not ready to shake off my fear and emerge from the closet. By now I had ended my relationship with Heidi. The intense years of stress from the tabloid incident had not just taken their toll on me, they had affected our relationship. So while we decided to continue to play in Ceremony together, we ended our romantic involvement. And in the fall of 1992 I fell madly in love with someone I had known since I was a child: Joan.

I'd had a crush on Joan for years — ever since she appeared at my mom's Christmas party when I was thirteen. Joan was around when I first realized I was gay and since that time had made a consistent effort to comfort and support me. For years, she had been the only adult with whom I could be open about my sexual orientation. After returning to L.A., I was able to pick up my relationship with Joan; I was soon more than shocked to realize that our friendship had metamorphosed into a love affair.

My childhood crush had become my lover.

Aside from the strong sexual attraction between us, it was the nurturing, mature quality of our love that affected me, and that ultimately laid the foundation for me to fully embrace my lesbianism. Sadly, this wasn't going to happen without enormous pain and loss.

When we got together, I was twenty-three and Joan was in her midforties; she was beautiful, vivacious, and very outgoing. She was an extremely giving partner and enjoyed making things for me — cooking a nice dinner, creating a romantic setting in which to have it, or planning a trip. She was extremely generous with her self and her time. She was a fun-loving spirit, with a real love of life, and I was totally drawn to her. I think, too, that her being older gave me comfort in the wake of the tabloid ordeal. By that summer we were living together in Joan's house in the San Fernando Valley. Thankfully, Heidi and I were able to navigate that complicated but sure path from former lovers to friends, and to this day we are the closest of friends.

It was within my relationship with Joan that I started to question the boundaries that I had set up for my life. In a very direct way, Joan began to question my need to be in the closet. Joan was extremely comfortable with the fact that she was gay, and it began to bother her that I was so vigilant about staying in the closet. At home I was still shutting the blinds, and I wouldn't accompany her dancing. I was still so paranoid about the press proving that I was gay that the only night of the year I would go out publicly to a gay bar was Halloween, because I could disguise myself with a costume.

At this point in time, the band was in the midst of finishing recording the album. Both Heidi and I were still convinced that our music career would be ruined if the press ever proved that we were lesbians.

I wasn't able to appreciate Joan's sense of freedom and

how my own self-imposed strictures were limiting our life together. Then suddenly our entire life changed.

The Honeymoon Ends

After living in a kind of honeymoon bliss for about nine months, Joan learned that her nonaggressive lymphoma, which had been diagnosed several years earlier, had become active. Although Joan had known this was a possibility, her condition changed immediately and drastically — and no one is prepared for that.

It was July 1993. My album was coming out in September. Heidi and I were planning on going on a promo tour for the second half of August, so Joan and I wanted to spend time together before I had to leave and life got crazy. My mom said we could use her house in Aspen. Joan had not been feeling well. She had been complaining of flulike symptoms — she had a low fever and was very achy. She suspected that the cancer had returned. The symptoms seemed to subside, so we decided to leave for Aspen. We packed up the car, put our bird, Jude, in the backseat, and started the two-day drive to Colorado. When we got to my mom's house, Joan began to feel sick again. We thought it could be the altitude, but Joan called her doctor, and he thought maybe it was the cancer. He found a doctor in Aspen to run some tests, and we quickly discovered that Joan was no longer in remission. The cancer had spread from the lymph nodes to the bone marrow.

I called my mom, hysterical with the news. My mother told me not to worry, that she'd get us airline tickets and send someone to drive our car back to L.A. As usual, my mother stepped up to the plate in a crisis.

Joan and I flew back to Los Angeles, and Joan started chemotherapy immediately at Cedars-Sinai in Beverly Hills.

The doctor was optimistic about the effectiveness rate for this type of chemo. Joan began the first round and felt better after a day or so, but the flulike symptoms continued off and on.

After a while of this, I talked to her doctor, who now wasn't as confident as he had been. They did a few more rounds of chemo, in the same cycle. It seemed obvious to me that it was not going well. I thought they should do another bone marrow test; if the chemo were working, the cancer should have lessened in the bone marrow. They did the test; the cancer had worsened.

In October, Joan was hospitalized at Cedars. She was very sick and in a lot of pain. She had to stay in the hospital for about a month, and I stayed with her every night. Her blood counts were very low, so she was in constant, grave danger of infection and had to be monitored closely.

Joan started a round of another type of chemo. One of her doctors told us that if this round didn't work, there would be nothing more they could do. But this second type of chemo worked and got her into remission. Then they wanted to go ahead and do a stem cell transplant, but after yet another round of chemo, Joan seemed to be in remission and came home. She began feeling a lot better; though her body had been through the wringer, she seemed to be mending.

In the hospital everyone seemed to know we were a couple. I didn't have the time or energy to think about hiding the nature of our relationship; I became completely unconcerned with the issue of being gay. I remember one of the nurses said to Joan's doctor, "Joan's daughter sure looks like Chastity Bono." Even I laughed at that.

Then Joan's doctors decided to do the stem cell transplant, a treatment that knocks out the whole immune system so the body will rebuild itself with healthy cells. It's a painful, dangerous, and debilitating process that takes about five weeks.

Meanwhile, Heidi and I had to continue to promote our

album and began discussing coming out publicly, as a band. It was becoming apparent that all the press we'd done for the record was boring because we were so guarded about ourselves. A number of the more sophisticated publications wouldn't even interview us because they knew we wouldn't reveal anything. We kept saying the same things over and over again.

Heidi and I talked to *The Advocate* about coming out. But I was still hesitant. Our album was not selling well, and I didn't want it to look as if we were coming out as a publicity stunt to boost record sales. I thought we should wait and come out for our second album. We did, however, make the decision to cultivate more of the lesbian audience.

In early January of 1994, we played an L.A. lesbian club, Girl Bar, for the first time. This act marked my first conscious step toward coming out. I was playing lesbian bars and open at the hospital. I wasn't yet announcing it to the world, but I wasn't going out of my way to hide it either.

I remember once Joan was hooked up to several machines to do stem cell harvesting, which is a long process that filters blood every few hours. We were in the blood donor room, and I was sitting on the end of her bed, holding her hand, when a woman doctor came up to me and asked me to move. She said, "This is a public place, and we don't tolerate this kind of behavior here." And although I was angry at this blatant display of homophobia, I didn't refuse to move. This was a rare instance of encountering homophobia at the hospital; most everyone there treated me appropriately as the significant other. But looking back, I can't say I am proud of my behavior at that moment.

At the end of January, Joan was released from the hospital, and we went home. All the tests showed she was in remission, and we were optimistic. But once at home, she seemed to deteriorate; the doctors kept telling us this was normal, that it took the body a long time to recover from the procedure. I was consumed with taking care of her: I administered all her medications, her IVs, and her catheter.

Without recognizing my own transformation, I had become her primary caretaker. She'd become addicted to Delaudid, one of the strongest pain medications, and I had to constantly battle with her to contain her intake of the pain meds. This was enormously stressful. She'd lost all the hair on her body, which had dwindled. She started to get very disoriented; she got confused about the time and couldn't tell if it was night or day. Then she began to hallucinate. She'd hear a neighbor's lawn mower and imagine it was a friend on his motorcycle.

The doctors couldn't figure out what was going on because of the various side effects of the chemo, the medication, and the illness itself. To this day, I don't know why they didn't bring her back into the hospital then.

We had been home for a week when I went in to donate blood. I had also organized our friends to donate blood and platelets. When I returned from Cedars, there was an ambulance in the driveway. Joan was having trouble breathing and had begun to hyperventilate. At first I thought she was having an anxiety attack, so I gave the paramedics her anti-anxiety medication. It didn't work.

They soon rushed her to the hospital nearby in the Valley. There, doctors did a bunch of tests but couldn't find anything wrong, so they sent her to Cedars. That night she was admitted to the ICU.

I couldn't stay the night in the ICU, so I returned to the hospital in the morning. Joan was a mess. Her doctor informed me that she had developed pneumonia, which was why she had been so disoriented the previous week — she hadn't been getting enough oxygen to her brain. The doctor told me at that point that she might not make it. I didn't fully understand what was happening. Part of me knew what was going on, but I was in denial.

Meanwhile, Joan was getting more and more delusional, with only moments of lucidity. Heidi came by and suggested that I stay at her apartment that night. Later I realized that Heidi knew Joan was going to die, and she didn't want me to be alone.

That night the phone rang, and the doctor told me that Joan had died. She'd had a cardiac arrest. They had put her on a respirator, and shortly after, her heart had stopped.

I was standing at the side of the bed, and my legs went out; I fell to the ground. My knees just buckled. I called my mom, and she and my aunt drove down from Malibu and met me at Heidi's. They got to the house at four A.M. and stayed up with me throughout the rest of that night and the next day.

Joan died on a Tuesday, and the funeral was that Sunday.

The same week, Ceremony, our band, was dropped from the Geffen label.

After that, insanity hit.

I stayed in our house until after the funeral. Then I began to unravel. Heidi, who was staying with me, sensed that my behavior was becoming irrational and that I was becoming dangerous to myself. She called my mom, and my mom demanded that I come home.

Staying at my mom's house for a few days was probably a good idea, but I got so sick of being treated like an invalid that I left and went to Heidi's while I looked for my own place to live.

As the acute pain of Joan's death began to subside, something miraculous happened. I began to feel a much stronger sense of who I was; with distance, I saw how my behavior and actions during Joan's illness had transformed me into an adult. I had never before accomplished something as meaningful as taking care of her and not worrying about myself. Although Joan's absence from my life is still a source of pain, I learned an invaluable lesson as a result of her dying: I learned to like myself and feel committed to living life fully. This meant living life out of the closet. I finally had the courage to be truly myself.

Be Who You Are

BEN

Ben, the minister, who had been certain that he was gay since he was eleven or twelve, came out slowly and steadily. The steps he took are a good example of a very cautious approach to coming out. "The very first person I told was a woman friend in college who I was really drawn to emotionally. She came out to me as a lesbian, and then I came out to her. I was in shock, because she'd been in a relationship with a man for about six years, and they'd been talking about getting married. In hindsight now, I should have been suspect of her passion for Olivia Newton-John. She was explaining to me how difficult it was for her to deal with her realization, and I felt relieved because I had still not yet come out to anyone in my life."

Ben admits that the next time he took the risk of coming out was when he was in divinity school. "I came out to a professor of mine at Vanderbilt. She was a New Testament scholar. I had a real strong sense of feeling safe. But I remember feeling that it was the biggest thing in the world. Her reaction was pastoral and considerate and mine was that this was so earth-shattering. I needed a promise from her that she would tell no one. I would enumerate [to myself]: now Margaret knows, and Professor Talbot knows, etc. I was always keeping a mental fence around the people I told, swearing them to secrecy. But I continued to tell people. Then I'd go through a period of panic — 'Oh, my God, I can't take it back. I've told too many people.'"

Ben's panic is common; you take a big step, and yet it doesn't quite quell the fear. Ben had still not come out to his parents, and he explains himself this way. "I came out to a lot of people before I came out to my parents, which was sad for my mother. She thought the process should work in the opposite way, that I would start with the people I was closest to and work outward. But I feel that you start with those you don't care to risk losing; if my seminary professor had said, 'Get out of my office,' I'd still have my mother. I find that as I counsel young gays and lesbians, I encourage people not to go through their inner circle, but to work up their courage by telling people they are less close to.

"The first thing my father said was, 'I love you, and this is difficult for me.' I told him that it was difficult for me too; then we hugged each other. But for my parents, the process was just beginning. They had to redefine what my life was going to be about and change the mental pictures they had of my life. There were some practical things too. I now had graduated from Vanderbilt, and I had big student loans to repay. I remember my father saying, 'If you knew you were gay before you went to Vanderbilt, why didn't you choose a career that wouldn't be affected, like being a hairdresser?'"

In coming out to our parents, many of us confront our parents' fear — and our own — that since we are gay or lesbian, we will not be successful in the world or in our lives. As Ben points out, "I began to have an enormous fear of the future. I had always been the man with a plan. From the time I was a kid, I was thinking about becoming an adult. I had finished college in two and a half years. I had never identified with people who took a year off; I always thought, 'I've got to hurry and get my degree so I can become an adult to be successful and do incredible things for other people.'" Ben's idea that being gay canceled out the possibility of success is one of the greatest myths about homosexuality to throw out and make obsolete. He admits frankly, "I did not equate success with being gay. I thought it was a vocational or career hindrance, and I didn't think it was possible for people to esteem you if you were gay." This view is yet another demonstration of internalized homophobia.

"The summer after the church study [on homosexuality] was published, I bought a book that was me to a T: John Reid's *The Best Little Boy in the World.* Reed was a Yale graduate, and he talked about the psychological process that a lot of gays and lesbians go through of being extreme overachievers. That we hope that if we win enough awards or enough affection from other people, the fact that we are gay becomes inconsequential. I remember buying the book and sitting in the mall and reading the entire thing in one sitting.

"A lot of people wanted to reassure me about things that I was already comfortable about — religious aspects, but I had already worked through that; they would say, 'You're not bad, you're not going to hell,' but I had worked that through too. What I was concerned with was, Am I going to be happy? What is my life going to be like? Am I going to be successful? In my house, success was really a value; my parents were professional educators, and they had very definite ideas about how their children should be successful. It wasn't just a gay issue. For years my sister had always identified with teaching; she'd tutored younger students. But any time she mentioned to our parents that she wanted to be a teacher, my father would say, 'You should be an engineer; you'd make more money if you become an engineer' (which she'd been studying) — it was a value to be successful, but it felt like pressure. My sister did become a teacher. But before she felt okay about doing what she wanted, without my parents' approval, she had to go through this transformation process. Both of us went through the process of redefining what it means to be successful, which is not based on how much money you make or how much people esteem your profession. It's an inner value."

The ability to define your own sense of success reflects a strong sense of identity and self-worth that is essential to feeling free and positive about coming out to others or deciding not to censor the fact of your homosexuality.

Eventually, Ben was faced with a conflict that involved both his profession and his personal life. Being a minister, he was in a unique position to reconcile his belief system with his work in the world. "I was serving as a student pastor and my church [the United Methodist] had just finished a four-year study on homosexuality in the church; there was a lot of conversation about it — mostly negative — so I felt really vulnerable. How is it going to affect me? I was also really torn between my value system [honesty, integrity, and not being ashamed] and practical concerns [the church implied that it was necessary for homosexuals to be dishonest]. It was the weird, schizophrenic position that most denominations take: on the one hand they welcome the gifts of gay people as long as they remain closeted. At the same time, they encourage truth-telling and say that the truth shall set you free."

But Ben was able to turn it around. "As I came out more and more in the seminary community, I began to come out to everyone. The next year I was elected president of the student body — that was a moving experience for me. Before I would tell someone that I was gay, I would imagine the worst, and then the worst wouldn't happen. I began to realize that I didn't have to live my life in the worst-case scenario. I was exploring alternate forms of pastoral care, which is what a lot of gays and lesbians do; they try to choose forms of ministry not directly involved with parish life, so they will avoid the scrutiny a congregation puts on their pastor and his or her personal life. I was waiting for the 1992 general conference of the United Methodist Church, where they would hear the report of the four-year study about gays and lesbians in the church. The study had voted seventeen to four to change the language to allow ordination of gays and lesbians in the United Methodist Church. However, the conference refused to hear the study. When that happened, I decided there was no place for me in that church, and I left."

Ben didn't leave the ministry. He found a church that openly acknowledged and supported its gay and lesbian constituents. But this confrontation with the church in which he'd been raised enabled him to finally live a completely out life. "Our fears are so much greater than the reality. I believe firmly that the bleakness of the closet is much worse than the reality of being out. I'm not dismissing the violence against gays, or the discrimination in the workplace, but as I continue to come out to people, not only do they say, 'I love you still,' but afterward our lives go on and things don't change."

Those Special People

NINA

Like Ben, one of the first straight people Nina came out to was a woman, a former coach and teacher who had been a mentor for her during and since college. Telling someone she loved and respected enabled Nina to take a few more steps toward being open and truthful. As an athlete throughout college, she had formed a close relationship with her basketball coach. "I really had difficulty coming out to straight friends or colleagues. Word kind of got around — people telling other people — but I knew I had to resolve the issue on my own, and that I couldn't control who found out and when. The first straight person (other than my parents) I told was a former coach and teacher. I had moved to Maryland to go to graduate school, and we'd continued to stay in touch. And since that time, we'd become friends and remained connected. One day when she was in town visiting, we had lunch. She hadn't heard from me in a while, and she was concerned that something bad was going on. I realized that it was time I talked to her. At lunch, an hour passed before I finally said something. I kept wondering, 'Should I, shouldn't I?' She was a mentor. I told her I was in a relationship with a woman that I would really like her to meet someday. I didn't say I was 'gay' or 'lesbian.'

"She looked at me and said, 'Why did you feel the need to tell me that?'

"'Because you've known me all these years, and I know that you have a lot of love and respect for me, and I felt like I wasn't being truthful to you about who I am. It's important to me.'

"She said, 'Nina, I asked you that because it doesn't make any difference to me. I love you for who you are. I imagine it may have been hard for you, and I respect the fact that you told me. I just hope that you are happy.'

"I thought, 'This is awesome.' Her response made me realize that if people are true friends of yours who love and respect you, then it's not going to matter. Telling my coach was a learning experience for me; it was instrumental in making me more comfortable with myself. I stopped censoring myself. It's not that I went around telling everyone, 'Hey, I'm gay' — but for people who were close to me, it was okay to tell them about my partner. When people would talk about their husbands, I'd say, 'I have a partner too.' I'm a much better person now.

"I finally told my friend Meredith from elementary school.

I was going out to Boulder, where she lives with her husband and two kids, for a conference. I hadn't seen her in over ten years. I kept asking myself why I hadn't told her yet.

"We had lunch, and I said, 'There's something I want you to know. Remember my friend Richie who I've spoken about? Well, she and I are in the process of breaking up after being together for eight years. I really wanted you to know.'

"She said, 'I thought you might be, but I thought I should leave it up to you if you wanted to share that with me.'

"I thought it was pretty cool."

What's interesting is that what motivated Nina to finally tell her old friend was the importance of ending a relationship. She didn't feel comfortable sitting across from her friend with the wide gap between them. How could Nina feel honest if she couldn't speak frankly about what was going on in her life at the moment? Each of these tiny steps can have a momentous effect on our self-esteem, our image of ourselves, and our ability to feel free and comfortable with who we are as we engage in the world around us. And yet, as Nina says, "I'm still on a journey."

Nina's reference to her journey underscores how coming out is a continual process of testing our comfort level, risking our boundaries with other people, pushing our expectations for our own happiness, and taking that leap of faith by being honest with others about who we are. With each new person, we gain a stronger sense of ourselves, increasing our self-esteem and dislodging our residual homophobia.

BRUCE

After Bruce withdrew from school, his life settled down. He liked correspondence school, which enabled him to live and study at home. His environment was safe and nurturing, which was a necessity after the trauma of the harassment and abuse he suffered in school. But he was still cautious about his homosexuality. As he says, "I didn't come out to my sister, Tonya, and half-brother until a year later. My sister was one of the last people I told. I had always been very aware of her telling gay jokes; she'd call me 'faggot' when we'd argue. I knew if I told her she'd have negative criticism. I am also really fond of my niece, and I was afraid that Tonya would withhold my niece from me."

But Bruce continued to reach out in a positive way to the gay community. At the time, he was only fourteen and still had not had any sexual experiences. For him, exploring meant attending the gay and lesbian youth group. "I continued going to youth group faithfully, and my parents drove me for two and a half years, until I got my driver's license. At first I went to a group in Bloomington, where I made friends and even had a crush on one guy. One summer I went to a gathering in Louis-ville and cried because I didn't want to go back: I came out at such a young age, most of the guys ignored me. They were older, and they didn't want to be labeled as pedophiles if they hung out with me. Most of the youth there ignored me, which made me question myself. I'd say to myself, 'These are gay people and they won't accept me? What the hell is wrong with me?'"

This interesting reaction shows, in part, the homophobia of some of the other kids that Bruce encountered. That these young men were afraid they'd be perceived as pedophiles is an example of how pervasive the stereotype of gay men as promis-cuous and not in charge of their sexual feelings is. This reduc-tive image of the gay man as representing only sex has played a large role in fueling homophobia.

But regardless of this initial rejection, Bruce continued to attend the group and eventually felt more accepted and there-fore more comfortable. As he says, "I still go — now they know me and my sense of humor."

DAVE

Dave also battled with this negative image of gay men, and the process of overcoming his internalized homophobia continues to happen over time. After Dave navigated the Silver Cloud Motel snafu with his parents, he became much more conscious of trying to integrate his homosexuality into his life and dismantle his internalized homophobia. When I asked Dave how long it took until he was comfortable enough with himself that he could overcome the image of himself as sexually deviant, he admits, "I guess to a certain degree I'm still not entirely comfortable. I don't want to start living my parents' worst fears about what homosexuals do."

However, it is clear that this "worst fear" is really not his parents' but his own. This becomes obvious when Dave admits that he wouldn't feel the same way if he were bringing home different girlfriends every other month. "If I brought women home, I'm sure there would have been disapproval, with my parents saying something like, 'Oh, he's playing the ladies' man.' But I don't think there would have been moral judgment. The same actions in the straight community get a nod of disapproval, but in the gay community people are horrified."

Here we see how deeply rooted the stereotype of gay male promiscuity is in our culture, as well as the hunger for more positive role models, especially in terms of relationships. Gay people want to believe that their relationships are long lasting, but they don't seem to trust that this is a real possibility as much as it is for heterosexuals.

It's clear that this lack of concrete social example contributes to Dave's inability to trust the lasting nature of his relationships. Dave continues, "My parents have been married for almost forty-five years, and so I think there is a hope that I will find someone to grow old with — not that it isn't my hope too. I guess I'm a bit more realistic: my brothers and sisters have all been divorced. I'm now in an exclusive relationship with John, and I think we share the expectation of growing old together."

Dave insists he lives an uncensored, completely out life now. "After college I moved to Seattle and became a title examiner for an insurance company. The first person I worked with in the corporate world was also gay, and he was really out. He was my immediate supervisor, and that made me feel sort of protected. They couldn't fire him, because he was so good at his job. I know some people feel it necessary to make a proclamation as soon as they walk in the door, and I guess if people wanted to know something, I have nothing to hide, unless I felt threatened by someone. If the straight guys were sitting around talking about football and their sexual prowess, I guess I would just shut up and not volunteer any information. I'd probably play along at that point. I've found that the best strategy is to tell the biggest blabbermouths at the office, that way the information is out there, and I don't have to tell anyone. That way people can approach you on their comfort level, rather than stretching to your comfort level. For the past ten years my comfort level has been pretty high."

But there was an incident at a different job that made Dave take a leap of faith. "I was dating Ed, a guy I shouldn't have been dating. After the first three weeks, we realized we had nothing in common, but we dragged it out for a year and a half. We began to have these heated wrestling matches that got more and more intense and violent. He was also becoming verbally abusive. I had just started a new job with this hard-core Republican boss, a woman, who was tough as nails and a stickler for punctuality and keeping your personal life out of the office at all costs. Ed had threatened to come into my office and have me fired. He'd also threatened my niece and nephew. The first thing I did was call my parents and tell them what was happening. They told me to get the hell out of there. Unfortunately, I had just signed a lease, but I spent all my time elsewhere.

"I felt like I had to take his threats about getting me fired seriously, so I went in to my hard-core Republican boss after three days in a new department and shut the door, sat down, and said, 'I'm gay, I'm living with this guy, and he's threatened to come in and have me fired.' I was terrified, but I just had to lay it on the line.

"She looked at me for a while and said, 'First of all, you need to know that only I can fire you, and you're doing a fantastic job, so I have absolutely no reason to fire you. And if he comes here, we'll call security.'

"That was the real turning point. It was hard as hell to go in there and have to trust her. I was in tears; I had never cried at the office before. I may have inherited some stoicism from my dad, but I lost it that day. I felt if Andrea could handle this, anyone could handle it. The whole incident made me realize that I was good enough at my job, that I didn't have to worry about getting fired. Actually, I can say that I've never had any negative reactions from others about being gay."

Trusting people can feel dangerous, but the more we give the people we live and work with an opportunity to experience us as human beings, the less our homosexuality will feel like something that separates us from others; instead, we will feel closer to other people and in that way better about ourselves.

From Tolerance to Acceptance

The events leading up to living a truly out life take many forms, and often, as happened with me, we take three steps forward and then one step back before we spring from the closet for good. The tabloid ordeal made me run back into the closet. After waffling for a few years, hiding behind the veneer of heterosexuality, Erik pushed himself out at work and gained strength and purpose.

ERIK

"I had left St. Louis after freshman year and decided to go to the University of Delaware, where I became really involved with the lesbian and gay community. I started to do outreach programs, and that's when it all turned around for me. I was able to stand up in front of a group of thirty to sixty people and say, 'I'm gay and this is who I am and I'm proud of who I am.' Every time I would do that I would feel better about myself.

"I had started going to the gay and lesbian meetings on campus and meeting more people. It felt really good to educate people and talk to them about who I was and who we were as a community. The more and more I did it, the better I felt about myself, which was really important at that point in my life.

"After school I started working for a human services organization and came out to everyone there. I wanted to reach out to people who were homophobic and didn't know how to approach gay people and help turn around their fear. By the time I left that job, those people who had been obviously homophobic had taken a turn around. They'd realized that I was just a regular guy who happened to be gay. They were able to see that my being gay didn't affect my success at my job, and that I got along with everyone. It had been my policy to encourage people at work to ask me questions and begin a dialogue. Whether it's negative or positive, it is essential that people talk about it, and maybe later on down the line it will turn into a positive experience to them and change them in some aspect.

"When I left, everyone came up to me and congratulated me and said thanks, it was nice to work with you. Earlier in the job, some of these people, some of whom were very religious, wouldn't even talk to me. We still may have been different, but on a professional level there was an understanding and a mutual respect. It was such a wonderful feeling. Another gay guy at work told me that now he's really comfortable and his parents are now accepting. That made me feel that I was out for that reason.

"After school I moved to Washington, D.C., and immediately got involved with a gay group and became president. I picked up where I left off in Delaware, educating people, becoming involved with campus politics, educating the administration. That was my big push: I wanted the university administration to understand how important it was to start a gay and lesbian resource center. I then got involved in international lesbian and gay youth organizations and became director of operations in the U.S.

"Standing up and saying 'I'm gay' is a really positive experience. Each time a gay man or lesbian does this, it changes that image of homosexuals and broadens the definition of homosexuality beyond what we do in bed. For me it's been empowering."

Brothers Paul and Davis began their journeys from vastly different points, but their arrivals were ultimately very similar.

PAUL

When Paul returned to South Carolina after living in New York City for several months, the healing process for him, his parents, and the rest of his family was long and arduous. "After I went home I got an apartment with a girl friend of mine. I didn't see my parents very much. By that time, my mom had started to do a lot of reading on her own — she'd go to the library and bookstores looking for titles, and of course they weren't in stock; she'd have to order them. But my dad still didn't really get it; he was still having a really hard time dealing with my being gay. We would still have these intense, heated arguments in which neither of us would back down. So I just stayed away a lot. My mom would say things like 'Please be patient with him.' But I was really angry and resentful."

It wasn't until after he turned twenty-one, four or five years later, when Paul left South Carolina and moved to Florida to attend a fine arts college, that his father showed any signs of tolerance. "When my folks would come to visit, they'd take me out to dinner, and I'd bring the guy I was seeing at the time. My dad wasn't overtly hostile, but he also didn't really say anything to him — he wouldn't dare acknowledge that the guy was more than a friend to me. He wouldn't ask a single personal question."

When I ask Paul to explain why he thought his father had been so rigid and unable to try to understand, Paul says, "Well, my dad is an only child. And he was very religious. We used to get into violent fights about religion. I was as stubborn as he was, but I wasn't judgmental." It became clear that if Paul's father were to consider and accept his son's homosexuality, then he'd be forced to confront some of the set ideas that he grew up with. As Paul says, "Having to rethink this major part of his life made him look at other parts of his life. He's left the Southern Baptist Church since. Not that we don't still argue about religion, but now we can talk about it more reasonably."

Keeping in mind such people as Bruce and William, I wonder, given all this rejection and overt hostility, how Paul managed to escape feelings of self-loathing. He explains, "I ignored his hostility and tried to stay away from him. I had done a lot of reading, and I knew that my ideas weren't sinful or wrong — I didn't buy into that. I had real strong faith in my own ideas, and I clung to them unerringly." He pauses and then says with a laugh, "I guess I inherited my bullheaded stubbornness from him."

The turning point that finally pushed Paul's father from mere tolerance to active acceptance occurred after his brother, Davis, came out. "Now both of his sons were gay. He had a harder time disowning both his sons. I'm sure he was initially disgusted with Davis too." I was curious whether Paul's relationship with his father had truly, fully healed, and he said, "I don't harbor any resentment toward my parents. My parents are like heroes to me — even my dad."

Paul lives a completely out life, never censoring himself. He says he shares his story when he thinks it may help people. Then he told me about a friend of his who had gone home to see his father on his deathbed, and the father still denied him. "That was really horrible; I just want people to know they can try, and sometimes, maybe even often, it all turns out okay."

DAVIS

Davis returned home for six months after he came out, and then he joined the Peace Corps and was sent to the Dominican Republic. Before leaving for his two-year stint, he lived in Greenville with his parents. Davis assumed that since he was already out with his parents and living a gay life (he was in a relationship with a man and going to gay bars), he was comfortable with his homosexuality. However, he discovered that when he arrived in the Dominican Republic, he went back into the closet again without fully understanding why.

"I chose to keep it quiet from everyone. Looking back at it now, it was a totally stupid thing, because all the other Peace Corps volunteers were totally liberal; no one would have cared whether I was gay or not."

When I ask Davis to explain why his fears of rejection returned, he says, "I didn't want to be ostracized for being gay. It was just easier." But, he says, "if I could do it over, I would have been out, at least to my American friends. There is a cultural difference in South America that also played a part in my fear of being out. But that was two years out of my life that I lived back in the closet."

When he returned to the United States, Davis reemerged into gay life, working in a restaurant while he applied to graduate school. "In the restaurant there were a lot of gay guys. At first I was trying not to let them know I was gay, but Greenville is a very small town. They eventually found out I was gay. It bothered me at first when everyone found out, but no one had an issue about it." This is a good example of Davis's own shame about being gay surfacing. Two years after telling his parents, he was still struggling with internalized homophobia. "When I got accepted to graduate school in California and got back into the academic environment, I began to loosen up. It was a small school (six hundred students), and the environment was so much about broadening horizons. Also, California was more liberal. California helped me a lot in terms of getting comfortable with my sexuality."

Davis started to announce his homosexuality and use it as an opportunity to share himself with others. "I gave presentations in my classes concerning gay issues in the workplace today. I addressed such topics as how business managers should deal with gay employees, blatant homophobia, or harassment toward gays." As Davis began to put a positive spin on it, he began to feel a much stronger sense of self.

If being in the closet is living a double life, that means splitting your sense of self. Being out and fully accepting of your homosexuality means becoming whole, which is the building block to living a full, happy life — one that includes being out in your professional as well as your personal life.

Davis is living in Atlanta now and says he no longer censors himself at all. "It's so easy in Atlanta, they have such a large gay population. I took my first boyfriend to my last [company] Christmas party. I got my company to have a nondiscrimination policy. This was my first job out of grad school, and I wanted to make a good impression. But I also didn't want to lie. I was so sick of lying. Coming out at work was gradual. Every Monday people would say things like 'What did you do this weekend?' I'd start with 'Oh, I did stuff with my friends.' Then it became 'Oh, my friend Scott and I.' Next it was 'Scott and I,' and then I was finally able to say, 'My boyfriend and I.' "

A lot of people think they are out and are unaware that they still censor themselves, especially in the workplace. Davis's Monday morning example is a good litmus test for how we may censor the fact that we are gay in certain situations. In Davis's case, he needed to take the risk of possible negative reactions in order to have peace of mind. Sometimes we convince ourselves that coming out is not worth the risk, because then everyone will always think of us as purely sexual beings — as if all our other characteristics boil down to one thing.

Davis continues, "I'm sure other things were said behind my back, but I wasn't aware of it. There were a lot of young people at this company. It was basically very liberal and international; many people had worked abroad [it was an export company]. Their travel made them more aware of different ways to live; most people just treated me courteously."

When I ask him if he had any negative experiences, he says, "Once with a woman who had been attracted to me throughout college. I knew she always liked me, but I ignored it. A few years after college, we were talking on the phone, and she asked me if there was 'anyone special' in my life. I hesitated, and then she said, 'You're not going to tell me you're living one of those alternative lifestyles, are you?' I said, 'Do you mean am I gay? Well, yes I am.' At first she seemed to handle it pretty well, but then she started lecturing me on the Bible. She was judgmental and hurtful. I don't need to be around people like that."

This is a good example of how once we've established a strong gay identity and self-esteem, the criticism of others no longer has the power to affect us deeply. Davis was able to be objective about his friend's opinions and not take her hurtful comments to heart. Like most of us, Davis understands that we all have our own timetables for determining when to take the essential steps to living a fully out life. "I think it's different for each person. Everyone has their own fears about coming out. When I was at the export company there were several other gay people, but I was the only one who was out. Everyone knew they were gay, but they never spoke about their personal lives. I remember talking to one guy, and he said he just didn't need to talk about this [his homosexuality] in business. I pointed out that everyone else spoke about his or her personal life. Then I asked him, 'Why can't you have that same privilege — to say, "My partner and I did this," or "My partner is sick"?' I encourage people to come out, but I don't force it."

Coming Out at Work

JUDY

When I first talked to Judy, she told me that she was afraid to come out at work; when I talked to her last, both she and her partner, Lenore, were still complicit in their fear, making it harder to move beyond. I asked Judy how she felt about coming out in a more public way, and she said, "It scares the living shit out of me. I now work in a real estate company which is very conservative; many of the people are very religious. I don't talk about my life at work at all, and they don't ask me questions."

When I ask her to pinpoint her fear, she says, "I've only worked there seven months. I didn't want to go into the situation with a billboard saying, 'I'm a lesbian.' I wanted them to know me first. I know that the people who know me as a person won't have a problem with the fact that I'm a lesbian."

This is a common explanation of why people are afraid to

be open about their homosexuality. It makes sense that gay people want to be known first as people, then as people who happen to be gay. But remember, if there is no evidence of prejudice, your fears may be ill founded. When I asked Judy to articulate just what she was afraid of, she couldn't put her fears or their supposed consequences into words. This points to her own as-yet unearthed homophobia.

Sometimes It's as Simple As . . .

Sometimes a fully out life is achieved with seemingly casual events. Robin told me that recently she was invited to the wedding of a friend from high school. She deliberated over bringing her girlfriend. When the bride-to-be phoned and asked if Robin wanted to bring a date, Robin took the risk and said, "Yes, Beth* will be coming with me." Her friend didn't question Robin's decision. Although Robin had already come out to her friend, she hadn't yet taken a date to any social situation with this group of old friends from her past. And although she was nervous, she decided that the act was significant; she needed to know not only how these people from her past would respond, but how she herself would respond.

Richard never verbally came out at work, but he brings his boyfriend to functions such as the annual holiday party. "Everyone knows, but it's not like I made a point of announcing it." This way of coming out is more suitable to many gays and lesbians. All these small victories add up. Whether it's a social or a professional situation, it's important to distinguish between real risks and more vague, irrational fears.

It's true that only thirteen states in this country have antidiscrimination laws to protect gays against firing or other unjust treatment. However, the number of public and private companies that have instituted policies against discrimination, and extend insurance and other benefits to the partners of gay employees continues to grow. Companies including Nike, Levi Strauss, and ABC have antidiscrimination policies in place, and many companies are following their lead. The climate is changing, but many gay people still fear coming out at work. And while I understand their fears and empathize (I was convinced for a long time that my record deal would fall through if I was publicly out), I also think that it's a crucial barrier to cross.

There are a few steps to consider when planning to come out at work. First, find out about the state, city, and company policies toward gays and lesbians. If any of those entities has an antidiscrimination policy, then you are legally protected as a gay person. If you are not in danger of losing your job, then try to come out by *not* censoring yourself. For example, on Monday when people are talking about what they did over the weekend, don't change the pronoun of your partner; rather, mention his or her name in passing, just as your straight coworkers do with their spouses or partners. This lets others know you are gay in a casual, nonconfrontational manner and allows them to digest the information on their own.

If gays are not protected in any explicit way, focus on the climate in the company. Is there a prevalent attitude toward homosexuality? Do you know of any other out people in the company? How are they treated? Do you hear offensive or antigay comments? How do others react?

If there exists an overt antihomosexual attitude among your coworkers, then you may want to consider changing jobs if you want to continue the coming-out process at work. This may sound cavalier, but I am quite serious. Eventually, working in a homophobic environment is damaging to you as a person. Hateful and intimidating remarks will whittle away your sense of self. I believe a healthy work environment is essential to a happy life, and the trouble of leaving a job that undermines your belief in yourself is worth it.

Emptying the Closet

In the aftermath of Joan's death, I stayed out of the world. But several months later, I met a very special woman. I was still going through the grieving process, but this new relationship began to become serious: I began to fall in love. It was at this point that I made a conscious decision to not make the same mistakes with Laura that I had with Joan: I lived my life more openly, not hiding, being affectionate in public, throwing all caution to the wind, so to speak. From this point on, if asked, I never denied the fact that I was gay. Further proof of my progress in terms of truly accepting my homosexuality was when a tabloid came out with a story on Laura and me and it had absolutely no effect on me.

Around this time I met Judy Wieder, the editor in chief of *The Advocate.* Judy asked me if I were interested in telling my story and coming out in the magazine. We went to lunch. As I began telling her about my life, she pointed out how helpful my story would be to other people. I realized it would also put to rest rumors created by the tabloid frenzy.

At the time, I had decided not to continue my music career. I had become so disheartened after Ceremony got cut from Geffen that I found myself uninspired to continue writing and playing music. I had not yet decided what I should do career-wise. I was floundering and spent a lot of time in therapy, trying to get my life back in order. I had a number of odd jobs, including one as a bartender at Girl Bar for a while. But I basically felt adrift.

I didn't want to be on the cover of a magazine unless I had a life that I felt proud of and comfortable with. So I told Judy that I would do the story with *The Advocate*, but I wasn't ready yet. That was in late spring of 1994.

Every few months, Judy would check in with me. Finally I called her and told her that though I was still not ready, I'd love to work at *The Advocate* and asked her if there were any entry-level positions open. She said there wasn't anything like that, but asked if I would be interested in writing something for the magazine. I said yes immediately, and they assigned me a couple of "Buzz" items to write. Then they offered me the chance to write a feature on singer Melissa Ferrick. It was my first official byline.

This was a huge challenge for me. On the one hand, interviewing felt very natural because I had been interviewed so many times in the past. But I found the actual writing difficult. I had never been scholastically inclined and had little confidence in my abilities as a writer. It was scary for me to try to write something of any real length. But I was motivated to do it. It felt like it took forever — but I tried not to let my fear get in my way.

After I turned in the article, I was offered the writer at large position, and at that point I felt like I was ready to do the coming-out story for them. My life was starting to take shape again — this time within a framework based on honesty, self-worth, and a belief that I could be out *and* happy.

Chapter 8

The Final Frontier

I came out on the cover of *The Advocate* in April 1995. At the time, I had no idea how this action would alter and reshape my life. I thought that I'd come out and continue to write for *The Advocate* and that would be the extent of my political involvement in the gay community. I knew that my appearance on the cover would affect people and have ramifications outside myself, but I never dreamed that my involvement would grow to such an extent. My simple goal was to give back what had been given to me: when I read or heard about gays and lesbians being vocal and standing up for who they are, I felt stronger about myself. Now I wanted to see if I could help people struggling to come out and show them the rich rewards outside the closet.

After I appeared on the cover, I started getting calls from different gay and lesbian organizations wanting me to get involved. My very first speaking engagement was the welcoming ceremony at the California AIDS Ride. Soon after that, I got a call from the Human Rights Campaign (HRC) to come to Washington and participate in the reintroduction of the Employment Non-Discrimination Act (ENDA) to the 104th Congress, of which my father was a member.

Prior to this time, I had no idea that gays and lesbians could be fired from their jobs in forty-one states solely based on their sexual orientation. I was shocked and outraged by the information HRC had sent to me on job discrimination, and after reading many real-life case files, I decided to go to Washington, D.C., and participate in their event. I had a lot to learn, but it was this trip to the capital that jump-started my career as a political activist.

HRC had also invited gay and lesbian relatives of members of Congress, including Candace Gingrich and Sandi De Witt, to participate in a press conference following the reintroduction of the bill. The press conference was going to be held at the Capitol. Beforehand, a bunch of us were waiting in Senator Ted Kennedy's chamber. I can't describe the electricity and excitement: the environment was a complete turn-on for me.

When we arrived downstairs for the press conference, I was armed with a prepared speech from HRC. There were a lot of people there — more than expected — and I began to get extremely nervous. I hadn't been onstage since my days in the band, and I had certainly never given any kind of press conference based on my being gay.

Then something magical happened. I gave my speech and then began taking questions. All of a sudden I felt a rush, as if time slowed down. Here I was being fully myself, talking and answering questions about what it was like to be gay. The moment was incredible; never in my years of performing music had I ever felt so in sync with myself. I lost my self-consciousness and felt exhilarated.

After the press conference was over, I met up with my dad, and he took me to the floor of the House of Representatives, where he had to vote. All these congressmen and -women began coming up to me and thanking me for taking part in the press conference. My dad was clearly excited that I was interested in politics, even though our views were different. He enjoyed the attention I was getting and seemed proud that we had this interest in common. After that, I was hooked on politics.

It wasn't until I came out publicly that I really learned about the extent of antigay discrimination in this country. I also realized that I received deep satisfaction from fighting for our civil and political rights, and that I myself could really help.

In the late spring of 1995, I was asked to speak at the annual dinner for the Mautner Project, a lesbian cancer organization based in Washington, D.C. This time, I had written my own speech, and when I went up to speak, I felt nervous. Once I started speaking, however, I again had the sensation of time slowing — it was this tremendous high. I was talking about Joan, her illness and eventual death, and I was clearly connecting with the audience: the women, and the few men, were obviously moved by and relating to what I was saying. In all those years of performing onstage, I had never come close to this kind of fulfillment.

I was reminded again of playing and singing music, and how I'd always felt insecure, never losing the sense that people were out in the audience judging me. For the first time in my life, I felt like I was good at something. I was doing something for myself and others that had nothing to do with my parents.

For the rest of that year, I continued to write for *The Advocate* and did occasional speaking engagements. In January 1996, I approached HRC and said that I was interested in coming on as their National Coming Out spokesperson for 1996, and they offered me the position. I began to travel around the country and speak at different events for HRC, such as gay pride events in different cities and black-tie fund-raising dinners, as well as at coming-out workshops for gay and lesbian community centers. Since it was an election year, I also talked about the importance of coming out politically, voting, and being vocal.

As I began to visit other cities and parts of the country, I realized that there were many places much less tolerant than those I knew. This may sound naive, but it was unbelievable to me: talking and listening to such different people's experiences opened my eyes to things I had not been aware of. For example, I went to a gay pride event in Salt Lake City during the city's controversy about establishing a gay-straight club alliance in schools. The school board initially banned all extracurricular school clubs, and then limited their ability to choose their focus, excluding those that had to do with race or sexuality. This was a young, growing gay community that had just been dealt this blow, and it was fascinating for me to see its strength and commitment. In a year's time, I watched the community grow tremendously, doubling the size of its gay pride parade. Such fresh dedication, political awareness, and involvement felt enormously encouraging and reinforced my belief in the importance of the gay community.

I also went to the Democratic National Convention in Chicago; it was amazing to be on the floor listening to Clinton use the word *gay* in his speech. The inclusion of the gay and lesbian community made me proud to be a Democrat.

In the fall of 1996, GLAAD (Gay and Lesbian Alliance Against Defamation) asked me to be its entertainment media director, a position I happily accepted. This new job has allowed me to link my activism with my knowledge of the entertainment industry. I work with entertainment industry professionals as an adviser/consultant on projects with gay and lesbian characters or themes. For instance, when *Ellen* was planning its coming-out episodes, I consulted with the writers and producers of the show, including Ellen DeGeneres herself. I helped to make the scripts more realistic by clarifying gay issues and situations. (I also had a cameo on the show, portraying a social worker at a gay and lesbian community center.)

I work with such shows as *Hard Copy* and *Entertainment Tonight* on a regular basis. Any time they do a story that contains a gay issue, they consult with me on the best way to present the information. Recently I worked with Universal Pictures and producer Sean Daniels on the film *The Jackal.* The studio executives were worried because in test screenings audiences had cheered during a scene in which a gay man was murdered. I worked with the filmmakers on editing the scene in a way that made it clear why the Jackal character killed the man, eliminating any possible homophobic motives. I also worked with Jack Valenti, the head of the ratings board, and the producers of *As Good as It Gets.* The word *fag* was used in the trailer by Jack Nicholson's character, and Valenti thought it might be offensive. He called me for my opinion. After seeing the trailer and the film, I advised that based on the context in which the word was used, it wasn't problematic. Jack Nicholson's character is an all-around bigot, and throughout the trailer he used a number of defamatory slurs — not only about gay people. He was revealing his character rather than making a gratuitous antigay statement.

Speaking about myself and for other people has helped me to see my own coming-out process with more objectivity. In the past couple of years, ever since taking that first step and appearing on the cover of *The Advocate,* I began to realize how much strain being in the closet had put on my life. I no longer wanted to live within the false confines of the closet. In the next couple of months, the idea for this book began to emerge. I wanted to share my experience as well as those of others so that coming out to ourselves, friends, family, and coworkers would not seem so daunting.

I hope that by the time you've gotten to this place in the book, you've gained the courage, by reading about other people's experiences, including mine, to begin or continue your own coming-out process. Coming out is still a scary idea and an even scarier action, but as the stories you have read convey, no matter how frightening it can be, most everyone feels better after coming out. The relief, joy, and gratification that you can be truly yourself is astounding.

Many of us think that we are completely out when we still censor ourselves and hide the fact that we are gay in certain situations. Hiding this part of ourselves is a demonstration of the shame we still feel about who we are. I discovered how subtle and tricky this shame can be when I was outed in the tabloids: I retreated to the closet and used the excuse of hurting my career to hide my homosexuality. I was so afraid of the repercussions my sexual orientation could possibly have on my career that I curtailed how I lived. Finally I realized that I was living in a constant state of oppression. As a result, I felt like I had little control over my own life.

Once I confronted my worst fear and decided to come out on the cover of *The Advocate*, the shame that I had been harboring for those years began to melt away. Announcing publicly that I was gay enabled me to feel whole in a way I had never really experienced before. I suddenly understood that it was true: I could be out, happy, and proud of who I am.

But that was only the beginning. I next realized how important it is to become involved in the gay community. I had to turn around the angry, negative feelings that I'd experienced during my outing ordeal. By writing for *The Advocate* and then becoming politically active with HRC, I began to see how rich and diverse the gay community is and to meet gays and lesbians with whom I identified and whom I respected. The gay community is filled with a lot of very smart, successful people who are working for our civil rights. As we have seen in many of the stories here, we need role models: we need heroes.

Learning how to best navigate the difficulties of coming

out takes preparation: it helps enormously to first reach out to the gay community for support. A good way to meet people and discover the community is to volunteer for an organization. There are many local and national gay and lesbian organizations. Gay community centers and support groups also provide ways to meet people. There are many magazines (again both local and national), as well as many good books published in the last few years that describe gay and lesbian coming-out stories. The Internet has chat rooms and gay web sites that describe what is happening and keep you up to date on events in your area as well as in other states and cities. The more aware you are of the gay and lesbian community, the more you'll feel a part of something larger. As you probably see by this point in the book, the gay community is as diverse as the population of the United States. And no matter where your interests lie, you will find people with whom to identify. One of the ways homophobia works against gay people is that it can give us a sense that we are not normal, that we don't fit in with the society at large. Once you become involved with the gay community — either directly by joining a gay organization or indirectly through reading lesbian and gay publications — your sense of identification as a gay, lesbian, bisexual, or transgender will be stronger. You will begin to see yourself not only as a normal and healthy individual, but as part of a creative, vibrant, thriving community.

Once again, I caution you: before you begin to come out to other people, make sure you've done your homework as best you can and have a realistic understanding of the gay and lesbian community and movement, so that when you tell others, you are prepared to be able to talk about it. It's very important to educate yourself as to what is happening both locally and nationally.

In the same way that you educate yourself, you need to help, or at least offer to help, educate your parents, grandparents, siblings, and friends. It's important that before you tell your family, you have resources set up for them, such as the number of your local P-FLAG chapter and information on when and where they meet. Have literature for your parents to read that will help them understand their own reactions as well as the myths and inaccurate definitions of or associations with homosexuality.

In the next part of the book, we will look at the reactions of parents to their children's being gay, lesbian, and bisexual. Just as coming out is a process for us, parents go through an analogous process in which they confront themselves starkly. After Joan died and I began to regain control over my life, my mother made subtle, significant, and irreversible steps toward not only full acceptance of me but also a sense of empowerment in having a lesbian daughter. But as we'll see, this growth process was not without pain and suffering for her.

I think it's important that gay people *and* their parents read both parts of the book, so that together we gain both perspectives. The next part will give gays and lesbians insight into their parents' potential reactions and the journey that lies ahead for their parents and the rest of the people in their lives.

In hindsight it's clear that once we eliminate internalized homophobia, we are able to realize that our excuses for not coming out are really manifestations of shame and not based on any real threat. There are many ways to live your life out of the closet, whether it means moving to a different city or working at a different job. Once the shame is gone, the idea of hiding becomes intolerable.

If you don't feel ashamed of who you are, you will not hide. Once you feel comfortable about being gay, no one can make you feel bad about it: the negativity of other people will not have as deleterious an effect.

The Personal Is the Political

It was no coincidence that my political awakening fostered my growth as a person; it was no coincidence that my leaving the confines of the closet allowed me to fully love myself; it is no coincidence that my relationship with my mother, after years of emotional distance, was transformed by our mutual love and respect.

Coming out is a personal act of transformation. It is also a political act. As Mark Blasius points out in his book *Gay and Lesbian Politics,* in order to break society of the delusion that compulsory heterosexuality is the norm, which is the foundation for all homophobic attitudes, gays and lesbians *must* come out. "One does not come out once and for all," he says, "and coming out is not just a disclosure of one's gay or lesbian identity to others. Rather than being an end state in which one exists as an out person, coming out is a process of becoming, a lifelong learning of how to be (and of inventing the meaning of being) a lesbian or a gay man in this historical moment."

When we come out, our parents, family, and friends are asked to come out too. Together, we will take all gays, lesbians, bisexuals, and transgenders out of the closet to acceptance, and beyond to empowerment.

Part Two
Parents Come Out Too

Chapter 9

When Parents Come Out
The Struggle Begins

*"He who knows nothing, loves nothing. He
who can do nothing understands nothing. He
who understands nothing is worthless. But he who
understands also loves, notices, sees. . . . The more
knowledge is inherent in a thing, the greater the
love. . . . Anyone who imagines that all fruits ripen
at the same time as the strawberries knows nothing about grapes."*

PARACELSUS, as quoted by ERICH FROMM
in *The Art of Loving*

Suspicions

My mom had her own suspicions that I was "different" when
I was about six and began to choose my own clothes. She says:
"I was just observing, letting it unfold, not really knowing
what it was going to be. But I also remember feeling a little bit
nervous. It wasn't one thing, it was something I couldn't put
my finger on. It's an instinct, a motherly kind of instinct."

This kind of vagueness is common among parents who
suspect something is different about their child but don't have

a name for it. Similar to how gay people themselves sense that they are different but don't know how or why, parents don't necessarily have the language to express what they think is going on. But what's clear is that my mother definitely viewed my being different as a negative, and it generated a vague dread in her that continued to grow throughout my childhood and adolescence. As I've said, I felt that dread in her, and it made me anxious.

My father, who'd been divorced from her for two or three years when she first became concerned, seemed only to exacerbate my mother's sense of apprehension. She remembers feeling a lot of anger toward my father when he would dress me as a boy. As she says to me, "That really pissed me off. He gave you all sorts of perks for acting like a boy. I think he really wanted you to be a boy. He was El Primo, and you were El Primo Jr. I would see pictures of you and your father together, and I would get pissed. I didn't think he was thinking about what was best for our daughter."

When I tell her I thought she got angry because my father seemed to be provoking her, she says no; rather, she was concerned about my well-being. She says adamantly, "I didn't think he was thinking about what was best for you." Even at this point, before she had put the label 'gay' to me, she was worried about how I would be perceived by the public, wondering whether I'd fit in with the other kids and if I'd be all right in the world.

But the more I began to express myself, the more she became uncomfortable. "There were little things — like you always chose male characters at Halloween." Like most parents, my mom was very aware of even the most subtle changes as I grew and started to become my own person. As she explains, "If you're around your child all the time, then you notice the difference in the way she acts or looks."

When I remind my mother how completely natural it was for me to dress like a boy, that I was much happier in those clothes, she says almost sadly, "When you were tiny, you were so frilly and dainty. You were my little girl. That's what I wanted you to be."

My mother remembers clearly the first time she thought I was gay: "You were about eleven, and we were in Paris, and we all decided to play dress up and take silly pictures. You dressed up in my black leather jacket. You had slicked back your hair in fifties style, had a cigarette in your mouth and a switch-blade in your hand. I thought, 'Oh, my God.' I was frightened.

"I thought you might be leaning toward being gay, and it made me nervous. It was the last choice of how I wanted you to be. When you were a little girl, we used to play dress up and paint our faces together — we were like girls together. I wanted you to grow up to be a beautiful girl."

What was most frustrating and unnerving for my mom was that she thought she knew me, and then when I started dressing differently, acting differently, she felt like she didn't recognize me anymore. "If you're around a child all the time, and then you begin to notice differences, it's disconcerting. You have a baby, then you have a child, and you look at them, and all of a sudden the child starts changing." She pauses and says to me, "All of a sudden you weren't the same to me. You'd become this slovenly, masculine-dressed chick, and I thought, 'Oh, what is this — what happened?' I kept wondering why you found it necessary to make this physical change." All parents watching their children grow up are faced with similar feelings when their children start to move away from them and develop their own identities. For many parents, this can be anxiety provoking, especially if the child, like me, seems so different from the parent.

But my mom continued to push away her suspicions. "Between the age of eleven and you becoming a teenager, I had an uneasy feeling every once in a while. I remember that you weren't having a really good time with anyone in life then, and that's why I sent you to Strasberg." As I've said, getting involved in acting made me feel much better about myself, and this in turn made my mother feel better about me — she seemed less worried about me, less standoffish.

It was around this time, when I was thirteen and fourteen, that I began to see more of Joan and her friend Scottie. My mom had known both Joan and Scottie for most of her life, but seemed a bit uncomfortable when I spent time with them. What's interesting is that my mother has no recollection of my hanging out with Joan and Scottie, or her own discomfort about the situation at the time. I would go to the beach with them, hang out at their house. I can also remember helping them organize a couple of garage sales. A few times, my mother questioned me about why I spent so much time with them. I muddled through my reasons: I really like them, they're nice people. I gave the vaguest of explanations. Now she admits, "I don't remember you hanging out with them a lot. But obviously that must have made me very uncomfortable." Then my mother took me to a therapist.

When I ask her what she was thinking when she took me to a therapist, she explains, "It was such a long time ago, I can't remember. . . . Well, the first thing that comes to mind is that I was probably scared shitless. I thought it would be better if we had a discussion with a therapist so that I didn't become hysterical. Also, I knew the therapist could give me some insight into what was going on with you once we were talking."

It's clear that she was struggling both to deal with her own feelings, which were frightening to her, and mine. She was worried about me. I can imagine her questions: What did it mean that her daughter was hanging out with an older lesbian couple? That her daughter preferred wearing boys' clothes to girls'? The way I dressed became a red flag that reinforced my mother's fear that I would turn out to be gay. But she was also disappointed that I was not more feminine. She remembers, "I was just so disappointed. I didn't understand what had happened to my beautiful, sweet, lovely daughter. I didn't like what she was going to be, and I was afraid that I wouldn't even know what that was." My mom seemed afraid that she was no longer going to be able to relate to me, and that she would feel more distance between us. "I kept thinking it was a phase you'd grow out of, but it kept happening."

Many parents of gay or lesbian children who are struggling with the idea that their child may be gay try to assuage their anxiety by telling themselves that their child is going through a phase. This seems to be about trying to stave off their fear of homosexuality in general: they don't feel ready to confront the reality.

It's both ironic and telling that when my mom was young, she was a tomboy too. She admits freely, "I was a real tomboy, but I also liked to wear frilly dresses — everyone would joke because there's this one picture of me in this adorable little dress, and if you look down at my legs, they're totally black and blue. I was a walking dichotomy. I loved getting dressed up, and I liked getting funky too. I wore jeans from the beginning — they were the first clothes I ever put on myself. But I also liked nice clothes and new shoes. I was also into sports: I ran, I played ball — I was really athletic. But you can't really run fast in a dress. That's still who I am today. Mostly I'm in no makeup and in my sweatpants. But then if I go out, I might as well do it."

Perhaps if I had been more like her — if I had been both a tomboy and a frilly girl — my mom may have been more accepting of me. It was the fact that I was a tomboy through and through that was the problem. Although my mom may have related to the part of me that wanted to dress in jeans, she had a tough time understanding and accepting that I wasn't a dichotomy like her, that I was simply much more masculine than she. It's clear that she experienced my being so masculine as a negative reflection on her.

When I ask her if she ever talked to anyone about her fears or discomfort, she says no, adamantly. My mother is a very private person who relies on herself to solve most problems. She didn't even share her trouble with Georgeann. And she certainly didn't want to confront me with her suspicions: "I was too frightened of it — I was hoping I was wrong. One of the reasons I encouraged you to get into acting was because you were so lonely [at school in Los Angeles]. I thought maybe if you were adopted by a group of people, you would become a different person."

Like many parents, my mother actively censored herself, very consciously limiting what she said about me to her friends and the people she worked with. "I was worried about their reactions — for you and me. I didn't want to answer questions about you. What was I going to say, that you were marching around in combat boots?"

Both of us remember that my difference from her and who she wanted me to be put a huge rift between us. She says, "It was very painful for me, and it kept us from being really close at the time. I mean, we still did things together, but there was this one subject we couldn't talk about. A lot of the time I felt angry." Obviously "this subject" was my sexual orientation and all that went with it: sex and dating and my latest crush.

The turning point came when my mother walked in on me and Julie just before my seventeenth birthday. My mother remembers, "I knew what was happening. That's why I didn't go to your birthday party. I was so flipped out about seeing you with Julie; it was the first time I realized for sure you were gay. I felt all kinds of things — shock, embarrassment, guilt — all kinds of negative feelings, so I just thought you'd have a better time at the party without me."

Like those of most parents, my mom's guilt and even her embarrassment were tied to her feelings about herself. She felt guilty because she thought there might have been something she could have done to prevent me from being gay. As she says, "I think when something happens to your kids, you always take on the responsibility. No one brings up their children perfectly, and there are a lot of things in childhood that you suddenly think you could have done better. *It must have been that thing I didn't do. Or I wasn't there enough. Or I could have taken care of this. If only I had done this differently. If only I'd made this decision another way.* All those thoughts and questions were streaming through my mind."

This raises an interesting question. Why is it all right for other people to be gay, but not your child? As my mother says, "The parent-child relationship is much more intense than other relationships." But since my mother had always been so accepting of her gay and lesbian friends, including Joan, it was surprising to her (and to those around her, including my aunt Georgeann) that she was so agitated by her daughter's probable homosexuality. My mother's feeling of responsibility is common among many parents of gays and lesbians, but I think this contradiction also points to my mother's inability at the time to see me as separate from herself. As I matured, especially when I finally emerged from the closet after Joan's death as a much stronger, more self-confident person, my mother was more and more able not only to see us as separate but also to be proud of who I am. But this transformation would take years.

Back when I was seventeen, my mother was still steeped in her confusion and disappointment that I was not meeting her expectations. "After the birthday party, when you and I made up, I didn't want to talk about the incident, and you didn't want to talk about it. So we just didn't talk about it."

I Just Can't Put My Finger on It

It's common that before a gay person comes out to his or her family, a parent suspects that child is different. In some cases, the parents already realize that the child may be lesbian or gay. Parents who have been exposed to gay people in their lives, in a positive or a negative way, tend to interpret their children's behavior or gestures as indicating that they may be gay. These parents pick up signals that range from blatant to discreet. And in most cases, the parents tend to react by getting nervous, frightened, and sometimes angry. Those parents with little or no awareness of homosexuality tend to overlook or ignore the signals. They don't take particular notice that their child may feel different, alienated from his or her peer group, or be struggling with some dilemma. It is only in hindsight that they see that their son or daughter may have been trying to communicate something.

Suspecting Without Putting a Name to It

ELLIE (Erik's mother)

Ellie, Erik's mother, is a Jewish homemaker from Delaware. She "suspected long before [she] really knew the fact" that Erik was gay. She recalls that Erik liked to "play house, which I felt was a bit unusual for a four-year-old boy. And when he was eight, he asked me for a dollhouse. I was always the kind of mother that believed that you should give dolls to little boys just like little girls. I always treated my children fairly. If my daughter had wanted a truck, I would have given it to her. But at the time, I thought he was just interested in miniatures and found a plan for a mini general store and an entire village that I helped build for him, which is now sitting in my living room. But I do remember thinking that he might be embarrassed if I got him a dollhouse, so I got him the general store. When little boys came to the house, he was kind of embarrassed to say it was his."

Looking back, she says, "All these indications should have been like a lightbulb going off, but I guess I was in denial. I just thought Erik was a sensitive boy. He played with trucks, built things with blocks, and rode his bike. It wasn't like he only had feminine traits. His sister is four years older, and he always had enormous respect for her, so I just figured that he was trying to relate to her. He spent most of his time with me and her while his father was out earning a living."

But there did come a time when Ellie felt specific discomfort. "When Erik was in high school, a friend of mine told me her son was [gay]. One day, she was walking out of my house and said, 'Well, one day your son will come home and tell you he's gay.' I looked at her, and I thought, 'Why would she say that to me — Erik is very masculine, Erik likes girls. I don't know where she's coming from.' But then I began to see indications of what she was referring to. I tried to ignore them because I didn't want to see. He would hide things. Every time I walked by the computer, he would make it go dark, and I said, 'Why is it going dark like that?' and he'd say, 'Oh, it just does that when I stop typing, Mom.' And so I knew something was going on."

Like many parents, Ellie essentially tried to ignore the signals that there was something "different" about her child.

CAROL* (Richard's mother)

When I spoke with Richard's mother, Carol, she said that although she was aware of her son's lack of interest in sports, she never worried about him. "Richard was a city kid. I just thought he wasn't a jock, wasn't that type of kid." Carol reminds me of my own mother when she says of Richard, "He was my baby; I had four daughters before him, and I was so happy to have a boy. He was this sweet, lovely, towheaded boy. He was an angel. I didn't want to think that he was different from the rest. I just loved him."

But Richard's sisters were well aware that he was effeminate. Starting when he was eight or ten years old, they tried to encourage him to play sports. But Carol would intervene. She says, "I didn't care so much that he wasn't interested in the real physical sports like football or baseball. I encouraged him to swim or play tennis. I love sports, but I didn't really care that he wasn't that interested.

"Looking back, I guess I had my head a bit in the sand. Richard was definitely not your typical boy. But either way, he was my son." Carol seems to forget the pressure she did put on Richard, and yet he remembers it clearly. A lot of parents, including my own mother, tend to forget difficult or conflicted feelings, and it's only on suggestion that they will recall certain details. When prompted, Carol admits that she was a bit uncomfortable that Richard "put on cologne like it was perfume. I'd watch him dab it on his wrists and then rub them together. It made me cringe, but I knew that he was just mirroring me and his sisters. His father wasn't around much after our divorce, and he had no other male role models. But at the time, it certainly didn't make me suspect he was gay."

The first time the thought crossed her mind that he might be gay, she dismissed it. "It was when he was in college, and he'd come home for the summer. I remember noticing that he used his hands in an effeminate manner. It bugged me, so I told him that people would think something. I think I got a little embarrassed in front of other people."

It wasn't until Carol read an article about Simon Le Vay's biological theory of homosexuality that her first real suspicions that Richard might be gay were triggered. In his study, Le Vay noticed that gay men demonstrated significantly larger hypothalamuses than straight men, suggesting that gay men differ biologically from straight men. Carol remembers: "I was reading the article on the plane going to visit one of my daughters in California. Le Vay's argument made so much sense: that there was a big biological component to homosexuality. Suddenly I saw Richard in this new way."

It's clear to both Richard and his mother that she had

been in denial about the signals Richard was sending. His mother, who considers herself very open-minded and liberal, is unable to explain her denial, which was quite unconscious, but now readily admits to not paying attention. It's probable that once she read an explanation that made sense, her denial was no longer useful to her — she allowed herself to see her son fully and accept his homosexuality.

I think it's interesting that in my mom's case and that of Richard's mother, they did not judge homosexuality itself — rather, their reactions were more about their own discomfort and fears. Perhaps the lack of moral dimension to their reactions is related to their having been exposed to or known closely other gay people. Their reactions had more to do with how they saw themselves in their children than with being prejudiced against homosexuality. Nevertheless, all parents I spoke with, including my mother, regret that they were not, at this early stage in their children's lives, more knowledgeable about homosexuality.

Regretting Their Ignorance

While parents may have been aware that their child was not "typical" growing up, they didn't always associate this difference with the possibility of budding homosexuality. Carol explains it this way, "I knew gay people. My parents had friends who were gay. But as a young parent, I never learned anything about the subject per se. I was raised in a Catholic environment, and we just didn't talk about homosexuality as a possibility." This is a common explanation for why parents did not make a direct association between a child's behavior, manner, or appearance and homosexuality. But that's not to say they weren't aware of the little signals making them uncomfortable.

GLENDA (Ben's mother)

Some parents are able to admit in hindsight that they actively ignored their suspicions. Like my mother, Glenda suspected that her son, Ben, was gay, but she would always "dismiss it." Glenda grew up in Kentucky and was raised in the Methodist Church. Both she and her husband are educators and consider themselves very spiritual. "I would always say to myself, "Well, he had a crush on a girl back in the sixth grade. Then I found some heterosexual pornographic material when he was in high school, and I said to myself, 'No, he couldn't be gay.'"

But she admits that he was always different. "He was an activist from the time he was in the fifth grade. Ben's father was an athlete and did the college scholarship in baseball, and he also coached basketball. But Ben was never interested in sports. His father was great in the fact that he never pushed Ben to be in athletics. I encouraged him to join the YMCA basketball team, and he did that, and I insisted that he stay through the season, but I could see right away that it wasn't his thing."

In many ways, Glenda was proud of Ben for his difference. "He was so good in music and drama, and he was on the ecumenical council. I noticed that he only had girl friends, but I'm ashamed to say that I was so unaware." When I ask why she feels ashamed, Glenda explains, "I'm so aware now, but I'm embarrassed that I didn't think that was what was happening with Ben. But sexual orientation was just not discussed." Glenda didn't share any of her thoughts with her husband, however. As she admits, "Well, I thought homosexuals couldn't be happy."

RHEA AND BUTCH (Bruce's parents)

For some parents, the idea that their child may be gay can be utterly terrifying. Rhea, Bruce's mother, explained it this way: "As a child, I grew up as a Nazarene, which is a fundamentalist Christian religion. In our church, the idea of homosexuality was just so horrifying and so disgusting that it was never given a forum to be spoken about. It went unspoken."

When she first suspected Bruce was gay, he was a toddler. "I would watch Bruce and my stepson, who is older, play, and they would play Hot Wheels and stuff like that together. Bruce seemed to like boy things, but he also liked to play with dolls and do things like play house and be the mother.

"I remember him having his first crush in kindergarten. It wasn't a sexual thing; it was just that his heart beat a little faster when this particular boy would walk in the class, and if he got to sit next to the little boy, it made him happy. Up until the second grade, he had both male and female friends, and then the boys started to ostracize him. There wasn't a peer group he could fit into.

"I very consciously pushed the thought that he was gay aside, because it terrified me. I had spent my whole life in a town with a population of eight thousand, and I hardly ever ventured past the city limits. It is a real small community, and on the surface the people seem to be warm and friendly, but underneath they are very cliquish and fearful of strangers or anybody who is different."

The combination of Rhea's religious background, the small size of her community, and her own fears of whether she could "handle it" further ostracized Bruce. And even though Rhea recognized that her son was experiencing peer rejection and obvious emotional trouble, she waited until he was fourteen before she took action to help him.

Bruce's father, Butch, had long suspected that his son was gay. Butch grew up in a small rural town in Indiana and was not raised in a religious environment. But his father was "a real bigot." As soon as he left home and joined the U.S. Army to serve in Vietnam, Butch made a conscious effort to be openminded and unprejudiced. Butch had always noticed things about Bruce that weren't the same as most little boys. "Bruce liked his trucks and cars, but he also liked to play with dolls. His heroes on TV were always female characters. I thought it was a possibility, and typical of many parents, I also thought he might grow out of it. In my heart I knew it was a very strong possibility that he would turn out to be gay; that was okay. The only thing that bothered me was I knew he'd have a hard time in society, because I know how redneck guys can be; they look down on anyone who is different or feminine. They think everyone should be macho and a jock."

Ignoring the Signs

BETTY AND PAUL (Judy and Dave's parents)

As mentioned earlier, Judy and Dave's parents, Paul and Betty, are both active Methodists, though Paul recently retired as a Methodist pastor. Among the four children, Judy and her younger brother Dave are gay. As pastor of several large congregations throughout his career, Paul was very familiar with gay people. But neither Betty nor Paul had any idea that Judy was gay, and neither attributed her "restlessness" and poor grades to anything out of the ordinary. Her father describes her as "very pretty, tall, and slender — striking. She was a tomboy, but there wasn't anything masculine about her." Was this a subtle form of denial? Were Betty and Paul perhaps reluctant to investigate Judy's emotional distress during high school for fear of what they might discover?

When it came to Dave, their suspicions were harder to ignore. Betty remembers that from the time Dave was small, he "was different from other boys I knew. He was interested in drama, music, and reading. The other boys in the neighborhood wanted to roughhouse, and Dave didn't want any part of it. He'd rather pursue quieter activities. I remember at four the neighbor kid would come over, and Dave would say, 'Let's play pretend.' But we didn't think anything was wrong; we just thought he was different."

There were indications later that something was troubling Dave. He'd always been a strong student, but when he entered high school, his marks began to go down — and then he flunked out of journalism, his favorite class. Betty remembers Dave coming home from school and saying, "I just don't fit in, I just don't fit in." She says regretfully, "I remember saying to him at the time, 'If you just weren't so effeminate, the kids wouldn't tease you.'" Later, when Dave was in college, Betty and Paul recall, "We knew he was struggling heavily with something. He was seeing a counselor and seemed depressed." Again, his parents seemed willing to avoid further inquiries as to what was troubling Dave.

Paul emphasizes, "I had always known gays in my congregation. I had placed gays in positions of leadership, and we treated them as we would any family. I remember a lesbian couple who got inseminated and were expecting a child together. We were totally accepting. The only difference with our kids was that they were our kids." As with my mother and other parents, Betty and Paul seemed to feel comfortable with other people being gay, but less comfortable with their own children.

Denial

Some parents are so frightened of what may lurk behind their suspicions that they deny even the most blatant of hints.

MARGE AND LARRY (Paul and Davis's parents)

For some parents, the idea that their child may be gay can be utterly terrifying because it takes on a moral dimension. Marge says this about Paul, her elder son: "I think deep inside

I felt my son may be gay, but I didn't think I could handle it. I remember thinking, 'If he is, I don't know how to deal with it, so I'm just going to put it out of my mind and just pretend it's not there.'"

As mentioned earlier, both Marge and Larry were Southern Baptists who grew up in a very strict religious environment. They were very active in their church and held positions of leadership. "Of course, we had always been taught that homosexuality was wrong, so that played a big part in the way I felt. I did not want my child to be gay. Basically, we just didn't want to face it."

Both Larry and Marge say that up until the seventh grade, Paul was an excellent student, interested in reading and gardening. "He loved flowers and growing plants." But otherwise he didn't seem that different or effeminate to Marge. In this way, her early sense that he might have been gay sounds like it was a subtle instinct.

Marge dismissed the idea, but Larry definitely suspected Paul might be gay. "Even at an early age, I noticed that Paul didn't have the same interests and play patterns that I had as a young boy. I did not notice it in Davis." As Paul got older, Larry became more concerned. "I would think back to how when I was twelve or thirteen, I had been interested in girls. I didn't see that in him, so that made me feel perhaps he was gay. I did mention it to Marge, and she disagreed with me."

What's interesting is that they knew something was going on with Paul by seventh grade; he'd always been a straight A student, and he'd begun failing classes. "He was being very rebellious in general." But at the time, they didn't question his obvious change in behavior.

Their lives were very much ordered by their religious beliefs, and within their church there was overt homophobia. "I felt that if he was gay, that he was wrong. I didn't know anything about homosexuality; all I knew were the myths and stereotypes I had heard all my life. The few that I knew of in our community were folks out cruising in their cars to pick up people; they were out for a sexual experience." This is a common and widespread stereotype: a definition of homosexuals as solely sexual beings. Again, we see that part of the reason parents fear their child's being gay is a lack of knowledge about the nature of homosexuality. And underneath the lack of awareness still lurk the negative, value-laden associations that historically defined homosexuality in this culture. But as parents get in touch with their love for their child, often the most concrete of false beliefs crumble.

VIVIAN AND HERB* (Sarah's parents)

Some parents, like Sarah's, are confronted with very tangible, self-destructive evidence that their child is in some sort of trouble and still purposefully turn away. Sarah describes her family as a Jewish Brady Bunch. "We were very close, very Long Island Jewish." Vivian is a housewife, and Herb is a businessman. They raised their three daughters in a wealthy, gender-specific manner. Her parents were quite aware that Sarah had gotten involved with drugs. But when her guidance counselor at school informed them that Sarah was cutting classes and hanging out with a crowd known for drug use, Herb and Vivian tried to punish her into submission. They grounded her and took away her car privileges. As her mother recounts, "Sarah just got angrier and more removed from us. We felt like we couldn't reach her, that there was no way of talking to her. Her two older sisters had never gotten into any trouble; we just didn't understand why Sarah was different."

Sarah didn't know how to begin to explain how she felt to her parents. "I definitely escaped into drugs so I wouldn't have to think about myself. My sisters were total squares. I could barely relate to them, and they thought I was from Mars." By this point, communication between Sarah and her parents had completely broken down, so her parents decided that Sarah should see a psychiatrist. Her parents recall that Sarah "went to see the shrink, but she didn't trust him. She didn't trust anyone." It would be years before Vivian and Herb would be able to be more open with Sarah and begin to accept her homosexuality.

Celebrate the Child's Difference

Some parents never suspect that their child might be gay, yet they are not alarmed when they find out. This seems to be more true of parents who have more open expectations of their children. Early on, these parents experience their children as both separate and different from them. When their child shows him- or herself to be different from either parental expectation or accepted gender roles, the parents applaud their child's specialness rather than regret their child's difference.

COLETTE (Nina's mother)

As an African-American woman married to a Caucasian man, Colette was used to conflict and standing out among her peers. Against the wishes of family and friends, Colette and Jim married and had four children in four years; they have now been married almost forty years. When I ask Colette, who has been active in the women's movement since its inception, if she had any inkling that Nina was different from other girls or that she might be gay, Colette says, "I noticed that Nina was always a tomboy, but she had dated guys. A good friend of mine told me that when our kids played together growing up, I once remarked to her that I thought there was something different about Nina, but I couldn't put my finger on it. But in those days, there really was no talk about lesbians and gays."

KARIN (Kari's mother)

Karin, Kari's mother, is a licensed psychologist and family therapist. Despite her professional knowledge and experience dealing with issues of identity and sexual orientation, Karin was not attuned to the idea that her daughter might not be heterosexual. "Both my kids are very unique. I also have a son four years younger than Kari. Both of them were brought up to be their own people. Now in hindsight I could say how did I miss that, she was a little jock from the time she was in elementary school, but so was I. Being a jock didn't mean lesbian. When she was a teenager, I noticed she didn't date, and I was delighted. I felt, 'Oh, good, when she's old enough, or when she's ready, then the more years on her the better.' She had lots and lots of male and female friends; she'd always been really popular." Oddly, at the time Kari was first coming out, Karin was teaching a course called "Alternative Lifestyles."

Colette and Karin, both of whom are open-minded and liberal, may not have paid attention to indications that their daughters were somehow different from other girls or young women because they weren't distressed by these signs.

Whether they suspect, ignore, deny, or simply overlook behaviors or characterstics in their children, most parents do not confront them; Bruce's mother did, but she's an exception. This points to how dangerous it feels for parents to approach their expectations of their children and their fears about them. Perhaps in a more open environment in which homosexuality is talked about and defined, both parents and their children will not be afraid to voice their concerns and will choose to speak directly with one another.

Chapter 10

The First Stage
You Are Still Who You Always Were

"Love is like childhood, caught in trust and fear.
The statues point to omens in the air,
And yet the fountains bubble bright and clear."

ADRIENNE RICH,
from "Lovers Are Like Children"

Taking a Toll

Looking back, my mother admits that her suspicions of my being gay and her inability to deal directly with her feelings about the issue were very wearing on her — and me. She says, "I think it took a toll on both of us. We both wanted to be close, but there was this gigantic obstacle in the way in large parts of our lives. When I suspected something was going on, I would just withdraw and do something with my work, or just not be there. We could talk about all kinds of things, but we couldn't talk about that."

Of course, I would also withdraw. My mother remembers me this way: "There was a huge part of yourself that you were hiding. At that point I was also really angry with you a lot. I would think since you're not being truthful, we can't talk about it, so I wouldn't have to deal with it. Of course, at first I didn't really want to know about it either." My mom rationalized our distance and her not wanting to deal with her suspicions that I was gay by blaming my own avoidance of the subject. As she explains, "A lot of times I just removed myself from different parts of your life and therefore became removed from you as a person."

But eventually my mother was unable to avoid it any longer, when I met Heidi. I was in love and wore it on my sleeve. My mom got up the nerve to call my father, and he confirmed that I was gay — and also said that he'd known for a while. As my mom remembers, "Then I found out that my assistant knew and that my sister knew — everyone knew except me. I went ballistic and began screaming and yelling at everyone around me. I was an insane woman. I couldn't believe it. I was embarrassed that everyone knew it but me, and I was furious that I had to find it out from Sonny. I hated your father at this time. He was a complete and utter asshole. He was so snotty about telling me, and I felt he was full of shit. At least my reaction was honest."

Much of my mother's anger stemmed from her sense of betrayal: I had told everyone but her. But underneath this anger was also tremendous hurt. As she says, "It was also the confirmation of something I had hoped wasn't true for a really long time. It was this awful secret that I had held on to for so many years, and now it was out and everyone had your confidence but me." She felt an enormous sense of rejection by me. When I ask her why, if her suspicions were so strong, she didn't confront me, she explains, "I just didn't want it to be true so bad. I thought if I didn't talk about it, it wouldn't be real. At this time, when you were in high school, I thought you seemed much more one of the girls. I thought maybe it was a phase that you were going through."

With the fact of my homosexuality confirmed, my mother's homophobia surfaced. She was afraid, convinced as she still was that being gay meant being unhappy. Before this time, she only had to deal with her outward acceptance of homosexuality in her friends and colleagues. Now she had to directly confront why she'd always been so afraid that I was gay.

In the two or three days after my mother found out, when she was steeped in intense painful, angry feelings, she was unable to really think about me. She says now: "I couldn't think of you being in pain at that time. I thought you were fine. I realized later, of course, that you weren't, but I wasn't thinking rationally at all. I'm not a screamer, but I'd become this banshee. My emotions were running wild. I was totally flipped out and upset and angry that you didn't tell me, angry that you would tell your father and not tell me. I was also angry that your father told me in a real snotty way."

Again, behind the anger was pain. "I felt helpless because I knew there was nothing I could do about it. Those aren't very good ingredients for anything but just hysteria."

Now that my mother could no longer ignore or avoid her fears and had to face the issue head-on, she summoned the strength she has always possessed in a crisis. "After I cried myself into a stupor for twenty-four hours, the reality was I had to figure out what I was going to do about it. Since you were my child and I loved you, I had to figure out a way to take what this was and turn it into something different."

Her shock and anger began to subside, and my mother recovered fairly quickly. "It was a big, big anger; everything was big and dramatic. But after a day or so, I wore myself out and then started to separate all the things that didn't have to do with the information that you were gay. That was the first and hardest part. I had to learn, very quickly, to take myself out of the equation, take everything out of the equation except just the idea that you were having sex with another girl and what that meant in society. At some level I knew that if I just narrowed the situation down to that equation, I would not feel so overwhelmed. Perhaps if I were religious in a Judeo-Christian way, I would have to consider the moral implications. But that wasn't the case. I tried to eliminate things that were bothering me, trying to figure out what was making me so upset. One of the first things I had to subtract was how you being gay reflected on who I was — who I was as a mother, as an entertainer, as someone in the spotlight. Of those, the biggest one to subtract was as a mother. I felt so responsible. I think that's what every parent thinks in the beginning: 'It's something I did.'"

My mother is right: many parents do immediately feel a sense of responsibility, which is soon followed by guilt. Since they see homosexuality as a negative, their sense of responsibility carries a negative connotation too: as if they have done something wrong to "make" their child gay.

But my mom couldn't let go of the complex range of her feelings right away. As she explains, "I didn't really let go of any of it; I just set it aside. You can't let go of it in that quick of a time period. I wanted to get to the part of what was the big deal for me, and mostly what I got to was that it reflected back on me in some kind of way; on my parenting skills, on who I was in the community, on who you were in the community. It was all pretty much an extension of me in some sort of way."

It took my mother only two days to gain a bit of distance and control. Then she asked me to come out to Los Angeles and talk to her. "If I had waited until I really let it go, it would have taken way too long; it was better to have you and Heidi come out so we could all talk about it. The thing that I really hung on to, that made it all fall into place, was that you were just you; you were still who you always were to me."

This is a significant recognition for parents: understanding that this new information about their child does not obliterate all the other ways they know and love that child. My mother's ability to separate her feelings from the fact of my being gay itself was an immense step toward not only healing her anger and hurt but also toward repairing our relationship and closing the emotional distance that had grown between us.

Many parents confront a similar choice in which they are almost forced to get in touch with their love for their child. My mother remembers: "I had to decide what to do with the information — do I turn my back or go, 'Fine, I have to understand this. This is a part of who she is and she's my child and I don't want to give up my relationship with her, and so I have to do this.' There had been this barrier between us for such a long time, for years and years and years, part of me wanted, needed for it to disappear."

As for me, I tried to explain and apologize for not having told her myself. Although she didn't let me off the hook at the time, she has since said to me, "I don't really blame you." She understands that my fear of her was in part warranted, given our rocky relationship.

She put aside her own feelings in order to deal with me and my feelings. After all, I was her daughter, and it was her love of and commitment to me that ultimately pushed her toward acceptance. But as my mother admits, this took enormous strength and determination. "I think my sister talked to me about it, and she said my reaction wasn't really like me. She thought I was being really closed minded. That's when I made a conscious decision to figure out a way to accept this."

I spoke to my aunt about what had happened from her point of view. Georgeann says, "Cher called me in the beginning and asked me whether I knew you were gay. And I said, 'Yes, I do.' And she said, 'Does everybody know but me?' and I said, 'Well, yeah, basically.' Cher was really upset."

Georgeann reminds me, "I didn't want to go to Cher to tell her; I didn't think it was my place. But I said to you, 'You're telling everybody in the family — you're confiding in Grandma.' You were too frightened, but I was worried about my sister. I felt it was between you and your mom — a mother-daughter thing. But I remember saying to you, 'Chas, please, tell her.' I really felt an obligation. It was a known thing, and yet Cher didn't know, so it was uncomfortable for me."

When my mom did find out, Georgeann was as surprised by her reaction as my mom was herself. "I think we were both surprised by Cher's reaction. There had been gay people around us our entire life. They were your mom's good friends. It was no big deal, so I don't think your mom expected to be that upset, and I certainly didn't expect her to be. Though I did know Cher would be upset about not having known and everyone else knowing. There was a lot of embarrassment, and that added to the negative reaction. My sister was hurt by that and rightly so; I understand your side of it and why you were so afraid to tell her, but I also understand my sister's side of it. If you were my daughter and everyone else knew, I'd be embarrassed and hurt. I'd wondered if I had failed in some way."

About the troubling period immediately following my mother's discovery that I was definitely gay, Georgeann says: "Your mom and I didn't have any big discussions at that point about being gay — was it a good or bad thing. It had never been a bad thing in our family, so it wasn't a topic of discussion in that sense. But I do remember in conversation where she was upset about it, and I always reiterated what a wonderful human being you were, what a great kid she has in you. And Cher would say, 'Yeah, I know.' When you're not the mom, it's easier to be in that situation, easier to be the aunt."

Although my mother's initial reaction to finding out I was a lesbian was hurtful, I was grateful for her quick turnaround. Some parents are more formidable.

Can You Change?

MARGE AND LARRY

It was Marge who found one of the notes that Paul had written when he was eleven and hidden around the house. "I found the note when he was fifteen. I was devastated. I didn't even want to share it with Larry. I thought Larry was going to have a very negative reaction, and I think I was trying to be protective of Paul. But I also didn't want Larry to be hurt. I knew that Larry would blame himself. I was already saying to myself that it was something we must have done wrong."

Marge assumed her parenting skills were to blame. Also similar to my mother, she admits, "My first thoughts were basically of myself, not yet of Paul. I was thinking about what are the people at the church going to say, are they going to ask us to leave the church? I immediately felt we had to keep it a secret, and it did stay a deep, dark secret for twelve years. We did not tell our parents or friends or anyone."

As Paul described, when his parents found his note, they took him out of school to confront him. When they found out he was gay, Marge says, "Our immediate reaction was to take him to a psychiatrist. We thought we could get him straightened out. We took him to several different doctors, and they all basically told us this is just the way he is and you and your husband are going to need to change."

That kind of response, however, did not help Marge and Larry deal with their own feelings, which were extremely intense and unmanageable. "We still thought he could be changed. I kept thinking, 'We're getting bad information. We just haven't found the right person yet.' We put so much pressure on him that he ran away."

Marge and Larry were beside themselves with worry, but they were still angry. They were concerned for Paul's welfare, but they hadn't really moved an inch toward changing their perspective on dealing with the issue. "We missed him an awful lot. We loved Paul very much, and we regretted that this had happened. We knew we had to do something toward coming to an understanding of homosexuality."

When Paul later ran away to Portland, his father went after him. "I contacted the police in Portland; the first woman I contacted told me that homosexuality was wrong. Well, I looked at her and I said, 'I don't give a damn how you feel about it. This is my son and I need to find him; he's fifteen years old.' I was very angry that she reacted this way when I came seeking help. She finally put me in touch with a police officer who took me around to all the gay hangouts, but we were not able to locate Paul. We found out later that he and a friend took a bus to New York City."

The lack of support and their general ignorance of how to deal with the situation exacerbated their fear, shame, and guilt. But in Larry's anger at the police officer, he was beginning to get in touch with his love and protective feelings for his son.

The Stats

Marge and Larry represent an extreme in the way parents can react to children, but there are still worse stories of parents disowning their children, kicking them out of the house knowing they have nowhere to go. This kind of treatment is reflected in January 1989 statistics put out by the U.S. Department of Health and Human Services Secretary's Task Force on Youth Suicide, which have been found to be still accurate in recent local studies across the country:

- One in ten youths are gay
- 500,000 young people attempt suicide annually
- Gay youth are two to three times more likely to attempt suicide than their heterosexual peers
- Suicide is the leading cause of death among gay and lesbian youth
- 30 percent of completed youth suicides are by gay youth

- The majority of suicide attempts by homosexuals take place at age twenty or younger, with nearly one-third occurring before age seventeen
- 28 percent of gay youth are high school dropouts
- 26 percent of young gays and lesbians are forced to leave home because of conflicts over their sexual identity
- Approximately 30 percent of gay youth have alcohol and drug problems
- 30 percent of all youth living on the streets in this country are homosexual, bisexual, or transsexual

Even the most brutal treatment by parents can be overcome. Indeed, some children bear their parents' negative reactions with inspiring strength and dignity.

VIVIAN AND HERB

When Sarah came out to her parents when she was twenty-one, her parents, specifically her mother, disowned her for over a year. Vivian remembers it this way: "Sarah just blurted it out one night. I couldn't take it. She was always a rebellious child. I felt like she was doing this to hurt her father and me.

"We went into the den, and I kept clutching my pocketbook and saying, 'What are you doing?' I'd had enough. Then I said, 'I thought you were going to tell me you were a heroin addict, and I wish you were, because that I could fix. I can't fix this, and I wish you were dead.'"

Although both Vivian and Herb now speak of their remorse and regret at how they handled Sarah's homosexuality, they explain that their expectations of all of their daughters, including Sarah, were so specific that they were overwhelmed with fear and grief.

Sarah was forced to leave home. She moved to New York City and became financially independent. "That was a good thing," Sarah admits. "I was forced to grow up and take responsibility for myself."

For many parents, learning of their child's homosexuality is a test of their trust and love of their child. And hearing the news and learning to accept their child can force parents to grow.

A Spiritual Awakening

RHEA AND BUTCH

Even the most inflexible religious beliefs can be overcome in response to a parent's love for his or her child. Rhea is a good example of a parent who struggled deeply with accepting her son's homosexuality. Rhea's entire world was organized around her church. After she noticed that Bruce was being ostracized and realized he was falling into "a deep, dark depression," Rhea thought it was time to do something. So she gave Bruce the article about the youth group for gay teens. "But the next day, when he went to school, I cried all day long. I was ripped in two — my mind said I was doing the right thing, but my gut was in a knot. I was hysterical. I would cry when Bruce was at school and scream into my pillow at night. This went on for quite a while. Sometimes I'd wash my face in cold water so he couldn't tell that I was suffering, because I could tell he was watching me. Finally, because I know I wasn't that good an actress, I looked at him and said, 'Son, I know that you are aware of the fact that I am struggling, but I want you to know that I'm responsible for my feelings. Have a little faith in me. I'll get through this.'" That was the beginning of Rhea's healing process, as well as her first steps toward fully accepting Bruce's homosexuality. Like my mother, Rhea needed to be able to separate her feelings from the issue itself. Once she was able to do that, she could begin to heal herself.

"I felt grief, fear, and guilt. I wondered if I had failed him in some way. I think the overriding feeling was fear, because we are never allowed to entertain the idea that we may have a gay child. We can entertain the idea that a child may be physically impaired, but not gay. So when you find out you have a gay child, you have no frame of reference. You have to process this in a total vacuum. There is no manual suggesting ways to parent a gay child."

Her guilt was exacerbated by her thoughts about how Bruce had always been ostracized at school and harassed by other kids. "I then thought of him having a whole lifetime like that — it was almost more than I could bear. I had no exposure to gays, so I couldn't envision a good life for my son."

As with any other crisis in her life, Rhea reached out to her faith in God. "I went to church, to an empty sanctuary, and begged and pleaded with God to change this, that it was more than I could deal with. Then I had a moment which to me was a spiritual awakening. It was in my bathroom, of all places. I was so upset with God because I had been a Sunday school teacher, a deacon, I had devoted much of my life to God. And I kept getting this crushing silence from him. Finally he/she decided to speak to me. I realized the reason I was hurting so much was because of the negative images of gays. God said to me, 'You know what a gay person is like; you lived with one for fourteen years.' From that moment on, I never shed another tear that my son was gay. I may have shed a lot of tears for how he was treated, but not because he was gay."

In order to let go of the powerful negative moral associations she had of homosexuality, Rhea had to examine her own conscience and talk to God directly. That moment of insight, as Rhea refers to it, was the catalyst for a review of her entire belief system.

Her husband, Butch, who had grown up without any religious training, "wasn't that surprised at all. I just thought,

'He's a nice boy, and I love him.'" The simple fact of his love for his son enabled Butch to discard any residual prejudice against homosexuals.

For most parents, the leap from shock to the first step toward acceptance occurs when they get in touch with their love for their child. As Rhea points out, she'd known and loved someone who was gay for fourteen years.

Turning on the Lights

GLENDA AND JIM (Ben's parents)

After many years of suspecting that Ben was gay, Glenda finally confronted her fears. But indirectly. "My daughter came to my house to tell me that she was going to get a divorce. She lived only two hours away, and I had always thought she had a very happy marriage, so I was surprised when she popped in the door and told me her plans. I got onto the subject of Ben, and I asked her if she had ever wondered if Ben were gay. Apparently Dana and Ben had already discussed the possibility of me asking her before [I asked] Ben himself. They agreed that if I asked Dana, she would say yes, he's gay. We waited for my husband, Jim, to come home, and then we talked everything through. I was hit by two shocks — first of all, my daughter's life had fallen apart, and the second was that my son is gay. Then Dana told us that Ben was in the neighborhood and he was going to drive by the house. We live in a big two-story white house with black shutters and white columns. Dana had promised to give Ben a signal of how we took the news: if we had taken the news really badly, she was to get the hell out of Dodge, and he'd see that her car was out of the driveway, but if we received the news fairly well, she was supposed to put a light on in his bedroom window. Kind of like tie a yellow ribbon.

"When I found that out, I just screamed. I couldn't stand the thought of Ben thinking that we wouldn't accept him. I said, 'Quick, help me,' and we turned on every light in the house — even those in the closets. When Ben drove up, even the lights in the back workshop were on."

The first thing Glenda asked Ben was if he was healthy. "This was in August 1991, and we were very much aware of the growing AIDS crisis. My second thought was why he would ever believe that we would reject him. But he told me that he had taken signals from me that made him think I didn't want to know, which of course I see now was true in part." Both Glenda and Jim express regret at the idea that their child would ever imagine them rejecting him.

Like gays and lesbians, parents too come out, and it's also a journey of self-discovery and self-acceptance. And like most personal journeys, this one is without end. As Glenda says, at that moment, she and her husband "started our journey."

CAROLYN AND BILL (William's parents)

Bill and Carolyn had been married for over twenty years and were living in a small town in Arkansas when their son, William, came out to them. Throughout their lives, they had known a number of gays, lesbians, and even a transgender person who was a babysitter for their two children, Holly and William. Both Carolyn and Bill had worked hard for many years, Carolyn as a registered nurse and Bill primarily as a technician. They had always thought of themselves as open-minded and liberal. Carolyn remembers first suspecting that William was gay when he was thirteen. "I was driving a bunch of William's friends home from school in our station wagon. And one of the kids had a magazine with Cindy Crawford on the cover in a bathing suit. I remember William's friends going on and on about how gorgeous she was, and I remember thinking I had never heard William say anything about girls. But having studied human growth and development, I just thought he might be slower than other boys to get interested in the opposite sex."

But like a lot of the other parents I spoke with, Carolyn and Bill overlooked other problems William was having that were strong indications that he was struggling with something. William tried to commit suicide at fourteen because of a severe clinical depression. And though his parents were very concerned about his mental and emotional health, their ignorance about homosexuality prevented them from helping William get to the root of his depression.

When he had been in a psychiatric hospital for three months after his suicide attempt, William informed his parents that he had something to tell them. "We both thought he was going to tell us he had some terrible drug problem; we were scared to death. When he told us he was gay, we said, 'Are you sure,' and he said yes."

Carolyn and Bill each took the news differently. Carolyn says she was "hit by a ton of bricks. I was saddened, real sad, because I feared for him. I began to imagine what his life was going to be like. As a parent you have this image of what you want your child's life to be like — it's a kind of fantasy. Then I began to see the dangers ahead for him, all the hurt feelings, the misunderstandings. My husband wanted to talk immediately about safe sex — I couldn't believe it. All I could think about was losing that image of a daughter-in-law, a beautiful wedding, bridesmaids, and grandchildren. The one thing I looked forward to was spoiling my grandchildren rotten."

Carolyn describes this time as similar to a period of grieving, and like so many parents, she questioned her parenting skills. "I had to find out if I had done something wrong. My husband and I had worked real hard to have a fifty-fifty relationship, so working the way we did, different hours, I suddenly wondered if that was what made William gay. This is when I became desperate for information. I had this intense craving for information; I couldn't get my hands on enough books, pamphlets, or videos."

Unbeknownst to Carolyn, Bill's identical twin brother had recently come out to him, so Bill had already started to become educated. By the time William announced his news, Bill was already fairly certain that his son was gay too — hence his safe sex concerns. Bill had already moved from his personal reaction to focusing more on his son and his state of mind. "I told him that I didn't care. I just want you to be safe. Then I told him that my brother, his uncle, was gay. Soon after that my brother came and visited with William. Having an adult gay person to talk to made a big difference for William. He began feeling much better, and soon he was released from the hospital."

Carolyn and Bill, however, decided that they "couldn't live where [they] were living" and moved to Fayetteville, a much larger town. Although they integrated the fact of their son's homosexuality into their lives, their lack of knowledge about their community and its prejudice against gays and lesbians would soon shock them.

There's Nothing You Can Do or Say

COLETTE

Nina came out to her mother and father while she was in college. Colette remembers it this way: "We were driving Nina to the airport at the end of Christmas vacation. We were living in Houston at the time, and she was returning to the East Coast. She had told me that she had to get back for New Year's Eve; she was going to a certain bar. Well, I knew about the bar from my lesbian friends; I knew it was a lesbian bar. I had been suspecting this for a number of years, but I was waiting for Nina to come out to us. I had assumed that because we were so-called liberal, she would feel comfortable telling us. But she really wasn't. At the airport I said to her as she was getting on the plane, I said, 'You know what, we know,' and she burst into tears.

"When I asked her later why she hadn't told us before, she said she had friends who thought that their parents would be accepting and weren't. She was just plain-out scared. She was trying to understand it herself and know who she was."

Colette had a positive reaction. "I was fine with it. I had met enough women that I really adored who were lesbians. It wasn't a problem for my husband either; he just wanted Nina to be happy. I don't know if it was because we had other kids who were straight. I don't think we'd have a problem with it even if she were our only child."

Colette attributes her lack of judgmental attitude to the fact that she had already encountered outside criticism for marrying outside her race. "All my kids know that there are going to be people who challenge you, question you, not like you. But that's okay, because there will be other people who do like you. I think we worked very hard on raising our kids. I told them they were going to have a tough time; they knew that from the time they were little. We were also a very communicative family."

But like all people, Colette did make some mistakes. "After I confronted her in the airport, I proceeded to go home and call my parents, my cousins, my aunts, and various other relatives. And tell them, 'Oh, guess what, well, we finally have a name for Nina: she's a lesbian.' Most of the family was fine, but others, like my mother, said, 'Oh, it's a phase.' Her sisters and brothers said they'd suspected, which I thought was interesting.

"But what I hadn't expected was that Nina was absolutely furious when she found out that I had told the entire family. I didn't realize that it wasn't my place. Nina didn't talk to me for a while; she felt betrayed. She still wasn't comfortable herself; she didn't even say the word *lesbian* for a long time. She felt very hurt that I had gone ahead and spouted her personal business. And again, because we are a family that communicates and I don't give up on my kids, I insisted that we sit down and talk about this. I apologized to her and told her I had no idea. I told everyone because I felt so good about her and I wanted them to accept every part of her. But she didn't see it that way. I eventually stood up in a Unitarian church service and publicly apologized to her."

Each family has its own distinct process. The fact that Nina felt more uncomfortable than her parents is not quite so typical, but it certainly is understandable given her mother's fierce openness and challenging personality.

KARIN

Karin's response to learning that her daughter Kari was a lesbian was equally as supportive. However, Karin still worried about her daughter, who had left her a letter and then gone away for the weekend. "I wanted her to know that even though I was naive and not tuned in to what she was going through, there was nothing she could do or be that would cause me to love her any less. I may get frustrated with things she does or doesn't do, but there's just no way my love for her would change."

Karin's concern extended beyond her own child. "What bothered me the most was that Kari was afraid to tell me. I thought, 'My God, if this kid was afraid to come out to me as a mom, what must it be like for other kids who aren't growing up in a supportive, nonjudgmental environment?' For me, parental love should override everything. But I was discovering that wasn't the case."

Karin points to the concern we should all have for gays and

lesbians, especially those who come out as children. Everyone needs to know that there is a loving community of homosexual sisters and brothers, as well as a supportive network of straight parents, across the country, so that we can all do our part in preventing gay teenagers from running away and hitting the streets. The more we educate ourselves and our parents, the more society will realize that a gay child is neither more special nor less special than any other child.

Chapter 11

Learning to Accept
Weeding the Garden

"All this was to the good. But no abundance of sensation or fineness of perception would avail unless she could build up out of the fleeting and the personal the lasting edifice which remains unthrown. I had said that I would wait until she faced herself with a 'situation.' And I meant by that until she proved by summoning, beckoning, and getting together that she was not a skimmer of surfaces merely, but had looked beneath into the depths."

VIRGINIA WOOLF,
from *A Room of One's Own*

Put One Foot in Front of the Other

Meeting with my mother and her therapist was a good step in the direction of healing our relationship and helping her to accept my homosexuality. I was quite nervous flying out to L.A. I still felt rattled from my mom's asking me to leave our New York apartment. I was also feeling guilty. I felt I was the one who was wrong, that I was the only one who had a "problem."

By the time I arrived in L.A., my mother had calmed

down a lot. This time, the therapy session was not about 'Are you gay?' but about helping us both deal with the reality and what it meant for us.

For the first time, I felt hopeful. I could tell that my mother was there because she cared about me, and that she was trying to work on the issues surrounding my homosexuality as a family. That's not to say she was totally comfortable with my being gay.

When my mom first met Heidi, she was very suspicious and looked Heidi up and down. At that time, Heidi was kind of militant, and I think that made it harder on my mom. But I began to feel more at ease with her anyway. After so many years of tension between us, when I could barely sit in a room with my mom without feeling as if I were going to jump out of my skin, I was beginning to relax a bit. This was a huge improvement.

But there were still some hurdles to jump. Things between my mother and me were getting better, but I knew she was still leery of letting other people know about me. She wasn't open and honest with other people. Her needing to censor the fact that I was gay from other people points to her struggle to fully accept my homosexuality. She was still questioning her skills as a parent. She says now that she thought that "part of it was that I failed as a parent, that happy, healthy people don't grow up to be homosexuals. I guess I thought that if you were gay, then I must be a failure. I felt like I must have done something." Since many parents of gay people have internalized the negative stereotypes associated with gays — specifically that gay people are unstable and promiscuous — they imagine that there is something wrong with their child and that the "wrongness" is a reflection of not being raised correctly, or properly.

Like many parents, my mother was searching for an explanation, and the first place she looked was herself. "I think when something happens to your kids you always take on the responsibility, because no one brings up their children perfectly. There are a lot of things in childhood, and a parent automatically thinks, 'Oh, it must be that thing that I didn't do, or I wasn't there enough, or I could have taken care of this if I had only done this differently, if I'd only made this decision another way.' "

But one of the first lessons parents need to learn is that being gay isn't a problem. And that's what learning to accept means: throwing away the stereotypical associations that define homosexuality and replacing their negative view of their child's sexual orientation with the positive qualities in their child that they are proud of. This isn't easy.

My mother's exposure to gays didn't seem to help her with her discomfort when she first suspected I was gay. This is a clear testament to the power of stereotypes. When I ask my mom directly how she reconciled having such negative feelings about my being gay and having so many positive relationships with gay people, she says, "Well, they were not my children. It's a different thing that happens with your child — it's not the same. None of those people had successful home lives or successful relationships. I saw John go from this one to that one and not have a real decent life. That was part of my fear and worry for you."

I counter her stereotypes by pointing out that I can't think of anyone growing up, gay or straight, who had a stable relationship. I want her to acknowledge that she seems to be associating unstable relationships with gay people. She still insists on her knowledge of gay people: "Most of the people I knew, even though I loved them dearly, were way fucked up — especially the gay men. Their lifestyle just seemed so much more promiscuous, and as for lesbians, it's only been lately that the stereotype of lesbians seems to be changing. You don't have to be either a butch or a femme. Lesbians can look like any other woman, and I think that's really important. I don't really care whether it's right or wrong: people have an idea of who you are and what you are from what you look like. When you had your hair really short, didn't wear any makeup, and wore really masculine-style clothes, I just didn't think it was a good way to be a messenger of the church. I think it keeps people from accepting you."

Like my mother, most parents are afraid that their child might be rejected. These sorts of fears can often lead parents to censor themselves about their child's being gay. Of course, at the time my mother is referring to, I didn't dress all that differently from the other kids my age who were straight. We were all kind of slobs — it was during the punk era. At the time, I felt my mother just didn't get the current style.

But as she continued to struggle with her feelings, my mother did not want me to tell certain people. At one point, when I was about nineteen, I had to be treated for dysplasia and needed laser surgery. I was still living in New York, and my mother wanted me to use her doctor in L.A. I had told her that I had come out to my doctor in New York, and she made it very clear that I wasn't to tell her doctor that I was gay. She said, "Tell him whatever, just don't tell him that." This kind of bothered me, and I tried to push her to deal with it. I was also going through a phase during which everything I wore had a pink triangle on it. She said to me once, "Why do you have to wear that shit? Why does it have to have a triangle on it?"

When I ask her today why she felt so much internal pressure to censor herself about me, she said, "I just really didn't talk about your being gay. It was still a secret, so it was still a negative thing. I wasn't comfortable, and what I did was choose to ignore, and no one chose to confront me with it. When anyone would ask me about you, I would try to walk around the subject and give other descriptions or statistics about you, staying away from that one specific point, and hopefully people wouldn't talk about it."

Of course, once I was outed in the tabloids, she was no longer able to pretend that I wasn't gay: the secret was out, despite my going back into the closet. My mom was nervous when I began to record, because she didn't think I was "tough enough." As she says, "You need to be tough in this business, and you had gotten in bed with a bunch of snakes." The tabloid debacle just exacerbated her worries about me. "I was also really proud of you, and proud of your music, but I didn't want you to get hurt by the slimy press coverage. At the time, I thought it might be better if you just came out. I knew that you weren't going to be able to escape it, because I was always too much in the limelight in that particular readership. You were Chastity Bono, after all, and there would be a lot of mileage in that. But I felt bad for you because there is nothing those people won't do or say."

Having been in the public eye for over twenty years by that point, my mother understood how nasty, vindictive, and malicious the press could be — especially the tabloids. She thought my career would be ruined before it even started. She was also concerned about the effect of my being outed on her own career. She knew she was going to be asked a lot about me, and she had always made it a policy never to lie to the press. But suddenly, faced with my record deal being canceled, I wanted her to lie. This put her in an awkward position.

Slowly but surely, my mother moved toward full acceptance. But like anyone going through a process, she had to do everything in her own time. She explains her process in this way: "At first I thought I was a failure as a parent; then I felt that you were going to be the failure, and that you wouldn't be able to succeed and have a normal life." My relationship with Heidi, during and after the tabloid debacle, was becoming unhealthy and a bit destructive, and my mother was worried about me. She took the status of my relationship as a sign that being gay wasn't good: if my relationship wasn't working, then I wasn't okay, and that meant being gay wasn't okay. My mother's criticism of my relationship with Heidi (and the others that followed) demonstrates her discomfort with my homosexuality and the power of the negative stereotypes of homosexuality in general.

She says, "At the beginning I liked Heidi; I thought she was great and really smart, which made me feel better about your being gay. But then I started to really dislike her. You didn't seem happy in the relationship, so it was harder for me to feel okay about the gay issue. I thought I was doing pretty well at accepting it, and then all of a sudden I wasn't doing well with it at all. It seemed to me that it was really unhealthy, and I blamed it on what your relationship was. I love Heidi now, but at the time I thought not only is my daughter gay, but she's made this horrible choice of a lover and now she's in this sick relationship. I didn't go beyond, it could be either sick homo or hetero — I was still blaming it on the homo."

At the time, my mother was fighting against her sense of loss and disappointment. She needed to blame my being gay on someone, something. This period, when parents are struggling with many complex feelings — anger, hurt, disappointment, loss — is very disconcerting, and often parents feel overwhelmed. As my mom has said to me about that time in our relationship, "I went ahead three steps and went back four."

But often the turning point for parents, what really allows them to separate their experience of their child from negative images of homosexuality, is when they see their child happy, healthy, and strong. As I began to feel better about myself after I came out of the closet and emerged with a stronger sense of myself, my mom responded and became much more accepting of my being gay. As she admits, "It made me feel better about you as a person, and so therefore anything you got involved in, you would be choosing that thing from a position of strength and not weakness, not neediness. From that place, you wouldn't make the wrong decision."

She began to let go of the negative stereotypes. As she explains, "The stereotypes are not there by accident; they are there because they happen a lot. And sometimes I still worry about you getting into relationships or situations that seem to be not so good for you, but now we can talk about it, and I can say to you, 'Don't go there, don't fall into the things that are stereotypical or cliché; be the person you are and keep going and discovering who you are; it's not enough to say "I'm gay" and stop there.' "

This kind of dialogue not only breaks down the stereotypes, it has brought my mother and me closer.

My mother continued to process my homosexuality for a number of years. "It was part of my therapy, for sure; I was already in it anyway, and it certainly did present a nice new wrinkle, and that's okay, because that's what therapy is supposed to fix is wrinkles." She pauses and adds with irony, "The other night was one of the most hysterical nights. Elijah was going out, and he wanted me to put makeup on him, and I kept thinking, 'What is wrong with this picture?' But we just have to accept our children as individuals, and we have to accept what their wishes are and who they are in their journey."

As for many parents, arriving at this place was not easy for my mother, but its difficulty didn't stop her from continuing to examine her feelings and learn how to grow. "It surprised me a little bit that I was as concerned as I was about what people would think of me, because I think people always think parents who are in show business are bad parents. The truth is, we do leave a lot to be desired, but you could be a homemaker and still leave a lot to be desired. But because I am so preoccupied with my career, and was so preoccupied the whole time you and Elijah were growing up, a lot of times I felt really guilty. Since then, I've also talked to other working mothers, and they have the same guilt."

The key that ultimately allowed my mother to accept me was first seeing and then accepting me as separate and different from herself. "A lot of it [her initial lack of acceptance] had to do with the fact that I saw you as such an extension of me, and I couldn't really separate the two of us and just go, 'Okay, this is your choice and it has nothing to do with me.'"

Again, we see the need for parents to look at their children as separate individuals; in this way, parents' expectations of their children can be realistic, not tied to what they want or lack in their own lives.

My mother also sees how the censoring was a by-product of her lack of acceptance. The shame she felt made her feel bad about herself. "There are certain things that are ridiculous, guilt-ridden things, because in our society some people still haven't accepted it and are still coming to terms with it; when you're in that place it's very difficult to be proud of it. If the majority of people in society didn't consider homosexuality a negative, I don't think anyone would care. Everyone would come out to their parents and life would go on."

And life did. As my mother came to terms with me, we became closer than we ever had been before. That's not to say she, like any parent, doesn't still worry about me. "I think I've let go to a great extent. When you see your child being happy in the thing they're doing and having a good relationship with somebody, and you're around them and they're very positive, you can kind of exhale a little bit. You can kind of relax. But mothers still worry about stuff."

My aunt acknowledges that my mom's willingness to confront the issues happened quickly. As Georgeann says, "I have to give her credit; my sister is a very introspective, intelligent person."

Many parents I spoke with talked about their sense of disappointment. This is linked not only to images parents may have grown used to of how their child's life would be in the future, but also to the negative images embedded in the stereotypes of gays and lesbians. Even the most open-minded parents, like my mother, still respond to the idea that gay people cannot be successful or happy.

When Kids Come Out, Parents Go in the Closet

RHEA AND BUTCH

As Rhea says philosophically, "When kids come out, parents go in the closet." After Rhea began to heal herself, with the utmost support of her husband, Butch, they still had to face the criticism and judgment of their community, in this case their church. It's often the case that parents retreat into the closet when they first encounter negative feedback from others, so it's important to feel grounded with your immediate family before telling others. Given her long relationship with her church, it was perfectly natural for Rhea and her family to turn to the congregation in their time of need. However, "love thy neighbor" didn't seem to apply to a family with a gay child.

"Our minister speculated that Bruce was gay and said something to other people in our congregation. We came under a lot of attack, and since it's a small community, this wreaked havoc in our lives. Bruce started getting death threats at school, and he was even harassed by teachers. We confronted our minister, and he admitted that he was afraid that no church would welcome us. I told him that after all these years of service, we were deeply hurt that now they could only fear us when they used to love us. I also told him how disappointed I was in the church: instead of being overwhelmed by love, we were overwhelmed by judgment. The congregation responded with verbal violence, and we left the church."

This was a tremendous personal loss for Rhea and her family. For the next few years, as they searched for a church that would welcome them, Rhea took her children to a wildlife refuge to pray. A year or so later, they joined an Episcopal church in town that was very embracing. Rhea says of that period in her life, "I call it free falling through the dark night of my soul; I didn't know what I believed anymore. When you have to rethink an issue or belief, it tends to have a domino effect." But the urgent optimism in her voice is a testament not only to her struggle but her victory over this issue that at one time seemed completely overwhelming. "I have a life that is so unreal now. Before I was so one-dimensional, all my friends were from the same small town of Seymour. That's why we had to drive over a thousand miles a month to get support. Once we branched outside of Seymour and got to know gay and lesbian people, that was what healed me. I began to see that gay people have good, productive lives. I was meeting wonderful people. I'll never forget my first P-FLAG meeting: two men got on their knees before me and took my hands and said, 'Thank you for being here.' It was the first time in my life that I ever experienced unconditional love. I think you have to experience unconditional love before you can truly understand it."

It wasn't until Rhea met other gays and lesbians that she believed the world was open to her son, and to her. She recalls another event with equal intensity: "When I took Bruce out of school after it became too dangerous for him, the principal said to me that 'a lot of doors won't be open to your son.' That night I made a promise to myself that planted the seed of an activist in my heart. So when I ventured out to show him a bigger world, I ended up doing it for myself as well. I started going to college. My number one fear had been public speaking, and now I do public speaking engagements all over the country. I had never flown before, and now I fly coast to coast. It's a totally different life."

The gains were not without losses. "It was difficult coming out to a lot of our family, and we lost a lot of our relationships, but whatever we lost, we doubled elsewhere. We call it a weeding of our garden; it only lets the most precious bloom. We have a more magnificent garden now. Some of the family had a hard time dealing with the issue, and even a harder time dealing with me because I'm so vocal. They wish I would just shut up and go away."

Rhea concludes, "The more gay people I had in my life, the more I realized the issue of homophobia was bigger than my family. I saw gays lose their homes, families, their relationships with their churches, lose their jobs; I saw gay teens trying to kill themselves. Now Butch and I deal with this personally in Seymour. I organized a P-FLAG chapter here. I get a lot of phone calls, one recently was from two lesbians who were homeless; they were only fifteen years old, and their parents kicked them out. They were living in a storage shed. I also dealt with a nineteen-year-old boy who tried to kill himself with an X-acto knife, another boy who swallowed drain cleaner. I witnessed these tragic stories, and I became convinced that I had to be a voice. I would plead with God, but sometimes I feel like I'm a lone wolf crying in the wilderness."

GLENDA AND JIM

Glenda and Jim both admit that they also went through "a little grief period." As Glenda explains, "I think most parents have a dream for their children: we envision what's going to happen in the future. I envisioned that Ben would marry and have children, and I would get to know his children. That dream died when we heard that Ben was gay. But I tried really hard not to let him see that I was mourning; I didn't.want him to know. Looking back, I realize I was in a bit of a depression for a while."

That parents grieve is natural; when a parent replaces his or her private expectations of a child with the reality, there is loss involved. But the key at this juncture is to realize that being gay does not preclude happiness or success. Sometimes it takes time for parents to fully understand and embrace this truth. Glenda says that she and Jim thought at first that all of Ben's undergraduate and graduate work at divinity school would "just go down the drain." "We had sent him to college and through Vanderbilt Divinity School, and he was preparing to be an ordained minister. He had told us immediately that he did not plan to stay in the closet. There are two questions the United Methodist Church asks before ordination: the first is 'Have you committed a felony?' and the second is 'Are you gay?'"

Initially for Glenda and Jim, Ben's decision to leave the church was upsetting. "The bishop of the Methodist Church had named Ben or had referred to Ben as the rising star in the Methodist Church, so he would have just climbed the ladder, so to speak, in no time. By coming out, he was giving up a very promising profession."

But then Glenda says proudly, "I remember him saying, 'How can I lie and be a minister?' He had already worked it out and taken the polity course for the United Church of Christ. He knew that's the only denomination that would ordain him."

After Glenda and Jim took in the information, they realized they needed to share the news about Ben with their community, especially their church, as it had supported Ben financially while he was at divinity school. "I made a list of forty people who I thought were really important to me and Ben. I knew that the leaders at our church would hear that Ben was leaving in a month. Many of the people were friends and family, and I called each one of them. This took lots of energy. I said, 'I have something I want to talk to you about, could I meet you for lunch or could I come to see you,' and they would say yes. I'd say, 'You are going to hear this; I want you to hear it from me, and I don't want you to think of Ben doing something behind our back and that we are not supportive. I want you to know that we are with him a hundred percent, and we are proud of him.' "

Although she was nervous making the calls, the more she did it the more comfortable she became. "I would say maybe seven or eight of those forty people I haven't had another conversation with; they just don't want to talk about it anymore. No one was rude to me, but some of them responded with 'Oh, you poor thing, I just can't imagine anything worse.' I wanted them to know that yes, there is some pain in there because Ben's going to have a hard life, but there is some joy in knowing that my child has that much integrity."

Glenda and Jim found that almost everybody they shared their story with would tell them about a sister's gay son or a lesbian aunt. Glenda recalls a recent story: "I sat down with a man on an airplane just last month, and he was telling me about his family. I told him I have a gay son, and he said, 'You know, I never told anybody, but my son is gay too.' He wanted me to send him some literature. He said that he and his wife had known for twelve years, but they just never talked about it and had never read anything. Then he said, 'I think it's about time we enlightened ourselves.' "

Glenda underscores the importance of celebrating, not hiding, the fact of a child's homosexuality. "If parents hide this, then they can't share the lives of their children with their friends, and we all love to talk about our children. I always try to tell parents that their hiding will make them as miserable as the gay person being in the closet."

Resistance

Some parents, like Larry and Marge, take much longer to reconcile their learned prejudices against homosexuality and their love for their children.

MARGE AND LARRY

Larry and Marge were terribly concerned when Paul ran away to New York. "The first thing we wanted to do was to get Paul home and get him back in school, because he needed an education. He was only fifteen. So after about six or seven weeks, through the efforts of a man who worked with Paul, Paul agreed to talk to us. We tried to get him to come home, and he said he wasn't ready, so we arranged to go to New York for a day trip. At the time, they had trips out of our local airport here; you could go up for a day for ninety-nine dollars and fly back that evening. Paul picked us up at the airport, and we spent the day with him in New York. We felt better after we saw where he was living and working. He was okay, and again we tried to get him to come home. It was a year later before he finally decided that he was ready to come home and get back into school."

While Larry and Marge were very concerned for Paul's welfare, they did not reach out for help. They were too afraid of their church's prejudiced attitudes toward homosexuals. Marge remembers, "We still internalized all of this judgment. We didn't go to our church for help; we just kept everything secret. It was a very difficult time of our lives — trying to keep the secret and love our son. It just was very difficult."

When Paul did come back to South Carolina, he was told

that he was too old to return to high school. "The school told him the best thing for him to do would be wait until he was seventeen and get his G.E.D. He was tested at a local technical college, and they said he could get his G.E.D. right away. He went to school for a couple of years and got his G.E.D. He worked for a couple of years, and then when Susan and Davis were going off to college, Paul decided he wanted to go back to school. He's very artistic, so we mentioned Ringling School of Art and Design in Florida. He got a B.A. down there and is now in computer graphics art."

When I ask Marge and Larry when they started to go through the process of reeducating themselves and learning how to accept Paul's homosexuality, they sigh and say, "We stayed in the closet for twelve years. We still didn't tell anyone even after Davis came out. It was only four years ago that we joined P-FLAG."

ELLIE

Like many parents, Ellie had convinced herself that she was "fine" with Erik's being gay. He had told her while he was in the hospital having surgery for Crohn's disease, which can be brought on by stress. Ellie recalls, "I had flown in from Louisville. After his surgery, Erik was lying in bed and he was very upset. He was in pain, and he said, 'Mom, we've got to talk,' and I said, 'Sure.' Then he said, 'I think I'm gay.' At that point I only clung to *think*, because if he thought he was gay then I could think that he wasn't. We talked about it for a while, but I kept thinking he was only seventeen, so I figured he was going to change. I thought perhaps it was the Crohn's disease, the stress. I talked to his father about it, and his father was really upset because he thought he had failed as a father and maybe he wasn't there for him enough, and it was a real threat to his masculinity. I was living in Des Moines at the time, and Erik was living with his father, which his father hadn't expected. It was definitely a stressful situation. But because I was in Iowa and he was in Delaware, it was easier for me to deal with because I didn't have to deal with the issue directly. I was able to go on with my life. I didn't realize at the time that I immediately went into the closet about this and never mentioned it to anyone for a number of years."

What's interesting is that, like my mother, Ellie had a number of gay friends. "It's funny to look back, because at the time, I supported my friends when they were having problems with their own families. I was always there for them, but I never once told them that I had a gay son. I had one female friend in Des Moines who was married and had two children. She and I were in a workshop together, and she shared with me that she thought she might be a lesbian and asked me if I thought she was. Right after that she came out." None of these friends or peers helped Ellie deal directly with her own homophobia.

She explains her retreat into the closet by emphasizing that Des Moines is in the Bible Belt. "I didn't think it was going to be something I could deal with out there. I was supportive of people when they talked about gay issues, but I just couldn't acknowledge that my son was gay." It seems that though she was intellectually and emotionally empathetic for other people, when it came to her son she couldn't overcome her negative definition of homosexuality. Again, as with many parents, including my mother, she had not yet separated her vision of her son from who he really was in the world. She explains her attachment by revealing that two years before she gave birth to Erik, she had a stillbirth. "When I was pregnant with Erik I was extremely emotional because I was so afraid I was going to lose another child, so the pregnancy with Erik was a stressful one. Of course, that's the first thing I thought of: I caused this because I worried too much when I was pregnant with him. Maybe I babied him too much. He was like the rebirth — the *Messiah*."

Again in the heat of the moment, parents search for answers. Ellie relaxes and says, "Well, it's funny, because I just came back from a regional P-FLAG directors meeting, and a few of us were sitting around the table talking. We all came up with these reasons why we thought our kids were gay when we first found out, and one of them was 'Oh, I must have breastfed them too long.' Now we can laugh, but at the time, I thought of all the negative things I could have done to cause it. I guess I beat myself up a little bit about it. I worried about his future and what it will be like. He's a nice kid, a wonderful boy, and I really wanted people to like him. All parents want their children to have a successful future, and I wanted that for him."

When Erik was in college, a young woman he had been dating approached Ellie and said, "I really don't want Erik to be gay." This made Ellie realize that Erik wasn't going to change. "At that point, I thought I had accepted it, that I was fine with it. I was supportive of him, but he wasn't living near me. I didn't know what effect I had on him by not telling people. I just figured it was enough to say, 'Erik, I love you. You know I support you. I'll do whatever you want, but I don't see any reason for me to shout it from the rooftops.' I didn't realize the impact that my not coming out had on him."

It took several years before Ellie finally agreed to attend a P-FLAG meeting. Erik had asked his mother to attend one, but she refused. "I said, 'I don't need support,' and he said, 'But Mom, you do,' and I said, 'No, I don't. I said I love you. I don't need to have somebody tell me that I'm OK. I know I'm OK and you're OK.' I wouldn't listen. But just to please him, I called P-FLAG to find out where they met. I found out they met at a church that most of my friends attend on Sunday. I was very active in the Des Moines symphony guild, and all of my symphony guild friends went to this particular church. On Sunday afternoon I just could not bring myself to go. How was I going to explain why this Jewish woman was walking into a church on Sunday?"

Ellie points to a concern of many parents: what will the neighbors think? Again, once parents feel comfortable with themselves and have examined and redefined their ideas of homosexuality, the opinions of others, especially those people with prejudiced or judgmental attitudes, will not be so significant. But learning not to care about others' opinions is difficult.

"When Erik visited Des Moines wearing this little pink triangle in his ear, I had a big problem. I kept saying, 'Erik, you know I accept you for who you are, but why do you have to wear that earring?' It was very hard for me, and he said, 'When you take off your wedding band I'll take out the earring.' We had a real hard time every time he came with the earring. That put me back in the closet for a little longer."

Ellie didn't see her reaction to Erik's pink triangle earring as a reflection of her homophobia. She claimed she "didn't want anyone talking behind [her] back." This kind of contradiction is common among parents as they begin to uncover the layers of homophobia and approach true acceptance of their child's homosexuality. "I was going to tell people I had a gay son, but I wanted it to come from me, not from somebody else. I wasn't embarrassed by having a gay son, but I was embarrassed by having people talk behind my back." Now Ellie admits that she just wasn't ready to be open. A few years later, she moved back to Baltimore. "I made a vague commitment to Erik that I would go to a P-FLAG meeting. I moved here in December of 1994, and in January of 1995 I went to my first P-FLAG meeting." Ellie's journey had begun, again.

Protecting Your Child

CAROLYN AND BILL

The turning point for Carolyn and Bill came when their son, William, was beaten by a group of students from school. But before the harassment at school started, neither Carolyn nor Bill had any idea what kind of danger their son was in because he was gay. "I hadn't even thought of it being a problem," says Carolyn. "I was ignorant of the fact that gays and lesbians had absolutely no legal protection. It was a planned, deliberate, organized attack on William specifically. Bill and I were at home when one of William's friends called. Bill answered the phone and, acting like there wasn't anything wrong, grabbed his billfold and keys and said he needed something at the store. I knew something was wrong, but I couldn't do anything. I'm in a wheelchair now. I called the hospital, the police station, and the school. No one could tell me what had happened; I had to do something. I was so angry that I couldn't get in my car and go."

Carolyn's frustration is palpable as she speaks of the day of William's attack. Again, she criticizes her lack of knowledge about the subject and refers to her "desperate craving" for information. She was an open-minded person, but she never thought such vicious attacks could occur against her child.

William had told her that there were other kids at school who were gay and afraid to tell their parents. After this incident, Carolyn "heard horror stories of parents rejecting or disowning their children." She asks indignantly, "Why aren't state agencies protecting these kids? Why aren't these parents prosecuted for neglect? That's another mission I have down the road."

■ ■ ■

I recognized an evolution of feeling in my mother's gradual but steady acceptance of me as her lesbian daughter. It was clear to me that she was trying to get over her hurt feelings. In the same way that I suggest gays and lesbians get involved in their community in order to find support and develop a better understanding of their sexual orientation, I also advise parents to reach out to both the gay community and other organizations that help parents deal with accepting their children's homosexuality. Parents and Friends of Lesbians and Gays (P-FLAG) is a national organization with chapters in many cities and states across the country offering support and outreach services for parents and other family members. Meeting other parents of gays and lesbians and hearing their stories and sharing your own can be enormously helpful in understanding and learning to accept and integrate this information about your child. You may not be ready to make a big announcement that you are the parent of a lesbian or gay child, but you will begin to see that there is nothing wrong with such a disclosure. Indeed, no longer censoring this information might well feel like a tremendous freedom. It will certainly be seen as a profound statement of your love for your child.

Chapter 12

From Acceptance to Empowerment
"So This Is Your Journey"

*"In these troubled, tumultuous times, the world
badly needs us. America could do well to learn
from our creativity, our inclusive approach to
problem-solving, our skills in building unity out of
diversity and in forging alliances and political
coalitions. Our families of choice are vibrant,
loving examples of how private life is being remade
in this complex world in wonderfully democratic
ways."*

TORIE OSBORN,
from *Coming Home to America*

Significantly, what really changed my mother's level of comfort with the issue was the same thing that pushed me out of the closet once and for all: my coming out on the cover of *The Advocate*. As she says, "When I read your *Advocate* interview, I was really proud of it. Then you started doing all that work with HRC, and you would call and tell me what you were doing. You were getting involved and telling me about the different bills. You were so enthusiastic, and that made me feel much better about you."

Clearly, the more comfortable I became, the more comfortable she became with me. Her direct involvement in gay issues, which began when I invited her to Washington, D.C., to speak at the 1997 P-FLAG ceremony, changed her perception of lesbian and gay politics. "We'd been talking a lot, and I got interested in what you were doing from an activist point of view. It had made such an impression on you. When I first started hearing those stories of parents having these awful reactions to learning that their child is gay, I was stunned. I was shocked to hear stories about parents who never talked to their children again, who let their children die of AIDS. No matter what, your child is still your child, no matter what they do. Even if they killed someone; it doesn't make a difference, you still have to stand behind your children. Hearing these stories of parents walking away from their children made me much more aware. I got closer to the issue from hearing from you, and that too made me listen more intently when I heard something on TV or the radio."

My mother also felt a sense of catharsis when she talked to some of the parents involved in P-FLAG and heard their coming-out stories. "I felt really comfortable around the P-FLAG people because nobody could know that feeling but a person who has gone through it and is making the attempt to deal with something that they don't know how to deal with. Maybe sometime it will be easy and commonplace to come out. That's one of the things I hope for."

My mother now sees that once the stereotypes are broken down and replaced with an accurate picture of lesbians and gays, coming out won't be life shattering for parents or children. "If people don't have to have an opinion about it, then discovering someone is gay will have the same impact as preferring red to blue." She agrees with me that once we take away the moral or religious dimension in viewing homosexuality, there will no longer be a negative value assigned to it.

But she admits, "It's a very difficult thing to root out and make a decision about. You can't accept it for what it is if you put any kind of Christian or Judeo-Christian religious connotation on it. It's really hard to be proud of something that so many people still consider a negative."

She also thinks the gay community itself needs to take responsibility for debunking the stereotypes. "There's a lot the gay community has brought on itself by not showing a serious face as far as relationships go. Wigstock and the parades — that's not all there is, but that's what gets a lot of coverage. The coverage gays and lesbians need is about couples who are adopting children, who live together and own their homes and are the pillars of their community. You need role models so you no longer feel ashamed."

She realizes that activism is necessary, because discrimination still exists against gays and lesbians. "I don't like people to be repressed in any situation. As far as I'm concerned, everyone should have the same rights. When I realized that you guys didn't have the same rights as everyone else, I thought that was unfair, and you shouldn't have to tolerate the prejudice. I have my own concept about right and wrong. If I hear someone with racial, hateful views I react."

She believes that in order for gays and lesbians to be treated equally in our society, "we have to go from thinking of [homosexuality] as a negative to thinking of it as a positive. And we have to learn how it is a positive. We've got to get involved if we're really going to accept it. It's probably not something we want to get involved with, but we've got to — we have to do things like join P-FLAG, even if we just want to complain."

My mother has this advice for parents who are still in the midst of their struggle, their own coming-out journey: "Take a breath and sit back, because you're going to go all over the place. You're going to be everywhere at once. Just take a breath and remember that the child you are talking to is the child that you love, and that he or she is going through something that's really hard. Try not to take it personally and try to stay calm. Keep the lines of communication open and don't get so frightened that you block yourself off."

And now my mom can say to me, "After living this much of my life, I realize it's not important to push yourself. It's just something that people do. The most important thing is to enjoy yourself. Whatever either you or Elijah decide to do, I wouldn't really care, as long as you were doing something that gives you a sense of fulfillment and not be on social security at the same time. I realize that a lot of money and fame isn't the thing that makes us happy."

In the spring of 1996, I asked my mom if she were interested in doing an interview with me for an *Advocate* cover story. She had an album coming out and was looking for press. She told me the only way she'd do it is if I did the interview and wrote the piece. I assured her that I would and then asked, "Well, when could we do it?" and she said, "Now!"

My mom's appearance on the cover of *The Advocate* in the August 20, 1996, issue was a public statement of her acceptance of me. But it doesn't mean the process has ended. "I see it as ongoing and evolving; that's the way I see everything. I'm still a mother, and I'm still bossy with you, and we still have our never-ending arguments about clothes in which I say, 'Where did you get those awful shoes?' and you say, 'They're men's shoes,' and I'll say, 'Goddamnit Chas.' I think we'll always fight little battles, but they're not specifically about you being gay. I never liked the way you dress, and you don't really like the way I dress. So it's okay, it's less about you being gay; eventually you've got to get off that issue."

I may not hear too much praise directly from my mom, but Georgeann is still there to be the voice of the family. She lets me know that Mom is proud of who I am and what I have done with my life. "Your mom couldn't be more proud of you," she says. "Every time she can, she says her daughter is the best person she knows — that's a famous Cher quote."

Turning Another Corner

I think it's important to keep in mind that each family, each situation, is unique. Both parents and children need to be aware of each other's feelings and circumstances and help each other learn about what being gay is all about — and it's different for everyone. Again and again we see that it's often the negative stereotypes that inflict the most damage and create the biggest source of pain. Once these stereotypes are dismantled and parents as well as their children are able to replace outdated definitions of homosexuality with accurate, life-affirming images, parents and their children will have reached the final frontier.

Parents turn the final corner at different times. My mother's initial shock and anger were powerful, but they didn't last long. Other parents, like Marge and especially Larry, continue to reject their children's homosexuality for years before finally releasing themselves from their prison of secrecy. Marge and Larry spent twelve years in the closet before they had the courage to come out. This liberation enabled them not only to embrace their sons' homosexuality but accept themselves as well.

MARGE AND LARRY

It was joining P-FLAG that enabled Marge and Larry to fully accept their son's homosexuality. Larry says, "Our P-FLAG chapter was organized by two ladies in Greenville who had gay sons. They had met while working for crisis hotlines and discovered that they had gay children; that's when they started P-FLAG. We read about it in the paper and went to the second meeting. We've been going ever since. That's what really caused us to start coming out and to start being willing to tell friends and family. That really was a growing process for us."

Their love for their children eventually made Marge and Larry renounce their former church. "We left our church about four years ago. Our church was very conservative, and the Southern Baptist Convention leadership at a national level has been taken over by ultraconservatives — all called right-wing extremists, if you will. We had not only served in leadership positions but we also had supported the church with our money. But then we felt we could no longer give our money to people who were teaching and preaching hatred at a national level. It was very difficult because we had been lifelong Baptists. All we knew was the Baptist faith. But it was the right thing to do in our minds. We refused to give our money to extremists who were preaching hatred and bigotry against our children."

Like my mother, Larry and Marge are still coming out. They see it as necessary to be active and speak out against hateful or discriminating views and actions against homosexuals. "We speak at the colleges and have been in a couple of churches. We also work the crisis line all the time and train volunteers. We will speak anywhere they will ask us. What we try to do is put a face on homosexuality and let the public know that gay people are real people who are deserving of your love and respect just as any other human beings."

Reexamining Religion

There is no doubt that religion plays an important role in many of our lives, and coming out can often challenge views that we previously thought were written in stone.

BETTY AND PAUL

In explaining what pushed them from tolerance to full acceptance, Betty and Paul point to their children's assertion that being gay wasn't a choice for them. They describe how both Judy and Dave "really struggled with being gay. They both tried to be straight, and finally each of them, in different settings, came to the conclusion that they were [gay]." And while at first both Betty and Paul typically blamed themselves for the homosexuality of two of their four children, it didn't take them long to realize that their homosexuality was no one's "fault."

As Paul says, "I had to put a new paradigm on the issue. I immediately began wondering about environmental factors: was it something I did, did I travel too much when they were young, was I out of their lives too much? Then we thought about heredity and ancestors. We talked to a number of our relatives, and each of us had speculated or heard about someone in the family who was gay. Our learning curves increased exponentially."

"Dave admitted to us that he had contemplated suicide, then Judy told us the same thing. This was astonishing to us. A real wake-up call." Betty and Paul continued to educate themselves. "We kept the conversation open with the kids, listening to them and trying to understand. Second, we made sure that we were their support system, whatever they were going through. We began seeking reading materials. I had a file on homosexuality that I used for people in the congregation who discovered their kids were gay. I went back through it with a whole new attention to it. After that, we started a church group. A number of our friends were already in P-FLAG, and there was a meeting at the United Methodist Church in Bellevue. We were scared to go the first time. It was a wonderful group, and we got their mailing list. By our third meeting, our family was the guest group."

Something that helped Paul and Betty accept this information into their lives was literally integrating it into their work. As a minister, Paul had always addressed social issues in his sermons. "I'd talk about child abuse in one of my sermons, and afterward people would approach me, saying, 'I've experienced child abuse.' I began to talk about homosexuality in that way, and the same thing happened. Very cautiously I began making more allusions to homosexuality or using illustrations about these people. Little by little I tried to deal with it, opened it up to discussion within my congregation. I wanted to deal with it in a positive way; I didn't want to cram it down people's throats."

When he retired, Paul's church gave him a formal retirement party. Both Judy and Dave asked their parents if it was okay to bring their partners. "We said, 'Of course, bring your partners; they're part of the family, along with everyone else.'"

Paul and Betty admit that they came out very fast. "But others come out more slowly. I think it's important to tell people first, it's not your fault; then move on to understanding that it's not their choice; then begin cautiously talking to your friends, monitoring their response and attitudes." Despite his retirement and a move to Olympia, Washington, both Paul and Betty are very active in gay issues in their community. And they both continue to push for gay rights within their church as well. "The teaching in our denomination is that homosexuals as well as heterosexuals are both children of God and deserving of the full ministry of the church. But unfortunately, it goes on to say that homosexuality is incompatible with Christian teaching. It's been an issue of 'Let's be vague' since 1972 in church," Paul says dejectedly.

But Paul remains hopeful. "Little by little we're gaining votes to have that disclaimer deleted from our social creed. It's still about sixty-forty, and all we need is a majority." Paul says those congregations that have not yet dropped their bigoted, exclusionary views come from the southeastern states. But there is a concerted effort to change their minds and reach an accord. Paul continues, "It is my belief that homosexuality is not a religious issue but a prejudicial issue. I think some people use it to advance their own issues. If you look at church history, you will see that the church radically changed its position on slavery, on the vote for women, and on divorce. It will change on this, but it will take time."

When I ask him to define the motivating factor for change, he says, "The primary catalyst is knowing someone gay, knowing a family of someone who is gay, and seeing the normality of their lives. The knowing comes from inside." He points out that knowing homosexuality only from a secondary source, reading about it in the Bible, for instance, often leads to misconceptions. The Bible contains some passages that refer to homosexual practices of Hebrew men as being immoral. Specifically, such passages as this one from Leviticus 18:22: "You shall not lie with a male as with a woman; it is an abomination."

Paul points out that Hebrew law condemned homoerotic acts within its particular historical and cultural context. *What the Bible Really Says About Homosexuality*, written by a Roman Catholic priest, Daniel A. Helminiak, Ph.D., addresses similar issues. Helminiak says, "What is the point of the Genesis story of creation? What was the author intending to say? Well, the Bible intended to give a religion lesson, not a science lesson. The seven-day story of creation is just a way of making the point: God created the universe with wisdom, care and order. If science determines that the universe actually evolved over millions and millions of years, there is no conflict with the Bible."

Some people insist that if the Bible says something (such as homosexual acts) is wrong, then it's wrong: no argument. But Helminiak asks us to consider this: "A thing is wrong for a reason. If the reason no longer holds and no other reason is given, how can a thing still be judged wrong? Simply that 'God said it is wrong' is not a good enough answer, for the point remains even in the case of God: God also says things are wrong for reasons."

Helminiak says we must keep in mind as we begin to reconcile the religious views of homosexuality with our knowledge of those who are homosexual that "in biblical times there was no elaborated understanding of homosexuality as a sexual orientation. There was only a general awareness of same-sex contacts or same-sex acts. . . . Our questions today are about people and their relationships, not simply about sex acts."

Like Marge and Larry and my mother, Betty and Paul speak publicly every chance they get. As Paul says, "I never thought I'd retire and become an activist. But somebody has to stand up and counter the myths of the right wing that they continue to propagate; they are lies. My strong feeling is that people in mainline churches don't hear anything else, so they have to hear this. Many pastors are so scared to death, they're silent. I think straight people will have a lot more influence in some arenas than gay people."

RHEA AND BUTCH

Although Butch and Rhea were victorious in reaching an acceptance of Bruce's homosexuality, there were still challenges ahead. Butch remembers an instance before he and Rhea took Bruce out of school. "One night a few years ago, back before we actually started the P-FLAG group in our town, when Bruce was still in high school, a vanload of boys harassed him when he was with us. Bruce knew the boys, so I wound up calling their fathers. Surprisingly, those fathers said that they would talk to their sons. Those boys didn't harass Bruce anymore. I feel in that way something positive came out of a negative experience."

Like Paul and Betty, Butch is hopeful. "Yes, I think times are changing. It's going to be very slow, but I think education has a lot to do with it, because most people, like ourselves, don't know anything about the gay community other than negative images that come out a lot on TV. My old image was that homosexuals were just sexual beings. I didn't understand that they had personal relationships just like we all have. Since then I've learned so much. After the local news did a spotlight on the gay parade, everyone in town knew Bruce was gay. At work no one really came up and gave me a hard time, but I got cold shouldered. One guy who is really into religion started arguing with me about it. He even got his Bible and showed me where it said homosexuality was a sickness. I told him in a friendly way that if we were going to stay friends, we best not talk about this subject. He has a right to believe his way, but I have a right to believe my way. We kind of let it rest. Since then, I have changed workplaces. I have gone back to the R&E, where I basically started as a young man.

"Since we have come out in public, I've had many people come up to me and congratulate us as a family for what we are doing. As a matter of fact, even some people that I thought were very redneck guys told me how great it was that I would stick by my son and all. A lot of the engineers said they'd give me support, even if they are not from our area. For a while there we kept waiting for the other shoe to drop. But it really made me feel so good that the people at my workplace supported me the way they do now. Well, it's going to be a long road nationally and culturally, but it is so clear to me that the work with P-FLAG is really having such a positive effect. So much of it is about education."

As for Rhea, she is still counting her blessings. "Our social circle is not back to where it was before, and I don't know if it ever will be. I used to have all my eggs in one basket: the church. Now I have friends around the world of all different ethnicities and educational backgrounds. After having been through this experience, I would never want to be mainstream again. I find the higher-quality people are in the margins."

Free at Last

ELLIE

Before Ellie became an activist, she had to finally and completely let go of her homophobia. Ellie explains, "I was raised Jewish, in a family that was trying to assimilate. I just go back to my childhood and the childhoods of most people and how we were raised. Nobody ever really told us there was such a thing when I was growing up; you really had to make up your own mind, and because of gay jokes and the negative names, we formed this opinion that it must not be okay to be gay. For me, it wasn't just admitting that my son was gay; it was about assimilation. I grew up with the understanding that 'you don't have to tell people you are Jewish; it's not important that you tell people you're Jewish.' I was raised to not be really open about myself to people because I didn't want to be judged. I think my initial response to Erik's being gay reflects my background in that way."

"I think parents come out too," Erik says of his mom. "It took me eighteen years to come out; it only took her ten years to come out and acknowledge that she has a gay son and be proud of it. She had to realize that it's something that she needs to fight for — not just for me but for the gay children who don't have parents who are fighting for them. Sure, she went through that whole grieving period. But I think the biggest stepping stone for her was realizing that she had a gay son for a reason. There were so many people against gay people, and she felt she had to do something about it. She wanted to spread the word that being gay is not a choice my child has made; it's natural. People shouldn't be putting my child down or firing him from his job or treating him poorly because he's gay. The more she saw, the more upset and angry she became."

Ellie corroborates, "I need to be out there and shout it

from the rooftops that I have a gay son, and he's okay, and it's okay with me. Suddenly I really needed people to know because I don't want people to have to be in the closet anymore. The closet is a terrible place to be. I've been there, and I don't want anybody else to be there. At P-FLAG I could help other people come out of the closet and help Americans in general find out what it's like to be in a closet.

"Erik feels that being gay is a gift. At first when he said that, I thought, 'How could it be a gift?' But now I have accepted it as my gift as well, because this has certainly made me a better person — a more educated person and a more enlightened person. It really has been a growing experience for me, and I can't imagine not having a gay son now."

As Ellie says in conclusion, "I'm free at last."

My mother also sees how vital it is for parents to be open and direct about their children's being gay. "I think it's important for every parent to be public in whatever their arena is, because if you hide it, then it is still making you embarrassed. We only hide things that we're ashamed of. Being ashamed will only make us feel worse about the situation."

As always, my mother is ready for a challenge. She looks at me and says, "So this is your journey: making being gay or lesbian commonplace."

Epilogue

My reasons for writing this book have always been very personal. Because my coming-out journey has been such a profoundly positive life-changing experience, I wanted to help others attain the personal freedom and closeness that my family and I have experienced. My hopes are that by reading my story and those of others, you will realize that coming out really is a family affair.

I felt qualified to write a book on this subject because I had personally grown from a scared, closeted lesbian to a happy, openly gay activist in my community. I was also inspired by the fact that my mother and I were able to turn a distant and cold relationship into one that is close, loving, and spilling over with mutual respect. Unfortunately, that is only half the story. The other half is not a success story with a happy ending: instead, it is the most difficult life lesson that I have had to learn.

In the past, when people were having particular trouble coming out to their parents, I would suggest they read a memoir entitled *Prayers for Bobby*. This is the true tragic story of a fundamentalist family with a gay son, who, after unsuccessfully trying to gain his family's acceptance, kills himself by jumping off a freeway overpass. It took Bobby's suicide for his family to realize that their problem was not Bobby's sexual orientation but rather their own homophobia, as well as that of their church. Since Bobby's death, his mother has become an effective gay rights activist. But no matter how much she now gives back to her son's community, the void left by his death cannot possibly be filled.

I have never wanted to use scare tactics to convince people to begin or continue their coming-out process. But if by sharing my difficult lesson, I can prevent someone from making the same mistake, then I'm willing to be more adamant. As I've said from the beginning of this book, coming out is a continuous process that goes beyond simply telling someone that you are or a family member is gay. Indeed, as I've said, the coming-out journey is often three steps forward and one step back. But no matter how many steps backward we take, we must always continue to move forward.

Throughout this book, I've tried to emphasize the importance of coming out by sharing different family outing triumphs, including my mother's and mine. However, I purposefully did not include a lot about my more recent relationship with my father because I wanted the book to reflect the experience of those who have fully accepted either their own or their child's homosexuality — privately and publicly. And though my father was wonderfully supportive when I came out to him at eighteen, in the last few years, since he became a Republican congressman and I became a high-profile gay activist, we often found ourselves on opposite sides of heated political issues. My father and I had fundamental differences in the way we viewed various personal and political topics, and these differences created distance in our once very close relationship.

This in and of itself does not seem that tragic or out of the ordinary. All relationships go through periods of distance and disagreement. And children and parents especially are not exempt from strong disagreements, or even anger. When my dad cosponsored the Defense of Marriage Act (DOMA), I became very angry with him, feeling that his sponsorship was, in a way, a personal betrayal. Yet I never confronted him directly with my anger. If I had, I may have at least understood his reasons for cosponsoring the bill; in that case, we could have agreed to disagree. Instead, I just swallowed my feelings and let more space develop between us.

My father died in a fluke skiing accident in Lake Tahoe on January 5, 1998. I hadn't spoken with him in almost a year, and now I will never talk to him again. Whatever differences were between us prior to his death do not seem that important now. Instead, I find myself left with other truths: all that we shared and how much I truly loved him. My dad was not always an easy man for me to love, but I am full of regret that I didn't put in the effort to be closer to him. I guess I assumed we would work on our relationship in the future.

I allowed my anger over my father's political stance to stop me from pushing our personal relationship forward. I don't know if I ever could have convinced my dad to publicly support and vote for gay rights, but I do know that if I had been honest with him about my anger and made an effort to keep the lines of communication open, I would have spoken to him before he died.

Gays and their families often have more obstacles to overcome in building and maintaining close relationships than straight people do. Acceptance of sexual orientation can be a painful process that requires work and commitment. However, upon completing *Family Outing*, I hope readers will conclude that living openly, honestly, and out is far more rewarding than the false security of the closet.

Life can be tenuous, and no one knows what the future holds. I personally have lost two people I loved: Joan died three hours after I was last with her, and my dad died almost a year and a half after I had last been with him. For those of you who are as stubborn as I have been, let me leave you with one final thought: loss can be a powerful motivation to overcoming obstacles, but it shouldn't be the one we rely on. Take it from me: try to work out difficulties with those you love, for as hard as it seems, the rewards will be that much greater.